Malte Liesner

Sanskrit – Historical Phonology Workbook

I0643887

Reichert Verlag Wiesbaden 2025

Sanskrit

Historical Phonology Workbook

Malte Liesner

Reichert Verlag Wiesbaden 2025

Bibliografische Information der Deutschen Nationalbibliothek
Die Deutsche Nationalbibliothek verzeichnet diese Publikation in der Deutschen Nationalbibliografie; detaillierte bibliografische Daten sind im Internet über http://dnb.dnb.de abrufbar.

Tauernstraße 11, 65199 Wiesbaden
info@reichert-verlag.de, www.reichert-verlag.de
ISBN: 978-3-7520-0844-9 (Print)
eISBN: 978-3-7520-0347-5 (eBook)
https://doi.org/10.29091/9783752003475

Preface

रसोऽहमप्सु कौन्तेय प्रभास्मि शशिसूर्ययोः ।
प्रणवः सर्ववेदेषु शब्दः खे पौरुषं नृषु ।। ७ ८ ।।

पुण्यो गन्धः पृथिव्यां च तेजश्चास्मि विभावसौ ।
जीवनं सर्वभूतेषु तपश्चास्मि तपस्विषु ।। ७ ९ ।।

Bhagavad-Gīta 7.8/7.9

The German version of this book was published by me in 2019. In 2020 I translated the book into English and then in 2021 Jared S. Klein wrote a review of the German version. After reading the review I felt so bad and ashamed that I did not touch the English version for almost three years.

I had put in my best effort to produce a user-friendly modern workbook on historical phonology, the third in a row (after publishing the same on Latin and Greek), using the same format in order to make it really easy for the learner to get aquainted with historical phonology in an easy and playful way. The books are designed for beginners in the first semester at universities or self-learners. That was my intention.

It is not about the errors I made in my book. I can gladly accept all the linguistic corrections which were presented in Mr Klein's review. But it's the sound that makes the music, as we say in German. The style of language in which the review was written is so arrogant that I can hardly describe it. Mr Klein used the following words: infelicities, embarrassing, blatant error, sloppiness, absence of concentration, less than stellar command, inexcusable, outrageous footnote…. And he was perfectly right when he said that I do not have „full command" of the Sanskrit data. I really do not have that.

I took a few Sanskrit courses because of my deep yearning for spirituality which was indeed saturated after finding the beauty and deep wisdom of the Bhagavad Gita. I travelled to India and met spiritual people. Therefore, I do not really feel guilty for not having read one specific linguistic article from 1993 from a specific person about which fact Mr Klein was so „outraged" that I had not cited it. The arrogant style of his review can also be seen in the use of phrases like „éclat de nouveauté" or „caveat lector" which I had to google to understand them.

Unfortunately, in some cases an increase in intellectuality is accompanied with a decrease in empathy and humanity. We should treat people in this world with respect and modesty. Mr Klein's review took away all the motivation I had to continue my hobby which was designed to help students not having to use dusty undidactic material like me during my time at the university from 2000–2005.

So, dear professors, learned scholars, educated high-level people, who „know-it-all", this book is not really for you but for students and learners. But of course, feel free to use it with respect and modesty. You can now start searching for the mistakes I made in order to increase your publication list. But please, don't be too kleinlich. Thank you!

February 2025
Königsberg, Germany

Malte Liesner

Contents

1 Sanskrit in Space and Time

In India, Sanskrit has the same significance as Latin, Greek and Hebrew have in Europe and it is extremely important for historical comparative linguistics because this language has been handed down to us with an enormous text corpus. The word Sanskrit means 'constructed, put together' and in a broader sense 'sophisticated, refined, highly elaborated'.

Classification of Sanskrit within the Indo-European languages

The Indo-European languages go back to Proto-Indo-European, a theoretical language which has been reconstructed through sound correspondences and of which we do not have written documents. One of the major branches of the Indo-European languages is Indo-Iranian, which itself is divided into Iranian, Indo-Aryan and Nuristani. Indo-Aryan is the ancestor of the varieties Vedic and Sanskrit (Old Indo-Aryan) and Prakrit/Pāli (Middle Indo-Aryan). The following classification is adapted from Kümmel 2007:37/38.

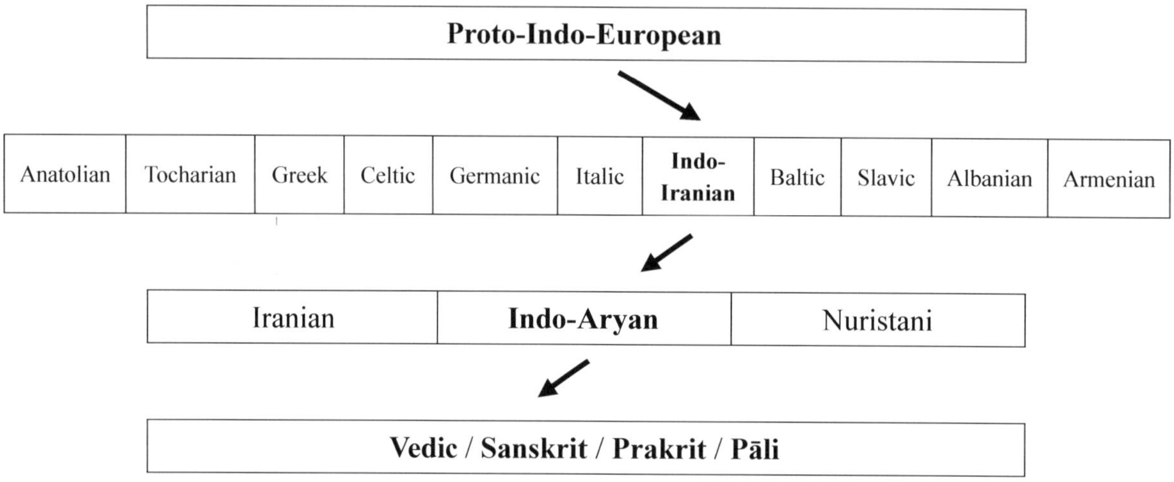

Loan words in Modern English

Some Sanskrit words have found their way as loan words into Modern English. Among these are *mantra*, *ashram*, *yoga*, *tantra*, *guru*, *karma*, *avatar*, *mandala* and also *swastika*, which is regarded as a lucky symbol in India. The self-designation of the Sanskrit speaking population was *arya-* 'Aryan', a word which was used wrongly as a designation of a superior human race especially during the Nazi era in Germany.

Varieties of Sanskrit / Language periods of Indic languages

Vedic: The four Vedas Rigveda, Samaveda, Yajurveda and Atharvaveda are the oldest holy writings of Hinduism. The oldest of these is the Rigveda with average datings between 1500–1300 BC. It is a collection of 1028 hymns and sacrificial poems which are directed at several different deities. The word Rigveda is composed of the Sanskrit words *ŕ̥c-* 'song of praise, stanza, verse' and *véda-* 'knowledge' and can be translated with 'knowledge composed in hymns'. The Vedic language is richer in morphology compared to classical Sanskrit whereas their phonology is almost identical. The four Vedas, which are also called Samhitas, are the starting point of Indic literature and accompanied by further writings which are called Brahmanas, Upanishads and Aranyakas.

Lit.: Ziegler 5–8.

- **Sanskrit:** It was the grammarian Pāṇini who documented and in this way defined the rules of Sanskrit which was the standard language of science, theatre, jurisdiction and religion in ancient India. He presumably lived in the 5th or 4th century BC and wrote the oldest and most important Sanskrit grammar called *Aṣṭādhyāyī*. The grammar rules are formulated in aphorisms called *sūtras* which have the characteristic of being composed in a highly compact mnemotechnical verse language. Pāṇini made use of a complicated meta-language in order to describe all grammatical phenomena adequately. He arranged and defined the rules of Sanskrit grammar in such a way that Sanskrit could be used as a unified scientific and cultural language. While the upper classes spoke Sanskrit, the variety Prakrit had already started to emerge among the lower classes which is similar to the opposition of Classical Latin and Vulgar Latin. The Prakrit languages did not evolve out of Sanskrit directly but coexisted next to Sanskrit for a long time.

- Prakrit (~ 300 BC until ~ 600/700 AD)

Prakrit and Pāli: Prakrit languages or Prakrits are the designations of several Middle Indo-Aryan languages which differ from Sanskrit in phonology and morphology. The term Prakrit is also used as a cover term for languages which deviate from Sanskrit in any manner. The most important liturgical language of these languages was Pāli which is regarded as the sacred literary language of Buddhism. The most important phonological differences from Sanskrit were the following: the assimilation of consonant clusters which created a great number of geminated consonants: *dugdha-* > *duddha* 'milk', *karma-* > *kamma-* 'work', *utpāda-* > *uppāda-* 'birth', *pudgala-* > *puggala-* 'beautiful', *śabda-* > *sadda-* 'sound', *varṣa-* > *vassa-* 'rain', *kalpa-* > *kappa-* 'rule'. In the initial position, simple consonants arose: *prāṇa-* > *pāṇa-* 'breath', *grāma-* > *gāma-* 'village'. The formerly separated Sanskrit sibilants *ś*, *ṣ*, *s* merged into *s*: *śaraṇa-* > *saraṇa-* 'cottage, hut', *doṣa-* > *dosa-* 'mistake'. Sanskrit *r̥* became *a*, *i* or *u* depending on the phonological environment: *kr̥ta-* > *kata-* 'done', *r̥ṣi-* > *isi-* 'seer', *r̥ju-* > *uju-* 'straight'. Similar to the outcome in the Vedic dialect, we find Sanskrit *ḍ* and *ḍh* emerge as Pāli *ḷ* and *ḷh* between vowels: *rūḍha-* > *rūḷha-* 'grown' (SC 29.3) and also the sandhi rules s4.3 and s4.6 seem to be anticipated Middle Indo-Aryan developments because we find these regularly in Pāli, too: *bhavati* > *hoti* 'is', *dhārayati* > *dhārēti* 'he carries' (SC 21). Furthermore, we find palatalizations, e.g. *adya* > *ajja* 'today'.

Lit.: Jain/Cardona 2007.

- Apabhramsa (~ 700 AD until ~ 1500 AD) / Modern Indo-Aryan Languages (from ~ 1500 AD)

The transition phase between Middle Indo-Aryan and Modern Indo-Aryan (also called New Indo-Aryan or Modern Indic) is called Apabhramsa. The old inflected system was lost nearly completely as it became supplanted by analytic forms. The loss of final vowels caused the emergence of many monosyllabic words, the vowels of which were often lengthened in the further development to Modern Indo-Aryan. What follows are some selected examples of language development from Sanskrit to Hindi: *dugdha-* > *duddha-* > *dūdh* 'milk', *karma-* > *kamma-* > *kām* 'work', *nāma-* > *nām* 'name', *adya* > *ajja* > *āj* 'today'. Many words also show nasalization: *grāma* > *gāma* > *gā̃v* 'village', *danta-* > *dā̃t* 'tooth'.
The Modern Indo-Aryan languages are mainly spoken in the northern part of India, in Pakistan, Nepal and Bangladesh. One of the most important languages is Hindi which, together with English, is India's national language with around 200 million native speakers. There also exist several other official local languages.

2 Basics of Phonetics

The Sanskrit grammarians were the first to classify human speech sounds according to their place and manner of articulation, which was the reason for the arrangement of the Indic alphabet. Please compare the phonetic terms of the two following tables with the arrangement of the Devanāgarī alphabet on the next page.

Fundamental places of articulation

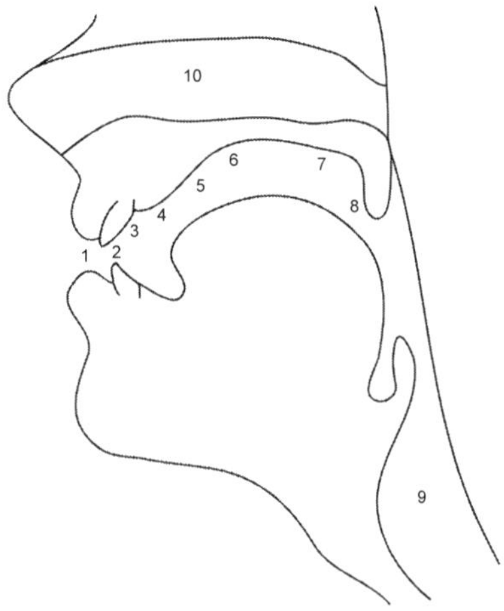

Place of Articulation		Description
1	**labial**	with the lips
2	**interdental**	between the teeth
3	**dental**	at the teeth
4	**alveolar**	at the alveolar ridge
5	**retroflex**	curled back tongue
6	**palatal**	at the hard palate
7	**velar**	at the soft palate
8	**uvular**	at the uvula
9	**glottal**	at the vocal folds
10	**nasal**	in the nasal cavity

Fundamental manners of articulation

Stop	The airflow stops completely due to an occlusion of the oral vocal tract. All languages have stop consonants, the most common are [p], [t], [k] and their voiced counterparts [b], [d], [g]. Sanskrit stops display a triple contrast of manner of articulation: voiceless (tenuis) vs. voiced (media) vs. aspirated.
Nasal	The airflow passes through the nose while there is an occlusion of the oral vocal tract which determines the resonant cavity of the consonant and therefore produces the sound of dental [n], labial [m] or velar [ŋ].
Fricative	A partial closure of the vocal tract causes the airflow to become turbulent which produces fricative consonants like [s], [f], [h]. Fricatives are also called spirants or stridents.
Approximant / Semivowel	The approximant consonants [w] and [j], which are also called semivowels, have an intermediate articulation between vowels and fricative consonants. The Sanskrit sounds *v* and *y* are classified as semivowels because they can be the non-syllabic variants of the vowels *u* and *i*. Sanskrit phonology also regards *r* and *l* as semivowels because they have the vocalic allophones *r̥* and *l̥*.
Vowel	Vowels are articulated with an open vocal tract. The airflow passes out of the mouth without constriction.
Diphthong	A diphthong is the combination of a vowel plus a semivowel. Sanskrit phonology also regards *e* and *o* as diphthongs although they were the plain long vowels *ē* and *ō* which originated out of diphthongs.
Aspirate	Aspirated consonants are pronounced with additional aspiration which is indicated by a postposed or superscript *h*.
Affricate	An affricate is the combination of a stop consonant plus homorganic fricative.
Lateral	During the articulation of the alveolar lateral /l/, the airflow escapes along the sides of the tongue while the tongue blocks the airflow in the middle. The sounds /l/ and /r/ are traditionally known as liquids.

Transliteration of the Devanāgarī-Alphabet

	Stop				Nasal	Fricative	Approxi-mant	Vowel		Diphthong	
	Tenuis		Media								
Guttural	क *ka*	ख *kha*	ग *ga*	घ *gha*	ङ *ṅa*	ह *h*		अ *a*	आ *ā*	-	-
Palatal	च *ca*	छ *cha*	ज *ja*	झ *jha*	ञ *ña*	श *ś*	य *ya*	इ *i*	ई *ī*	ए *e*	ऐ *ai*
Retroflex	ट *ṭa*	ठ *ṭha*	ड *ḍa*	ढ *ḍha*	ण *ṇa*	ष *ṣ*	र *ra*	ऋ *r̥*	ॠ *r̥̄*		
Dental	त *ta*	थ *tha*	द *da*	ध *dha*	न *na*	स *s*	ल *la*	ऌ *l̥*	ॡ *l̥̄*		
Labial	प *pa*	फ *pha*	ब *ba*	भ *bha*	म *ma*		व *va*	उ u	ऊ ū	ओ *o*	औ *au*

Sanskrit was written in the Devanāgarī script which can be literally translated as '(script of the) city of gods'. Even today this script is very common in India because it serves to write the modern Indic languages Hindi, Marāṭhī and Nepali amongst others. The Devanāgarī script goes back to the older Brahmi script and it is written from left to right below a horizontal line (नगरः: *nagaraḥ* 'city', जनः: *janaḥ* 'people') above which only vowel letters and the letter for *r* before consonant project. The frequent short vowel अ *a* is expressed within the consonantal sign (क *ka*, ख *kha*, ग *ga*, घ *gha*) and is only noted separately in the initial position (अनिलः: *anilaḥ* 'wind'). The other vowel letters आ *ā*, इ *i*, ई *ī*, उ *u*, ऊ *ū*, ऋ *r̥*, ॠ *r̥̄* and ऌ *l̥* are also written only in the initial position or within the word after another vowel, and they have another form if preceded by a consonant. Long आ *ā* is expressed by a vertical stroke (पा *pā*, दा *dā*, का *kā*), short *i* is written before the consonant (पि *pi*, दि *di*, कि *ki*) and long *ī* after the consonant (पी *pī*, दी *dī*, की *kī*). The letter *r* has a special form before consonants and is noted as a small semi circle above the horizontal line (कर्मन् *karman* 'deed, action'). If two or more consonants follow each other, their letters fuse together which is called ligature. For example the letters त *ta* and प *pa* fuse to त्प *tpa*. The vowel combinations are given in the following table and lists of ligatures can be easily found on the internet.

ka	*kā*	*ki*	*kī*	*ku*	*kū*	*kr̥*	*kr̥̄*	*kl̥*	*ke*	*kai*	*ko*	*kau*
क	का	कि	की	कु	कू	कृ	कॄ	कॢ	के	कै	को	कौ

Further Devanāgarī symbols

Anusvāra [◌ं] is a superscript dot and transcribed as *ṃ* (पं *paṃ*, तं *taṃ*). It was used to indicate the nasalization of a preceding vowel if the consonant following was *y*, *r*, *l*, *v*, *ś*, *ṣ*, *s*, *h*. Therefore, *siṃhá-* सहि 'lion' was pronounced [sĩha]. Anusvāra was also used to write the sandhi variant of *m* in the absolute final position as well as a homorganic nasal before a consonant in the middle of the word e.g. संधि *saṃdhi* instead of सनधि *sandhi*.

Visarga [:] looks like a colon and is transcribed with *ḥ* e.g. सः *saḥ*, तः *taḥ*. It is the sandhi variant of *r* and *s* in the absolute final position e.g. देवः *devaḥ* 'god' for देवस् *devas*.

Virāma [◌्] below a consonant designates the absence of a consonant following e.g. तत् *tat*, पत् *pat*, which needs to be explicitly noted because the Devanāgarī consonant letters by default contain short *a*.

Avagraha ['] is an apostrophe which is used to describe the "loss" of initial *a* according to sandhi rule s6.3 e.g. in *kaḥ api* > *ko 'pi* को 'पि 'someone'.

Daṇḍa [|] is a separator which is used to separate sentences, paragraphs or hemistiches from each other.

Anunāsika [◌ँ] does not appear in words but only in sandhi rule s15.4. It is transcribed as *ṃl* in this book.

Lit.: Stiehl 300–304; Ziegler 2012:12–23; Lehmann 2013:1–15; Thumb 1905:34–38.

3 Basics of Historical Phonology

Phonemes and allophones

If phonetic sounds are used to differenciate words e.g. *m* and *p* in *tá**m**as-* ‘darkness’ and *tá**p**as-* ‘ascesis’, these sounds are called **phonemes** of that language. The total number of phonemes is called the **phoneme inventory** of the language. If different sounds are just positional variants and not used to differenciate words, they are called **allophones** which occur in Sanskrit mainly in sandhi variants, that is in changes of final sounds before initial sounds of the following word. The original etymological final consonant *s* of *devas* ‘god’ remains as in *devas_tatra* ‘the god over there’ only before the voiceless dental sounds *t* and *th*. Before a following labial sound e.g. *devaḥ_punaḥ* ‘the god again’ we find *ḥ* instead of *s*. But, as this phonetic difference *s* ~ *ḥ* in the final position of the word does not change the meaning of the word, the two sounds *s* and *ḥ* are classified as positional variants or allophones in the final position.
In some cases the phonemic status of a sound is not absolutely clear, for example if we only have very few words which can be adduced as examples of this sound. Sanskrit does have some minimal pairs like *anu* ‘along’ :: *aṇu-* ‘atom’ which support the phonemic status of the retroflex nasal *ṇ* but usually nasals were homorganic allophones before following stops and no individual phonemes. Examples of allophonic homorganic nasals are: *da**ṇḍ**a-* ‘stick’, *pa**ñ**ca* ‘five’, *a**ṅ**ga-* ‘limb’.

Sound changes and derivation chains

The phonemes of a language are not static but subject to permanant changes which is called sound change. A sound change is expressed in phonological derivations through the derivation operator “ > ”. The number in the round brackets refers to the index in the back of the book which numerically lists all sound changes which are relevant for Sanskrit historical phonology.

Example 1: **lij́dʰá-* [lid̠ždhá] > (6.6) **liždhá-* > (23.2) **liẓdhá-* > (17.3) **liẓḍhá-* > (20.3) *līḍhá-* ‘licked’

This derivation states that the preform **lij́dʰá-* with its phonetic representation [lid̠ždhá] became **liždhá-* by sound change 6.6. Instead of writing 6.6 we can also directly put in the sound change **j́dʰ* [d̠ždh] > **ždh* which can be found in the index at SC 6.6. The process continues with the sound changes 23.2, 17.3 and 20.3. The asterisk in front of the word indicates that it is a reconstructed word and not an attested one. The last word of the derivation is the attested Sanskrit form which is the result of all the sound changes applied to the preform on the left side. The result on the right side is not furnished with an asterisk because it is an attested form.

Example 2: **du̯is* > (8.1) **du̯iš* > (23.1) *dviṣ* ‘two times’ = **du̯is* > (c24) *dviṣ*

It makes sense to summarize sound changes into a single rule when they always occur in the same sequence and have the same result. This is done in the case of the so-called ruki rule which states that **s* followed by *r,r̥,ū̆,k,ī̆* first becomes IIR **š* and afterwards SKR *ṣ*. The two sound changes PIE **s* > (8.1) IIR **š* and IIR **š* > (23.1) SKR *ṣ* are therefore expressed through the cover rule **s* > (c24) *ṣ*.

Consonants and Vowels

		Labial	Dental / Alveolar	Retroflex	Palatal	Velar	Glottal
Stop	**voiceless**	p	t	ṭ	c	k	
	voiceless aspirated	p^{h}	t^{h}	ṭ^{h}	c^{h}	k^{h}	
	voiced	b	d	ḍ	j	g	
	voiced aspirated	b^{h}	d^{h}	ḍ^{h}	(j^{h})	g^{h}	
Fricative			s ~ *[z]	ṣ ~ *[ẓ]	ś		h / [ḥ]
Nasal		m	n	ṇ	[ñ]	ṅ	
Lateral			l ~ [l̥]				
Tap / Flap				r ~ [r̥]			
Approximant		u̯			i̯		

- The stops *p, t, ṭ, c, k, ph, th, ṭh, ch, kh* and the fricatives *s, ṣ, ś, ḥ* are voiceless. All the other sounds are voiced.
- The sound *jh* appears only once in the Rigveda (*jájhjhatīḥ*, which is an epithet of lightning) and is otherwise restricted to some onomatopoetic Sanskrit words like √*jhaṇ*- 'to sound', *jharjhara*- 'drum', *jharā*- 'waterfall'. It is therefore unlikely that *jh* was an actual phoneme in Sanskrit.
- The retroflex sounds originated through the combination of palatal and dental consonants. A substrate effect of the indigenous Dravidian languages, in which retroflex sounds are common, cannot be ruled out.
- *r* and *l* have the vocalic allophones [r̥] and [l̥] if they form the syllabic nucleus between consonants.
- The grammarians also registered long *ḹ* but it does not appear in any word.
- Visarga *ḥ* is the allophone of *s* or *r* in the absolute final position and before *p, ph, k, kh*. The Vedic dialect also exhibits an additional allophone IPA [φ] called *upadhmānīya* before *p* and *ph* and an allophone IPA [x] called *jihvāmūlīya* before *k, kh*.
- The contemporary Sanskrit pronunciation in India repeats the vowel which precedes the visarga also after the visarga. Therefore, the standard pronunciation of *agniḥ* is *agnihi* and *devaha* is spoken for *devaḥ*. Visarga is pronounced as a voiced consonant.
- In phonological derivations the fricatives *s* and *ṣ* often become their voiced allophones *[z] and *[ẓ]. These sounds were very unstable and usually vanished with compensatory lengthening of the preceding vowel.

	Front		Mid		Back
Close	*i* / *ī*				*u* / *ū*
Close-Mid		*e* [ē]		*o* [ō]	
Open			*a* / *ā*		

- The exact phonetic value of *a* is unknown.
- The vowels *e* and *o* are in reality the long vowels [ē] and [ō] but their length traditionally does not appear in standard Sanskrit transcriptions. Sanskrit speakers regarded these sounds as diphthongs because historically they mostly go back to **ai̯* and **au̯*. Sanskrit also has the diphthongs *ai* < **āi̯* and *au* < **āu̯* which go back to the shortening of former long diphthongs.

Lit.: Allen 1953; Lehmann 2013:1–15; Mayrhofer 1978:15–17; Ziegler 2012:9–11; Stiehl 2007:307–308.

4 Sandhi / Roots / Word Stress

Pausa form / sandhi form / stem form / roots

Words are usually not spoken individually but in the context of sentences. If a word does occur individually and independently of other words, or it is spoken at the end of the sentence, this word is said to be in its pausa position or in the absolute final position.[1] This pausa form was taken as the default form by the ancient Indic grammarians and they used it as the starting point of their synchronic description of Sanskrit sandhi which in many cases did not match the diachronic development correctly. If a word is integrated into a sequence of words and not spoken individually, the initial sound of the word varies depending on the final sound of the preceding word which itself may also change. This process, which is very common in the world's languages, is called sandhi. The following examples show the changes of the example word *deva-* 'god', which changes its form depending on the initial sound of the following word.

The form	*devas*	stands before *t*, *th*.
The form	*devaḥ*	stands before *k*, *kh*, *p*, *ph*, *s*, *ś*, *ṣ*.
The form	*deva*	stands before a vowel except before short *a*.
The form	*devo*	stands before voiced consonants and before short *a*, which is omitted.

An English example for a sandhi process is the variant *an* of the indefinite article *a* before words with an initial vowel e.g. *an apple* or *an orange*. In this case, the variant *an* is indeed the older form, the final *n* of which corresponds to the *n* in MHG *ein* 'a'. Both words go back to Proto-Germanic **ainaz* < PIE **oi̯-no-s* which is related to SKR *eka-* 'one' < **aika-* < **oi̯-ko-*. Before words with an initial consonant, English *an* became *a* around the 12th century AD creating the present distribution of allomorphic *a/an*. This means that the sandhi form *an* preserves the historically older form and this is exactly what happened in Sanskrit in many cases e.g. SC s15.3 *devāṃs_tatra* 'the gods here' in which final **s* of the preform **devāns* remained in sandhi in contrast to its loss in the pausa form *devān* (cf. chapter 22).

Sandhi can lead to ambiguity e.g. *kāntān_na* in which the first word can theoretically be acc. pl. *kāntān*, abl. sg. *kāntāt* or acc. sg. *kāntām* of the word *kāntā-* 'spouse' because final *t*, *n* and *m* appear as *n* before *n*. The compound *mātāgacchat* could theoretically be translated as *mātā agacchat* 'the mother went' or as *mātā āgacchat* 'the mother came' because final vowels fuse with equal initial vowels in sandhi. In these cases, the correct translation can only be found through the context. You can find overview tables for all sandhi results in the appendix.

In order to have an unambiguous representation of the word, dictionaries list Sanskrit nouns according to their **stem form** e.g. *deva* which is an abstract representation of the word written with hyphen in linguistic notation *deva-* and often without hyphen in dictionaries. The ancient Indic grammarians also arranged words according to their underlying roots which are given in this book with the mathematical root sign √.

Lit.: Stiehl 2007:309; Ziegler 26–32; Mayrhofer 1978:26–32; Wackernagel 1896:301–343.

Differences and similarities between sandhi and morphological forms

The phonological rules of a language are in most cases valid for the junction of individual words (external sandhi) as well as for the junction of words with morphemes (internal sandhi). In Sanskrit, however, there is a crucial difference between these two. The rules of external sandhi do not apply to morphological formations before endings that start with a vowel, a semivowel or a nasal. Let us take a look at the example *marut-* 'wind' with the nom. sg. *marut* which is identical to the

1 In this position we usually only find vowels or one of the following eight consonants *k*, *ṅ*, *ṭ*, *t*, *n*, *p*, *m*, *ḥ*, and rarely *ṇ*, *y*, *l*, *v*. All the other consonants are not permitted in the absolute final position which causes their transformation into one of the before mentioned permitted consonants by deaspiration of aspirated consonants and devoicing of voiced consonants.

word stem. In external sandhi, we see voicing of final *t* before a vowel in e.g. *marut atra* > (s11.2) *marud_atra* 'the wind here'.
The other forms of the paradigm are acc. sg. *marut-am*, dat. sg. *marut-e*, instr. sg. *marut-ā* although we could expect ^{x}*marudam*, ^{x}*marude*, ^{x}*marudā* before the suffixes *-am*, *-e*, *-ā* which start with a vowel just like in external sandhi forms. But in order to avoid irregularities within the paradigm, the expected voiced allophone *d* was later analogically replaced by *t*.
Another example is root final *c* of the root √*vac-* 'to speak' which was preserved in the acc. sg. *vāc-am*, dat. sg. *vāc-e* of the word *vāc-* 'word' as voiceless *c* although we would expect voicing which we see e.g. in instr. pl. *vāgbhis*. But this form is a special case because the suffix *-bhi-* < **-b^{h}i-* of the instr. pl. as well as its extended form *-bhyas* < **-b^{h}i-os* of the dat. abl. pl. caused voicing of a preceding stops as we can see from instr. pl. **marut-bhiḥ* > *marud-bhiḥ*, instr. pl. *vāgbhis* and dat. abl. pl. *vāgbhyas*. This difference can be explained as follows: at the time when the morpheme **-b^{h}i-* was added to the word, it had not yet become a proper suffix which could only occur bound to another word but it was still an independent adverb. Therefore, the rules of external sandhi, which governed the junction of individual words, were applied to the above forms *vāgbhis* and *vāgbhyas*. We can finally conclude that in morphological forms in Sanskrit, the rules of external sandhi do not apply. But if they appearently do, like in *marud-bhiḥ*, this is the result of a recent univerbation.
However, in some morphological forms we find assimilations which also apply to external sandhi. These are formations with *d* and *t* before *n* and *m* e.g. **adna-* > (22.3) *anna-* 'food' from the root √*ad-* 'to eat', or **vidyutmat* > *vidyunmat-* 'equipped with lightning' which is a derivation of *vidyút-* 'lightning' through the suffix *-mat*, as well as **mr̥d-máya-* > *mr̥nmáya-* 'earthen' which is a derivation of *mr̥d-* 'clay' through the suffix *-maya-*. For the corresponding external sandhi cf. chapter 10.

Lit.: Thumb 1905:135.

Accentuation of Vedic and Classical Sanskrit

For centuries, the Vedic texts had been handed down from one generation to the next by oral tradition only, which meant that the teacher spoke aloud to the student who repeated what he had heard. This technique was still in use after the Vedic language had become antiquated and was no longer in use. At some point in time, manuscript tradition began and the scholars found it necessary to introduce the stress marks *udātta* 'raised pitch', *anudātta* 'low pitch' and *svarita* 'high falling pitch' into the manuscripts in order to indicate pitches which were not longer in use. Therefore, we can assume that Vedic had a pitch accent which means that words were stressed through a change in pitch level and not through the intensification of breath.
In classical Sanskrit this accentuation then changed into a system in which the penultimate syllable was stressed if it was a long syllable, and the ante-penultimate syllable was stressed if the penultimate syllable was short. A long syllable needed to have a long vowel or a diphthong (*bhar**ā**maḥ* 'we carry') or it had to be a closed syllable (*bhar**a**nti* 'they carry'). A syllable was closed if its offset (which is the optional final consonant of a syllable) consisted of at least one consonant. In case of a short penultimate syllable, the ante-penultimate syllable was stressed (*bh**a**rati* 'he carries'). In case of both a short penultimate and a short ante-penultimate syllable the stress could also fall onto the fourth-to-last syllable if it was the root syllable (acc. sg. *d**u**hitaram* 'daughter'). This system is similar to the accentuation of Classical Latin with the exception that the accent could also fall onto the fourth-to-last syllable if the penultimate and ante-penultimate syllable were short which was not possible in Latin.

Remember
penultimate = second last / the last but one
ante-penultimate = third from last / last but two

Lit.: Mayrhofer 1978:26; Ziegler 24–25; Wackernagel 1896:278–300; Thumb 1905:43–45.

5 Vowel Changes

PIE *e and *o became SKR *a* and PIE *ē and *ō became SKR *ā*

The Sanskrit vowel *a* was very frequent because both PIE **e* and **o* merged into this sound whereas they regularly remained unchanged in Greek and Latin if they were not influenced by other developments. We can compare VED *dám-* 'house' < **dóm-* (GR *dómos*, LAT *domus*) as well as *jánas-* 'race' < **ǵenh*$_1$*os-* (GR *génos*, LAT *genus*) or *páti-* 'husband' < **póti-* (GR *pósis*, LAT *potis* 'mighty'). Similarly, we find the development of long **ē* and **ō* to *ā* in *ā́śu-* 'fast' < **ōḱu-* (GR *ōkús*) as well as in *dā́nam* 'gift' < **dṓnom* (LAT *dōnum*) or *rāṭ* 'king' < **rēǵ-s* (LAT *rēx*).

Lit.: Thumb 1959:49–52.

> **INFO:** The sound changes 10.1 **e* > *a*, 10.2 **ē* > *ā*, 10.3 **o* > *a* und 10.4 **ō* > *ā* are highly frequent and affect nearly every word. Therefore, these sound changes are sometimes summarized as SC 10 in order to save space in this book.

Brugmann's law

Brugmann's law states that PIE **o* became SKR *ā* in open syllables before a resonant: *dā́ru-* 'wood' < **dóru-* (GR *dóru*) and *jā́nu-* 'knee' < **ǵónu-* (GR *gónu*). This sound change explains the difference between the stem formation of kinship terms in nom. pl. *pit**ar**as* < **ph*$_2$*teres* 'fathers' (GR *patéres*), *māt**ar**as* < **māteres* 'mothers' (GR *mētéres*) and *bhrāt**ar**as* < **breh*$_2$*teres* 'brothers' (GR *phrā́teres*) with short *a* < **e* in the suffix *-tar-* < **-ter-* in comparison to *svas**ār**as* < **su̯esores* 'sisters' (LAT *sorōres*) with long *ā* because word final *āras* goes back to **ores* whereas the other words go back to a formation with **eres*. However, this sound change occurs also in other contexts like **sod-éye-ti* > SKR *sādáyati* 'causes to sit' (GOT *satjan*) where we do not find a resonant next to **o*.

Monophthongization of IIR *ai̯ > e and *au̯ > o

The above described developments of PIE **e* and **o* to SKR *a* led to the merger of the originally separate diphthongs PIE **ei̯*, **oi̯*, **ai̯* > IIR **ai̯* as well as PIE **eu̯*, **ou̯*, **au̯* > IIR **au̯*. The vacant positions of **e* and **o* were filled again through the monophthongization of IIR **ai̯* > SKR *e* and IIR **au̯* > SKR *o*. Examples for **ai̯* > *e* are **h*$_2$*éi̯dʰos-* > IIR **Hái̯dhas-* > **ái̯dhas-* > (11.1) *édhas-* 'firewood' (LAT *aedēs* 'house' < *'fireplace', GR *aĩthos* 'fire'), as well as **toi̯* > (10.3) **tai̯* > (11.1) *te* 'these' (GR *toí*) and 3. sg. **u̯oi̯de* > (10) **u̯ai̯da* > (11.1) *veda* 'he knows' (GR *oĩde*). Examples for **au̯* > *o* are **h*$_2$*éu̯ges-* > IIR **Háu̯jas-* > **áu̯jas-* > (11.2) *ójas-* 'vigor' which is related to LAT *augēre* 'to increase', as well as **h*$_1$*éu̯s-e-ti* > IIR **Háu̯šati* > **áu̯ṣati* > (11.2) *óṣati* 'he sears'. This sound change also occured in sandhi forms, which is described in the next chapter.

Shortening of long diphthongs

The monophthongization of **ai̯* > *e* and **au̯* > *o* created gaps in the phonological system which were filled again through the shortening of the original long diphthongs **āi̯* and **āu̯*, which in turn go back to PIE **ēi̯*, **ōi̯*, **āi̯* and **ēu̯*, **ōu̯*, **āi̯* respectively. The diphthongs of *gaús* < **gā́u̯s* < **gʷōu̯s* 'cow' (LAT *bōs*) and *naús* < **nā́u̯s* 'ship' (LAT *nāvis*) can therefore be traced back to PIE long diphthongs as well as the ending *-au* of the loc. sg. of the *u*-stems like in *śatrau* < **śatrā́u* 'at the enemy'. This rule also explains the forms of the *s*-aor. **é-i̯ēu̯g-s-m̥* > *áyaukṣam* 'I yoked (an animal)' in which case the former long diphthong **ēu̯* was shortened to *au*: **é-i̯ēu̯g-s-m̥* > (22.1) **é-i̯ēu̯k-s-m̥* > (c24) **é-i̯ēu̯k-ṣ-m̥* > (15.4) **é-i̯ēu̯k-ṣ-am* > (10) **á-i̯āu̯k-ṣ-am* > (11.2) *áyaukṣam* 'I yoked (an animal)'.

Lit.: Thumb 1905:55–57.

Exercises

The development of PIE *ĕ and *ŏ

A LAT _novus_ :: *_néu̯o-_ > (10.1) ___________ > (10.3) ___________ 'new' **B** LAT _lubet_ :: *_lub^{h}eti_ > (10.3) ___________ 'he longs for' **C** GR _treĩs_ :: *_tréi̯es_ > (10.1) ___________ 'three' **D** GR _beltíōn_ :: *_bélo-_ > (10.1) ___________ > (10.3) ___________ 'strong' **E** AV _x^{u}afna-_ :: *_su̯épno-_ > (10) ___________ 'sleep' **F** LAT _fert_ :: *_b^{h}éreti_ > (10.1) ___________ '(he) carries' **G** LAT _iugum_ :: *_i̯ugóm_ > (10.3) ___________ 'yoke' **H** GR _nephélē_ :: *_nébhos-_ > (10.1) ___________ > (10.3) ___________ 'mist, fog' **I** GR _thūmós_ :: *_dhū́mo-_ > (10.3) ___________ 'smoke' **J** LAT _medius_ :: *_médhi̯o-_ > (10.1) ___________ > (10.3) ___________ 'middle' **K** GR _eruthrós_ :: *_rudhiró-_ > (10.3) ___________ 'red' **L** LAT _augēre_ 'to increase' :: *_ugró-_ > (10.3) ___________ 'big' **M** GR _hēdús_ :: *_su̯ēdú-_ > (10.2) ___________ 'sweet' **N** GR _títhēmi_ :: *_dhé-dhe-mi_ > (10) ___________ > (27.1) ___________ 'I put' **O** LAT _serpō_ :: *_sérpō-mi_ > (10.1) ___________ > (10.4) ___________ 'I crawl' **P** GR _phérō_ :: *_b^{h}érō-mi_ > (10.1) ___________ > (10.4) ___________ 'I carry' **Q** LAT _monēre_ :: *_monéi̯eti_ > (10.1+10.5) ___________ 'he honors' **R** GR _nõton_ 'back (of the body)' :: *_sónu-_ > (10.5) ___________ 'mountain's crest'

Monophthongization and shortening of long diphthongs

A O-LAT _loucos_ :: *_lou̯ko-_ > (10.3) ___________ > (11.2) ___________ 'clearing' **B** dat. pl. GR _lukois_ :: instr. pl. *_u̯l̥k^{w}ōi̯s_ > (4.1) ___________ > (9) ___________ > (10.4) ___________ > (12.1) ___________ > (28.3) ___________ **C** LAT _ūrō_ :: *_$h_1$éu̯s-e-ti_ > (c1) ___________ > (10.1) ___________ > (c24) ___________ > (11.2) ___________ 'he/it burns' **D** _sūnú-_ 'son' :: loc. sg. *_sūnḗu̯_ > (10.2) ___________ > (11.2) ___________ **E** GR _Zeús_ :: *_di̯ḗu̯s_ > (10.2) ___________ > (c24) ___________ > (12.2) ___________ 'sky' **F** LAT _octō_ :: *_oḱtṓu̯_ > (c13) ___________ > (10) ___________ > (12.2) ___________ 'eight' **G** _leípō_ 'I leave' :: *_é-lḗi̯k^w-s-m̥_ > (4.1) ___________ > (9) ___________ > (15.4) ___________ > (c24) ___________ > (10.2) ___________ > (12.1) ___________ 'I let (past tense)'

4.1: *_k^w_ > *_k_	**10.4:** *_ō_ > _ā_	**27.1:** _C^h...C^h_ > _C...C^h_
9: *_l̥_ > _r̥_	**10.5:** *_ó_ > _ā_ / _ _RV_	**28.3:** *_s_ > _h_
10: *_e/o_ > _a_ and *_ē/ō_ > _ā_	**11.2:** *_au̯_ > _o_	**c1:** *_h_1e_ > _e_
10.1: *_e_ > _a_	**12.1:** *_āi̯_ > _ai̯_	**c13:** *_ḱt_ > _ṣt_
10.2: *_ē_ > _ā_	**12.2:** *_āu̯_ > _au_	**c24:** *_s_ > _ṣ_
10.3: *_o_ > _a_	**15.4:** *_m̥_ > _am_	

6 Sandhi of Vowels I - Vowel plus Vowel

Final	**Initial**										
	a	***ā***	***i***	***ī***	***u***	***ū***	***r̥***	***e***	***ai***	***o***	***au***
a / ā	*ā*	*ā*	*e*	*e*	*o*	*o*	*ar*	*ai*	*ai*	*au*	*au*
i / ī	*ya*	*yā*	*ī*	*ī*	*yu*	*yū*	*yr̥*	*ye*	*yai*	*yo*	*yau*
u / ū	*va*	*vā*	*vi*	*vī*	*ū*	*ū*	*vr̥*	*ve*	*vai*	*vo*	*vau*
r̥	*ra*	*rā*	*ri*	*rī*	*ru*	*rū*	*r̥̄*	*re*	*rai*	*ro*	*rau*

- ## Final ā̆, ī̆, ū̆, r̥ before a similar vowel as well as ī̆, ū̆, r̥ before a dissimilar vowel or diphthong

The table shows that the sandhi result of short or long *ā̆* was always *ā*, the result of short or long *ī̆* was always *ī*, and the result of short or long *ū̆* was always *ū*. Examples are *jayā abharat* > (s1.1) *jayābharat* 'the woman carried', *asti iha* > (s1.2) *astīha* 'is here' as well as *sādhu uktam* > (s1.3) *sādhūktam* 'well spoken'. These rules also apply to composite forms and morphological forms like *hima-ālayaḥ* > (26.1) *himālayaḥ* 'literally: the place of snow', *ripu uras* > (26.3) *ripūras* 'chest of the enemy' and VED 3.sg.subj. **bhára-a-ti* > (26.1) *bhárāti* 'it can be expected that he carries / that he will carry' or VED 1.sg.aor. **á-aj-am* > (26.1) *ā́jam* 'I impelled'. Final and initial *r̥* merged to *r̥̄* like in *kartr̥ r̥ju* > (s1.4) *kartr̥̄ju* 'honest doer' but as final *r̥* is extremely rare, this rule can be regarded as being theoretical only. If final *ī̆*, *ū̆* and *r̥* were placed before an initial dissimilar vowel or diphthong, they were transformed into their corresponding semivowels *y*, *v*, *r*. Examples are *nārī aikṣata* > (s3.1) *nāry_aikṣata* 'the woman saw', *astu etat* > (s3.2) *astv_etat* 'this shall be' and *kartr̥ akarot* > (s3.3) *kartr_akarot* 'the doer did'.

Lit.: Allen 1972:30; Thumb 1905:125; Ziegler 26–27.

- ## Final ā̆ plus ī̆, ū̆, e, o

Similar to the monophthongization of **ai̯* > *e* and **au̯* > *o* described in the previous chapter, we find a merger of *ā̆* + *ī̆* > *e* and *ā̆* + *ū̆* > *o* in sandhi forms. Examples are *na icchati* > (s2.1) *necchati* 'he doesn't wish', *na īkṣate* > (s2.1) *nekṣate* 'he doesn't see' and *tatra uvāsa* > (s2.2) *tatrovāsa* 'he lived there'. At first, the initial vowel of the second word was transformed into its corresponding semivowel before monophthongization took place: *na icchati* > *na_ycchati* > *necchati* as well as *tatra uvāsa* > *tatra_vvāsa* > *tatrovāsa*.

The sandhi of final long *ā* before *i* and *u* in *rājā iva* > (s2.1) *rājeva* 'like a king' or *sā uvāca* > (s2.2) *sovāca* 'she spoke' requires the shortening of the final long vowel as a first step: *rājā iva* > *rāja_iva* and *sā uvāca* > *sa_uvāca*. Afterwards, the hiatus of the vowels was resolved by transforming initial *i* and *u* into their corresponding semivowels *y* and *v*: *rāja_iva* > *rāja_yva* and *sa_uvāca* > *sa_vvāca*, before monophthongization led to *rājeva* and *sovāca*. If this sandhi had already occured at the stage of *rājā iva*, the vowels *ā*+*i* would have resulted in a long diphthong *āy* which subsequently would have been shortened to *ay* so that *rājā iva* would have yielded *ˣrājayva*.

We can explain the sandhi results of *tathā eva* > (s2.4) *tathaiva* 'just like that' and *na odanaḥ* > (s2.6) *naudanaḥ* 'not the rice' in a similar fashion. In these cases, the starting points of the second words were not *eva* and *odanaḥ* but their preforms **aiva* and **audanaḥ* in which the initial monophthongization had not yet taken place. First, the vowels *ā* and *a* contracted to *ā* thereby creating the long diphthongs **āy* and **āv* which were then shortened to *ay* and *av*: **tathā aiva* > **tathāyva* > *tathaiva* and **na audanaḥ* > **nāudanaḥ* > *naudanaḥ*. As *r̥* and *l̥* are also classified as being vowels in Sanskrit, the sequences *ār* and *āl* are also regarded as long diphthongs which explains the sandhi of *yathā r̥ṣiḥ* > (s2.3) *yatharṣiḥ* 'like a seer' in which the newly created long diphthong **ār* was shortened to *ar*.

Lit.: Allen 1972:34–36; Thumb 1905:125; Ziegler 2012:26–27.

Exercises

E1 Insert the sandhi results

A *kā iyam* > (s2.1) ___________ 'Who is this woman?' **B** *tasya auṣadham* > (s2.7) ___________ 'his medicine' **C** *trīṇi etāni* > (s3.1) ___________ 'these three' **D** *na aikṣata* > (2.5) ___________ 'he didn't see' **E** *vinā īrṣyayā* > (s2.1) ___________ 'without jealousy' **F** *astu etat* > (s3.2) ___________ 'this shall be' **G** *asti iha* > (s1.2) ___________ 'is here' **H** *devī iva* > (s1.2) ___________ 'like a goddess' **I** *adya eva* > (s2.4) ___________ 'still today' **J** *bahūni ahāni* > (s3.1) ___________ 'many days' **K** *na īkṣe* > (s2.1) ___________ 'I don't see' **L** *tasya autsukyam* > (s2.7) ___________ 'his desire' **M** *narī īkṣate* > (s1.2) ___________ 'the woman sees' **N** *madhu iva* > (s3.2) ___________ 'like honey' **O** *sā r̥ddhiḥ* > (s2.3) ___________ 'this miraculous power' **P** *sā oṣadhiḥ* > (s2.6) ___________ 'this medicinal herb' **Q** *yadi icchet* > (s1.2) ___________ 'if he could wish' **R** *yathā aiśvaryam* > (s2.5) ___________ 'like the supremacy' **S** *sā uktvā* > (s2.2) ___________ 'after she had spoken' **T** *pitr̥ anuvartanāt* > (s3.3) ___________ 'out of obedience to the father' **U** *tena uktam* > (s2.2) ___________ 'is was said by him' **V** *sahasā utthāya* > (s2.2) ___________ 'standing up suddenly'

E2 Insert the historical development of the sandhi forms

A *adya eva* > (s2.4) *adyaiva* 'still today'

___________ > (26.1) ___________ > (12.1) ___________

B *na auñchat* > (s2.7) *nauñchat* 'he didn't gather'

___________ > (26.1) ___________ > (12.2) ___________

C *yathā r̥ṣiḥ* > (s2.3) *yatharṣiḥ* 'like a seer'

___________ > (12.3) ___________ > (12.3) ___________

D *sā uktvā* > (s2.2) *soktvā* 'after she had spoken'

___________ > (shortening of final *ā*) ___________ > (11.2) ___________

11.2: **au̯* > *o*	**s1.2:** *ī̆* + *ī̆* > *ī*	**s2.5:** *ā̆* + *ai* > *ai*
12.1: **āi̯* > *ai̯*	**s2.1:** *ā̆* + *ī̆* > *e*	**s2.6:** *ā̆* + *o* > *au*
12.2: **āu̯* > *au̯*	**s2.2:** *ā̆* + *ū̆* > *o*	**s3.1:** *ī̆* + *V* > *y*_*V* (*V* ≠ *ī̆*)
12.3: **ār* > *ar*	**s2.3:** *ā̆* + *r̥̄̆* > *ar*	**s3.2:** *ū̆* + *V* > *v*_V (*V* ≠ *ū̆*)
26.1: *ā̆* + *ā̆* > *ā*	**s2.4:** *ā̆* + *e* > *ai*	**s3.3:** *r̥̄̆* + V > *r*_V (*V* ≠ *r̥̄̆*)
	s2.7: *ā̆* + *au* > *au*	

7 Vowel Sandhi II - Diphthong plus Vowel

Final	**Initial**										
	a	***ā***	***i***	***ī***	***u***	***ū***	***r̥***	***e***	***ai***	***o***	***au***
e	*e* ’	*a ā*	*a i*	*a ī*	*a u*	*a ū*	*a r̥*	*a e*	*a ai*	*a o*	*a au*
ai	*ā a*	*ā ā*	*ā i*	*ā ī*	*ā u*	*ā ū*	*ā r̥*	*ā e*	*ā ai*	*ā o*	*ā au*
o	*o* ’	*avā*	*avi*	*avī*	*avu*	*avū*	*avr̥*	*ave*	*avai*	*avo*	*avau*
au	*āva*	*āvā*	*āvi*	*āvī*	*āvu*	*āvū*	*āvr̥*	*āve*	*āvai*	*āvo*	*āvau*

Final e, o before an initial vowel except before short *a*. Final *ai, au* before a vowel.

Final *e* und *o* before an initial vowel except *a* became *a* in sandhi forms, thus causing a hiatus between the final and the initial vowel: *yoge ālasyam* > (s4.1) *yoga_ālasyam* ‘idleness in yoga’ and *prabho ihi* > (s4.4) *prabha_ihi* ‘oh ye mighty one, come!’.

The synchronic state seems to be the result of a sound change *e* > *a* and *o* > *a*. But this is proven to be wrong when taking into account the diachronic development. The starting point of the synchronic sandhi was not *e* and *o* but their preforms **ay* and **av*. This original state of affairs was preserved in the unusual sandhi forms *yogay_ālasyam* ‘idleness in yoga’ and *prabhav_ihi* ‘oh ye mighty one, come!’ out of which the classic sandhi forms *yoga_ālasyam* and *prabha_ihi* can be deduced by assuming an intervocalic loss of the semivowels *y* and *v*.

This development also explains the sandhi result of *ai* before an initial vowel like in *devyai iha* > (s4.7) *devyā_iha* ‘the goddess here’. In this case, we also do not start explaining the synchronic state through a sound change **ay* > *ā* but by assuming the loss of the semivowel *y* in the preform **āy* which can still be found in the unusual sandhi form *devyāy_iha* which still displays the preform **āy* of the diphthong *ai* without the loss of the semivowel.

The development of *āv* was contrary to the above given examples because, in this case, it was the semivowel *v* which usually remained. Therefore, the regular sandhi of *nr̥pau ādiśataḥ* frequently yielded *nr̥pāv_ādiśataḥ* ‘the two kings commanded’ and the sandhi *nr̥pā_ādiśataḥ* was less frequent. The sandhi form *nr̥pāv_ādiśataḥ* preserved the original sounds whereas the less frequent *nr̥pā_ādiśataḥ* shows the loss of intervocalic *v*.

This loss of final semivowels after a long vowel can be also found in morphological forms independent of sandhi forms. Already in PIE, the preform of nom. sg. *sakhā* ‘friend’ < **sek*^{w}*h*$_{2}$*ō* < **sek*^{w}*h*$_{2}$*ōi̯* had lost its final **i̯* which can be found in the reflex of dat. sg. *sakhye* < **sek*^{w}*h*$_{2}$*-i̯-ei̯*. Another example is the coexistence of the forms *aṣṭaú* and *aṣṭā́* ‘eight’ which both go back to the preform **aṣṭā́u*. On the one hand, the loss of final **u̯* caused **aṣṭā́u* to become *aṣṭā́* while on the other hand, the shortening of the final long diphthong **āu̯* created the form *aṣṭaú*.

Lit.: Allen 1972:37–38.

Final e, o before short *a*

The sandhi of *e* and *o* before short *a* is written with an apostrophe *te abruvan* > (s4.3) *te ’bruvan* ‘those spoke’ and *prabho atra* > (s4.6) *prabho ’tra* ‘you mighty one here!’ which might create the impression that we are dealing with the elision of the initial *a*. Such a sound change is, however, very improbable as the elision of initial vowels is barely ever found in other forms. But, as we find the common developments **aya* > *e* (*bhājayati* > (21.5) *bhājeti* ‘he shares’) as well as **ava* > *o* (*avatāra* > (21.6) *otāra* ‘origin’) in Early Middle Indic, it seems very probably that this sandhi is an early example of a development which set in later at full scale. This can also explain the honorific form of address *bhavas* > *bhos* in Sanskrit. Therefore, in the preforms **tay_abruvan* and **prabhav_atra* we find the development of *ay_a* > *e* and *av_a* > *o* as a single sound change.

Lit.: Allen 1972:39–45; Thumb 1905:126ff; Malzahn 2001:134–136.

Exercises

E1 Insert the sandhi forms

A *mriyante iti* > (s4.1) ____________ 'they said so' **B** *dyotate avati ca* > (s4.3) ____________ '(the sun) shines and refreshes' **C** *nagare iha* > (s4.1) ____________ 'here in the city' **D** *te api* > (s4.3) ____________ 'even these' **E** *vane āste* > (s4.1) ____________ 'he sits in the forest' **F** *guro īkṣasva* > (s4.4) ____________ 'teacher, look!' **G** *tau ubhau* > (s4.9) ____________ 'these two' **H** *īkṣāvahai indum* > (s4.7) ____________ 'we two want to see the moon' **I** *gr̥he agaccham* > (s4.3) ____________ 'I went into the house'

E2 Explain the historic development of the following sandhi forms

A	*mriyante iti*	> (s4.1) *mriyanta iti*	'they said so'
B	*tau ubhau*	> (s4.9) *tāv_ubhau*	'these two'
C	*īkṣāvahai indum*	> (s4.7) *īkṣāvahā_indum*	'we two want to see the moon'
D	*vane āste*	> (s4.2) *vanay_aste*	'he sits in the forest'
E	*gr̥he agaccham*	> (s4.3) *gr̥he 'gaccham*	'I went into the house'

E3 Derive the sandhi forms historically (additional exercise to the next chapter)

A Synchronic Sandhi: *āgatāḥ r̥śayaḥ* > (s6.4) ____________ 'the seers have come'

Historic Explanation: *āgatās r̥śayaḥ* > (22.2) ____________ > (20.1) ____________

B Synchronic Sandhi: *gīḥ rocate* > (s6.6) ____________ 'the voice pleases (someone)'

Historic Explanation: *gīs rocate* > (22.2) ____________ > (c25) ____________

> (20.1) ____________

C Synchronic Sandhi: *gataḥ araṇye* > (s6.3) ____________ 'gone to the woods'

Historic Explanation: *gatas araṇye* > (22.2) ____________ > (20.1) ____________

> (21.3) ____________ > (11.2) ____________

s1.4: *r̥̆̄ + r̥̆̄ > r̥̄*	**s4.7:** *ai + V > ā_V*	**11.2:** **au̯ > o*
s4.1: *e + V > a_V (V≠ ă)*	**s4.9:** *au + V > āv_V*	**20.1:** **z / ẓ* > Ø without CL
s4.3: *e + ă > e'*	**s6.3:** *aḥ + a > o'*	**21.3:** Ø > *u̯*
s4.4: *o + V > a_V (V≠ ă)*	**s6.4:** *āḥ + G/V > ā _G/V*	**22.2:** *K > G / _G*
s4.5: *o + V > av (V≠ ă)*	**s6.6:** *Vḥ + r > V̄_r (V ≠ a, ā)*	**c25:** **z > ẓ / r,r̥,ŭ̄,k,ĭ̄ _*

8 Visarga-Sandhi before Voiced Sounds

Final visarga before voiced initial sounds

Final	Initial				
	a	Vowel	***n/m/y/l/v/h***	***r***	***g/gh/j/jh/ḍ/ḍh/d/dh/b/bh***
***as > aḥ**	*o '*	*a*	*o*	*o*	*o*
***ās > āḥ**	*ā*	*ā*	*ā*	*ā*	*ā*
***(V)s > (V)ḥ**	*r*	*r*	*r*	*V̄*	*r*

Loss of final voiced *z after a and ā. Preservation of original r.

The explanation of the sandhi forms *narāḥ īkṣante* > (s6.4) *narā_īkṣante* 'the people look' and *naraḥ īkṣate* > (s6.1) *nara_īkṣate* 'the person looks' starts by tracing visarga *ḥ* back to its preform **s*. Final *-s* after long *ā* was lost in sandhi forms before voiced sounds. First, an assimilation of voice **s* > **z* took place before voiced **z* was lost: **narās īkṣante* > (22.2) **narāz īkṣate* > (20.1) *narā_īkṣante*.

We see a parallel development of the singular form **naras īkṣate* > (22.2) **naraz_īkṣate* > (20.1) *nara_īkṣate* if not followed by short *a*. As the loss of final **z* should have been accompanied by a compensatory lengthening of the preceding short vowel (cf. chapter 12), the sandhi result *nara_īkṣate* was probably not regular according to sound laws but due to an analogical reshaping with the preservation of short *a*. The result of the lengthening of short *a* > *ā* in the sandhi of nom. sg. *nara_īkṣate* would have otherwise phonologically coincided with the sandhi result of the nom. pl. *narā_īkṣante*.

If the final visarga *ḥ* does not go back to **s* but to **r*, which is also possible, this sound *r* remained. The sandhi of *prātaḥ gacchati* > (s7.1) *prātar_gacchati* 'he walks in the morning' was therefore not *ˣprāto_gacchati* because *prātaḥ* goes back to *prātar* with original *r* which was preserved in the sandhi form. The sandhi of *pitaḥ īkṣasva* > (s7.1) *pitar_īkṣasva* 'father, look!' and *dvāḥ dṛśyate* > (7.2) *dvār_dṛśyate* 'the door is seen' can be explained likewise because *pitaḥ* goes back to *pitar* and *dvāḥ* goes back to *dvār*, both with final *-r*.

Lit.: Stiehl 2007:314; Ziegler 30–31.

The developments *-as > *az- > -o and *-asa- > -o-

The sandhi of *Nalaḥ nāma* > (s6.2) *Nalo_nāma* 'by the name of Nala' can be explained by the development of **s* to voiced **z* with subsequent loss of the sibilant starting from its preform *Nalas nāma* > (22.2) **Nalaz_nāma* > (20.1) **NalaØ_nāma*. This loss was then compensated by the insertion of the semivowel **u̯* in order to keep up the syllabic structure. This created the sequence **au̯* which developed to *o* regularly: **NalaØ_nāma* > (21.3) **Nalau̯_nāma* > (11.2) *Nalo_nāma*. We see this development also in morphological forms like the instr. pl. *manasbhiḥ* > (s6.4) *manobhiḥ* of *manas-* 'mind' in which we find the sequence *-as-* before the ending *-bhiḥ* which begins with a labial sound. This sound change, in which a labial *u̯* compensated the loss of final *z*, probably originated before labial consonants and was then analogically transferred to other contexts as well.

The sandhi of *nadyaḥ avahan* > (s6.3) *nadyo 'vahan* 'the rivers flew' is synchronically described through the elision of the initial *a* similar to the explanation of *prabho atra* > (s4.6) *prabho 'tra* described in the previous chapter but in both cases, we are actually dealing with the same sound change. Starting with the preform **nadyas avahan*, final **as* became voiced **az* before **z* was lost, but in order to compensate this loss, the semivowel **u̯* was inserted. This generated the sequence **au̯a* wich developed to *o*: **nadyas_avahan* > (22.2) **nadyaz_avahan* > (20.1) **nadyaØ_avahan* > (21.3) **nadyau̯_avahan* > (21.6) *nadyo 'vahan*.

Lit.: Malzahn 2001:135.

- **Analogical restitution of *r* for lost *-ẓ after *u, ū, i, ī***

The sandhi of *guruḥ īkṣate* > *gurur_īkṣate* 'the guru looks' can be explained from the preform **gurus* in which **s* was first voiced to **z* and then became retroflex **ẓ* according to the ruki rule: **gurus_īkṣate* > (22.2) **guruz_īkṣate* > (c25) **guruẓ_īkṣate*. Also **ẓ* had to vanish according to regular sound changes analogous to the development of **z*. But at this point, the formerly lost **ẓ* was reintroduced as *r* in analogy to the structure of the nom. sg. Likewise, the final short vowel was preserved in analogy to its preform although the loss of **z* or **ẓ* was normally accompanied by compensatory vowel lenghthening: **guruẓ_īkṣate* > (20.1) **guruØ_īkṣate* > (21.4) *gurur_īkṣate*. This sound change also occurs morphologically in the instr. pl. **cakṣus-bhiḥ* > *cakṣurbhiḥ* from *cakṣus-* 'eye'.
Before *r*, a lost **ẓ* could not be reestablished as *r* because the sequence of two retroflex *r*-sounds was prevented by dissimilatory effects similar to *usra-* 'bright' which should have developed regularly to *ˣuṣra-* via the ruki rule.
The initial *r* of *rohati* in *tarus rohati* 'the tree grows' > (22.2) **taruz_rohati* prevented the development of **z* to retroflex **ẓ*. Therefore, **ẓ* was lost regularly which led to a lengthening of the preceding short vowel: **taruz_rohati* > (c25) **taruẓ_rohati* > (20.3) *tarū_rohati*. After a long vowel or diphthong, we do not see any lengthening effect so that *r* was lost completely: *gopayos rathaḥ* > *gopayo_rathaḥ* 'the chariot of the shepherds'.

Exercises

E1 Insert the synchronic sandhi forms. Remember that *punaḥ* goes back to **punar* with *r*.

A *āgatāḥ ṛśayaḥ* > (s6.4) ____________ 'the seers have come' **B** *gīḥ rocate* > (s6.6) ____________ 'the voice pleases (someone)' **C** *śiśuḥ roditi* > (s6.6) ____________ 'the child cries' **D** *punaḥ rohati* > (s6.6) ____________ 'he grows again' **E** *kaḥ api* > (s6.3) ____________ 'someone' **F** *gataḥ araṇye* > (s6.3) ____________ 'gone to the woods' **G** *ānītaḥ dīpaḥ* > (s6.2) ____________ 'the lamp which has been brought' **H** *nṛpaḥ ādiśat* > (s6.1) ____________ 'the king commanded' **I** *naraḥ ayam* > (s6.3) ____________ 'this man' **J** *devaḥ api* > (s6.3) ____________ 'even the god' **K** *nṛpaḥ uvāca* > (s6.1) ____________ 'the king said' **L** *devāḥ ūcuḥ* > (s6.4) ____________ 'the gods spoke' **M** *vidhuḥ rājate* > (s6.6) ____________ 'the moon shines' **N** *dāsāḥ gacchanti* > (s6.4) ____________ 'the slaves go' **O** *vṛkṣāḥ rohanti* > (s6.4) ____________ 'the trees grow' **P** *punaḥ rogī* > (s6.6) ____________ 'ill again' **Q** *kaḥ ṛṣiḥ* > (s6.1) ____________ 'who is the seer?' **R** *bālaiḥ rūpavadbhiḥ* > (s6.6) ____________ 'with beautiful children' **S** *vṛkṣaḥ rohati* > (s6.2) ____________ 'the tree grows' **T** *nṛpāḥ jayanti* > (s6.4) ____________ 'the kings overcome'

s6.1: *aḥ + V > a _V* (V≠a)	**s6.4:** *āḥ + G/V > ā _G/V*
s.6.2: *aḥ + G > o _G*	**s6.6:** *Vḥ + r > V̄ _r* (V ≠ a, ā)
s6.3: *aḥ + a > o '*	

9 Visarga Sandhi Before Voiceless Sounds

Visarga before initial voiceless sounds

Final	Initial											
	Sanskrit							Vedic				
	k(h)	*p(h)*	*c(h)*	*ṭ(h)*	*t(h)*	*ś, ṣ, s*	##	*k(h)*	*p(h)*	*ś*	*ṣ*	*s*	##
ḥ	*ḥ*	*ḥ*	*ś*	*ṣ*	*s*	*ḥ*	*ḥ*	[x]	[φ]	*ś*	*ṣ*	*s*	*ḥ*

Synchronic sandhi rules vs. historical development

The description of synchronic sandhi rules takes visarga *ḥ* as the starting point whereas a diachronic description always starts with the preform **s* or **r* in order to explain all the phonological details correctly. Seen in a diachronic perspective, it is completely wrong to say that in the case of the classical sandhi of *devaḥ tatra* > (s8.4) *devas_tatra* 'the god over there' the visarga *ḥ* became *s* before *t* because we must start from the preform *devas*. It is true that this preform developed to *devaḥ* in the final position but in the case of *devas_tatra* the original final *s* was preserved before an initial *t*. This means that in this case there had never been a sound change **s* > *ḥ*. Respectively, the development of *kūrmaḥ calati* > (s8.3) *kūrmaś_calati* 'the turtle crawls' is not explained by assuming a sound change *ḥ* > *ś* before *c* but by positing that the original dental fricative **s* in the preform *kūrmas* had become the palatal fricative * *ś* before palatal *c* due to assimilation.

Classical sandhi of final -*ḥ* before voiceless consonants

Final visarga *ḥ* was therefore never original but always originated secondarily out of -*s* or -*r* (*devas* > *devaḥ* 'god', *punar* > *punaḥ* 'again'). In classical Sanskrit, visarga *ḥ* can be found in the absolute final position, before *k, kh, p, ph* (e.g. *aśvaḥ_khādati* 'the horse eats', *kapiḥ_pibati* 'the monkey drinks') and also before the sibilants *ś, ṣ, s* (e.g. *guruḥ_śapate* 'the teacher swears', *naraḥ_ṣṭhīvati* 'the man spits'). Before stops, visarga *ḥ* surfaces as a homorganic sibilant. Before palatal *c, ch*, it appears as palatal *ś* (*kūrmaḥ calati* > (s8.4) *kūrmaś_calati* 'the turtle moves'), before retroflex *ṭ, ṭh*, it appears as retroflex *ṣ* (*kapiḥ ṭīkate* > (s8.2b) *kapiṣ_ṭīkate* 'the monkey jumps') and before dental *t, th* it appears as dental *s* (*devaḥ tatra* > (8.2c) *devas_tatra* 'the god over there').

Emergence of classical sandhi

Vedic sandhi forms differ to some extent from the sandhi of the classical language and it is possible to demonstrate that the synchronic sandhi rules of classical Sanskrit are the result of a long development. Originally, *s* did not become *ḥ* before the sibilants *s, ś, ṣ* but was assimilated to the following sibilant, just like before the corresponding stop consonant (cf. s8 and s9). This can be seen in the Vedic sandhi forms *vaḥ śivátamo* > (s9.1) *vaś_śivátamo* as an example for *s* before *ś*, as well as in *dévīḥ ṣaṭ* > (s9.2) *dévīṣ_ṣaṭ* as an example for *s* before *ṣ*, and finally in *naḥ sapátnā* > (s9.3) *nas_sapátnā* as an example for *s* before *s*. Vedic manuscripts additionally show divergent writings of visarga *ḥ* before *k(h)* and *p(h)* which hints at different pronunciations before these sounds. As there were no corresponding sibilants in the guttural and labial series of stops into which original *s* could have developed, it was probably pronounced as a homorganic fricative. Before *k(h)* it was probably the allophone [x] similar to *ch* in *Loch Ness Monster* or German *lachen* 'to laugh' and before *p(h)* it was probably the allophone [φ], a bilabial fricative, similar to the sound when blowing out a candle, which appears in Japanese in the initial position of the word *Fujiyama*.

Lit.: Macdonell 1916:34.

Exercises

OVERVIEW: Historical development of final *s before voiceless sounds

Preform	Assimilation / Vedic Sandhi	Classical Sandhi
as_c(h)	> *aś_c(h)*	-
as_t̤(h)	> *aṣ_ṭ(h)*	-
as_k(h)	> VED *ax_k(h)*	> SKR *aḥ_k(h)*
as_p(h)	> VED *aφ_p(h)*	> SKR *aḥ_p(h)*

E1 Insert the sandhi forms

Preform	Vedic Sandhi	Classical Sandhi	Translation
puruṣas khanati			'the man digs'
kapis pibati			'the monkey drinks'
prathamas sargaḥ			'the first chant'
gurus śapate			'the teacher swears'
naras ṣṭhīvati			'the man spits'

E2 Visarga before voiced initial sound (additional exercise to the next chapter)

A *āgatāḥ r̥ṣayaḥ* > (s6.4) ____________ 'the seers have come' **B** *nr̥paḥ uvāca* > (s6.1) ____________ 'the king spoke' **C** *ānītaḥ dīpaḥ* > (s6.2) ____________ 'the lamp which has been brought' **D** *nadyaḥ avahan* > (s6.3) ____________ 'the rivers flew' **E** *vidhuḥ rājate* > (s6.6) ____________ 'the moon shines' **F** *guruḥ īkṣate* > (s6.5) ________ 'the guru sees'

s6.1: *aḥ + V > a_V* (*V*≠a)	**s6.4:** *āḥ + G/V > ā G/V*
s6.2: *aḥ + G > o_G*	**s6.5:** *Vḥ + G/V > Vr_G/V* (*V ≠ a, ā*)
s6.3: *aḥ + a > o '*	**s6.6:** *Vḥ + r > V̄_r* (*V ≠ a, ā*)

Historical development of final *s before voiced sounds

Preform	Voicing	Cerebralization	Loss	Restitution	Monophthongization
**ās_V/G*	> **āz_V/G*	-	> **āØV/G*	-	-
**as_V*	> **az_V*	-	> **aØ_V*	-	-
**as_a*	> **aza*	-	> **aØ_a*	> **au̯_a*	> *o*
**as_G*	> **az_G*	-	> **aØ_G*	> **au̯_G*	> *oG*
**u/is_r*	> *u/iz_r*	> *u/iẓ_r*	> *ū/ī_r*	-	-
**us_V/G*	> **uz_V/G*	> **uẓ_V/G*	> **uØ_V/G*	> *ur_V/G*	-

CONSONANTS

10 Assimilation I

Voicing of voiceless stops

We can see the assimilation of voiceless stops to adjacent voiced sounds in sandhi forms like *dik gajaḥ* > (s11.1) *dig_gajaḥ* 'world elephant', *āsīt rājā* > (s11.2) *āsīd_rāja* 'there was a king', *samrāṭ āsīt* > (s11.3) *samrāḍ_āsīt* 'there was a ruler' as well as in morphological formations like instr. pl. **vākbhis* > (22.2) *vāgbhis* of *vāc-* 'voice'. A pecularity is the sandhi of voiceless stops to adjacent *h* in examples like *suhr̥t hasati* > (s13.2) *suhr̥d_dhasati* 'the friend laughs', *madhuliṭ hasati* > (s13.3) *madhuliḍ_ḍhasati* 'the bee laughs', *vāk harṣayati* > (s13.1) *vāg_gharṣayati* 'language delights' in which the sequence of voiceless stop plus *h* was replaced by a sequence of voiced stop plus voiced aspirated stop. SKR *h* was regarded as a voiced consonant and therefore it caused assimilation of a preceding voiceless consonant. But the sequence *d+h*, which originated out of the assimiliation *t* > *d* / _*h* in words like *suhr̥t hasati* > (s11.2) **suhr̥d_hasati*, was regarded as a single consonant *dh* which violated the syllabification rules of the language because the sequence *t+h* had consisted of two consonants. Therefore, *h* was articulated as a homorganic aspirated stop which caused **suhr̥d_hasati* to become *suhr̥d_dhasati* in order to reestablish a phonological sequence of two consonants.

Deaspiration of aspirated stops

Aspirated stops were deaspirated in the final position and before all sounds except before a vowel, semivowels and nasals. This can be seen from roots like √*budh-* 'to become or be aware of' with a root final aspirated stop which lost its aspiration before morphemes that started with unaspirated stops. That is also the reason why *dh* became *t* before *s* in 3. sg. des. **bu-bhudh-s-a-te* > (22.5) *bu-bhutsate* 'he wants to get to know' and in 3. sg. fut. **bhodh-sya-ti* > (22.5) *bhotsyati* 'he will wake up'. Root final *dh* was also deaspirated before an aspirated consonant like in 2. pl. **rundh-dhve* > (22.4) *rund-dhve* 'you hold back' from the root √*rudh-* 'to hold back'. In other words, the aspiration of two adjacent aspirated consonants was transferred to the end of the consonant cluster and articulated only once for the whole consonant group.

Devoicing of voiced stops

The assimilation of voiced stops to devoiced stops can be seen in sandhi forms like in *āpad kāle* > (22.1) *āpat_kāle* 'at the time of misfortune' as well as in morphological formations like **bʰe̯id-tr̥* > (10.1) **bhai̯d-tr̥* > (11.1) **bhed-tr̥* > (22.1) *bhettr̥* 'splitter' which is from the root √*bhid-* 'to split'.

Progressive assimilation of retroflex consonants

The assimilation processes above can be classified as regressive assimilations because it is the second element that transfers its features onto the first element. The followings words are examples for progressive assimilations in which the first element transfers its features onto the second element. In **iṣ-ta-* > (17.1) *iṣṭa-* 'searched', which is related to *iṣa-* 'searching', we find dental *t* being assimilated to retroflex *ṭ* by the preceding retroflex *ṣ*. Another example of such an assimilation can be seen in **mizdhám* > (20.3) *mīḍhám* 'reward' which is cognate to AV *miždəm*. After the assimilation of **mizdhám* > (17.2) **miẓḍhám*, voiced retroflex **ẓ* was lost with compensatory lengthening but its retroflex articulation was preserved in retroflex *ḍh*: **miẓḍhám* > (20.3) *mīḍhám*.

Exercises

E1 Assimilations of stops in sandhi forms and before the ending *-bhiḥ*

A *apatat bhuvi* > (s11.2) __________ 'he fell to the ground' **B** *vaṇik bhāṣate* > (s11.1) __________ 'the merchand speaks' **C** *mahat dhanuḥ* > (s11.2) __________ 'big bow' **D** nom. sg. *marut* :: instr. pl. **marutbhiḥ* > (22.2) __________ **E** *kakup atra* > (s11.4) __________ 'this area here' **F** *ap jaḥ* > (s11.4) __________ 'water-born' **G** *nagarāt girim* > (s11.2) __________ 'from the city to the mountain' **H** *parivrāṭ ayam* > (s11.3) __________ 'he is a liar' **I** *suhr̥t dhāvati* > (s11.2) __________ 'the friend runs' **J** *suhr̥t ahasat* > (s11.2) __________ 'the friend laughed' **K** *parivrāṭ gacchati* > (s11.3) __________ 'the liar walks' **L** *abharat annam* > (s11.1) __________ 'he brought the food' **M** *sarit atra* > (s11.2) __________ 'the river here' **N** *samyak uktam* > (s11.1) __________ 'well said' **O** *tat hi* > (s13.2) __________ 'this indeed' **P** *āsīt hanuḥ* > (s13.2) __________ 'it was the chin' **Q** *tat hetuḥ* > (s13.2) __________ 'the reason thereof' **R** *vāk hi* > (s13.1) __________ 'the speech indeed' **S** *samyak hutaḥ* > (s13.1) __________ 'correctly immolated' **T** *kakup hi* > (s13.4) __________ 'the direction indeed'

E2 Devoicing and deaspiration in morphological formations

A √*pad-* 'to fall' :: 3. sg. des. **pid-s-a-ti* > (22.1) __________ 'he wants to fall' **B** √*dā-* 'to give' :: 3. sg. des. **dí-d-s-a-ti* > (22.1) __________ 'he wants to give' **C** 3. sg. mid. **dá-d-te* > (22.1) __________ 'he gives' **D** **da-d-tá-* > (22.1) __________ 'given' **E** √*nod-* 'to push' :: **nudtá-* > (22.1) __________ 'pushed' **F** √*syand-* 'flowing swiftly' :: **syand-tr̥-* > (22.1) __________ 'moving' **G** √*bhed-* 'to split' :: 3. sg. **bhinád-ti* > (22.1) __________ 'he splits' **H** √*mad-* 'to be happy' :: PPP **madtá-* > (22.1) __________ 'drunk' **I** √*bādh-* 'to vex' :: 3. sg. des. **bī-bhadh-s-a-te* > (22.5) __________ 'he finds disgusting' **J** √*labh-* 'to take' :: Fut. 1. sg. **labh-sye* > (22.5) __________ 'I will take'

s11.1:	*k + D > g_D*	**s11.4:**	*p + D > b_D*	**s13.4:**	*p +h > b_bh*
s11.2:	*t + D > d_D*	**s13.1:**	*k +h > g_gh*	**22.1:**	*G > K / _K*
s11.3:	*ṭ + D > ḍ_D*	**s13.2:**	*t +h > d_dh*	**22.2:**	*K > G / _G*
				22.5:	D^H *> T / _S*

11 Assimilation II

Stop before nasal

A stop consonant before a nasal became a homorganic nasal in sandhi forms. In the case of voiceless sounds before a nasal, we must assume voicing before the development of the stop to a nasal (cf. last chapter). Examples are *vāk me* > (s12.1) *vāṅ_me* 'my speech', *madhuliṭ nadati* > (s12.2) *madhuliṇ_nadati* 'the bee hums', *nagarāt nagaram* > (s12.3) *nagarān_nagaram* 'from city to city' and *kakup mr̥gyate* > (s12.4) *kapum_mr̥gyate* 'the direction is searched for'. In the case of dental *d*, we find this sound change also in morphological forms. Therefore, *anna-* 'food' goes back to **adna-* which can be seen by comparing it to *admi* 'I eat', and the PPP *nunná-* 'pushed' goes back to **nudná-* from the root √*nud-* 'to push'. After palatal *j*, the dental nasal *n* became palatal *ñ* which can be deduced by comparing *jñāti* 'he knows' < **ǵnéh$_3$-ti* to LAT *gnōscit*.

Nasal before stop / Anusvāra

A nasal consonant always assimilated to the place of articulation of the following consonant. In this manner, dental *n* of *tān* 'these' became palatal *ñ* in *tān janān* > (s14.3) *tāñ_janān* 'these people' and retroflex *ṇ* in *tān ḍambarān* > (s14.2) *tāṇ_ḍambarān* 'this noise'. Labial *m* became dental *n* before dental sounds e.g. **bhrāmtá* > (22.9) *bhrāntá-* 'confused' from the root √*bhram-* 'wandering around'. The same sound change also occurred before *v* in perfect participle forms e.g. **ja-gam-vān* > *jaganvān* 'having gone' from the root √*gam-* 'to go'. Before consonants, the sandhi of *m* was anusvāra *ṃ*: *svargam jagāma* > (s64.1) *svargaṃ_jagāma* 'he went to the sky' and *bhadram te* > (s64.1) *bhadraṃ_te* 'hail to thee!'. Nasals before homorganic stops as well as *m* before *s* could also be written with anusvāra e.g. **ǵ^{h}ans-ó-* > (c9) **hansó-* > (10) **hansá-* > (s64.1) *haṃsá-* 'swan' and **mēmsó-* > (10) **māmsá-* > (s64.1) *māṃsá-* 'meat'.

Rare sandhi of nasal before initial *l*

A rare sandhi form is the combination of a final nasal before an initial *l*, in which case the nasal becomes anusvāra and the initial *l* is doubled: *tān lokān* > (s15.4) *tāṃl_lokān* 'these worlds' as well as *amuṣmin loke* > (s15.4) *amuṣmiṃl_loke* 'in that world'. The starting point of this sandhi must be seen in the first element of compounds like **tāns* (*lokān*) with an etymological final double consonant, in which case **s* became voiced **z* before being totally assimilated to the following *l*. As a last step, *m* became anusvāra *ṃ* before a following consonant: **tāns lokān* > (22.2) **tānz_lokān* > (22.6) **tānl_lokān* > (s64.1) **tāṃl_lokān*. In this phonological context, Vedic manuscripts sometimes show anunāsika *m̐* for *ṃ*. Structurally, this sound change must be compared to the sandhi of *devān ca* > (s15.1) *devāṃś_ca* (cf. chapter 21).

Sandhi of dental stop before consonant

Final *t* or *d* in sandhi assimilated completely to following consonants. They became palatal before palatal sounds (*tat cakram* > (s10.1) *tac_cakram* 'this wheel', *tat jalam* > (s10.3) *taj_jalam* 'this water'), they became retroflex before retroflex sounds (*suhr̥t ṭīkate* > (s10.4a) *suhr̥ṭ_ṭīkate* 'the friend moves', *tat ḍayate* > (s10.4b) *taḍ_ḍayate* 'this thing flies'), and they became *l* before *l* (*tat lokāt labhe* > (s10.5) *tal_lokāl_labhe* 'that is what I receive from the world'). Before palatal *ś*, the consonants *t* and *d* first became *c* (*tat śrutvā* > (s10.7) *tac_śrutvā* 'having heard this'). But, as the sound cluster *c_ś* [t͡š_š] easily became *c* [t͡š] through the simplification of the sibilants, which were pronounced like a single consonant, the sandhi *tac_śrutvā* usually became *tac_chrutvā* in order to reestablish the former double consonant with the pronunciation *cch*.

Exercises

E1 Stop consonant plus nasal

A *manāk magnaḥ* > (s12.1) ____________ 'a little immersed' **B** *dik nāgaḥ* > (s12.1) ____________ 'world elephant' **C** *tat mama* > (s12.3) ____________ 'this is mine' **D** *vāk muñcati* > (s12.1) ____________ 'language liberates' **E** *kīdṛk naraḥ* > (s12.1) ____________ 'what kind of person?' **F** *prāk mukhaḥ* > (s12.1) ____________ 'eastwards' **G** *nagarāt nagaram* > (s12.3) ____________ 'from city to city' **H** *jagat nāṭhaḥ* > (s12.3) ____________ 'ruler of the world' **I** *yāvat na* > (s12.3) ____________ 'as long as not' **J** *ṣaṭ māsaḥ* > (s12.2) ____________ 'period of six months' **K** √*pad-* 'to fall' :: PPP **padná-* > (22.3) ____________ 'fallen' **L** √*bhed-* 'to split' :: **bhidná-* > (22.3) ____________ 'split'

E2 Assimilations of final dental consonants

A *mahat cāpam* > (s10.1) ____________ 'big bow' **B** *aharat śiraḥ* > (s10.6) ____________ 'he decapitated' **C** *mṛt chādayati* > (s10.2) ____________ 'the clay covers' **D** *tat chinatti* > (s10.2) ____________ 'he cuts this' **E** *etat ṭhakkuraḥ* > (s10.4a) ____________ 'this idol' **F** *tat jāyate* > (s10.3) ____________ 'this is born' **G** *tat ślokena* > (s10.6) ____________ 'through this verse' **H** *tat ca* > (s10.1) ____________ 'and this' **I** *abhavat jaḍaḥ* > (s10.3) ____________ 'it became stiff' **J** *suhṛt ṭīkate* > (s10.4a) ____________ 'the friend scuttles' **K** *tat labdham* > (s10.5) ____________ 'having taken this' **L** *tat ḍhaukate* > (s10.4b) ____________ 'it approaches' **M** *vidyut-lata* > (22.6) ____________ 'flash of lightning' **N** *mṛd-* 'clay' :: **mṛd-loṣṭa-* > (22.6) ____________ 'clod of earth'

E3 Sandhi of final nasals

A *arīn jayati* > (s14.3) ____________ 'he overcomes the enemies' **B** *bhadram te* > (s14.1) ____________ 'hail to thee!' **C** *tān jayati* > (s14.3) ____________ 'he overcomes them' **D** *yān jantūn* > (s14.3) ____________ 'which beings' **E** *svargam jagāma* > (s14.1) ____________ 'he went to the sky' **F** *kim karomi* > (s14.1) ____________ 'what shall I do?' **G** *pakṣin ḍīyasva* > (s14.2) ____________ 'fly, bird!' **H** *mahān ḍamaraḥ* > (s14.2) ____________ 'great turmoil' **I** *yachhan śrāddham* > (s14.5) ____________ 'handing out in the ceremony in honour of dead relatives' **J** *tān śaśāpa* > (s14.5) ____________ 'he cursed them' **K** *paśyan lokān* > (s15.4) ____________ 'seeing the people'

12 Loss of Voiced Sibilants

Loss of voiced *z with compensatory lengthening after a short vowel

The loss of voiced sibilants is a pivotal sound change in Sanskrit historical phonology which had tremendous effects on sandhi and morphology. The loss of a voiced sibilant was accompanied by compensatory lengthening of a preceding short vowel. This explains the long vowel *ī* in *sīdati* < **si-sd-a-ti* 'he sits' from the root √*sad-* 'to sit' which goes back to the short vowel **i* of a reduplicated verbal form. In this case, voiceless *s* became voiced *z*, before it was subsequently lost with compensatory lengthening of the preceding vowel: **si-sd-a-ti* > (22.2) **si-zd-a-ti* > (20.2) *sīdati*. Actually, we would have expected to find **z* become retroflex **ẓ* after *i* according to the ruki rule. This would have led to **si-zd-a-ti* > (c25) ˣ*siẓdati* > (17.2) ˣ*siẓḍati* via the assimilation of **ẓd* > **ẓḍ*, and this form should regularly have become ˣ*sīḍati* through SC 20.3. But in this case, retroflex *ḍ* was not retained, probably in analogy to other forms from the same root e.g. *sádas-* 'seat' with dental *d*. Voiced sibilants were lost completely after a long vowel or diphthong without any effect on vowel length. This can be exemplified by 2. sg. imp. **śās-dhi* > (22.2) **śāzdhi* > (20.2) *śādhi* 'command!' from the root √*śās-* 'to command' in which *s* became voiced **z* before *d*, before it was lost. More examples are 2. pl. imp. **ās-dhvam* > (22.2) **āz-dhvam* > (20.2) *ādhvam* 'sit down!' and **āz-daghná-* > **ās-daghná-* > *ā-daghná-* 'reaching to the mouth', the first element of which is the word *ā́s-* 'mouth'.

Lit.: Thumb 1905:118.

Loss of voiced *ẓ with compensatory lengthening after a short vowel

The loss of voiced sibilants also affected retroflex **ẓ*. This can be seen from *nīḍá-* < **nisdó-* 'nest' which is etymologically related to LAT *nīdus* 'nest' in which we find a similar loss of the voiced sibilant with compensatory lengthening. At first, **s* became voiced **z* before **d* and **o* became *a*: **nisdó-* > (22.2) **nizdó-* > (10) **nizdá-*. Then, **z* became **ẓ* according to the ruki rule and the *d* following was assimilated to *ḍ*: **nizdá-* > (c25) **niẓdá-* > (17.2) **niẓḍá-*. Finally, **ẓ* was lost with compensatory lengthening: **niẓḍá-* > (20.3) *nīḍá-*. In this case, retroflex *ḍ* preserves the place of articulation of the lost retroflex **ẓ*. This sound change also explains Vedic forms like *dū-ḍábha-* 'hard to deceive' from the root √*dabh-* 'to deceive' in which we find the variant form *dū-* of the prefix *duṣ-* 'bad' before voiced sounds: **dus-dábha-* > (22.2) **duz-dábha-* > (c25) **duẓ-dábha-* > (17.2) **duẓ-ḍábha-* > (20.3) *dū-ḍábha-*. Retroflex *ḍ* in *dū-ḍábha-* preserves the place of articulation of retroflex *ṣ* of the suffix *duṣ-*. After the voicing of *ṣ* > *ẓ* before the voiced initial of *ḍábha-*, the voiced sibilant *ẓ* was lost with compensatory lengthening.

Lit.: Thumb 1905:134.

The development *-as > *-az > -e before dental stops

The loss of voiced sibilants could also be compensated by the insertion of the semivowel **i̯* or **u̯*. The root √*as-* 'to be' has the 2. sg. imp. *edhi* 'be!' < **as-dhi* in which **as* first became voiced **az* before **z* was lost. Subsequently, the loss of **z* was compensated by the insertion of **i̯* creating a diphthong **ai̯* which monophthongized to *e*: **as-dhi* > (22.2) **azdhi* > (20.1) **aØdhi* > (21.2) **ai̯-dhi* > (11.1) *edhi*. This is a mechanical description of this sound change. Probably, the loss of **z* and the insertion of **i̯* are better to be described as simultaneous processes.
Likewise, we find a 3. sg. pfc. **sa-sd-e* > (22.2) **sazde* > (11.1) *sede* 'he sat' from the root √*sad-* 'to sit'. If the Rigvedic phrase *sū́re_duhitā́* 'daughter of the sun' goes back to **sū́raz duhitā́* < **sū́ras duhitā́*, this would be an example of this sound change in a sandhi form. If this is the case, also the Rigvedic junction *divé dive* 'day after day, every day' could be traced back to **diváz divé* 'from day to day'.

Lit.: Malzahn 2001:140.

Exercises

E1 The development *az > e

A AV *nazdišta-* :: **n̥sd-istho-* > (22.2) ___________ > (15.1) ___________ > (c24) ___________ > (10) ___________ > (c23) ___________ 'the nearest' **B** GR *mastós* 'breast, nipple' :: **másdes-* > (22.2) ___________ > (10) ___________ > (c23) ___________ 'fat' **C** AV *mazdā-* :: **mn̥s-dʰéh_1-* > (c2) ___________ > (22.2) ___________ > (15.1) ___________ > (c23) ___________ 'wisdom' **D** AV *pazdu-* 'beatle' :: **pasdú-* > (22.2) ___________ > (c23) ___________ name of a person **E** AV *dazdi* :: **da-d-dhí* > (2.4) ___________ > (6.5) ___________ > (c23) ___________ > (29.1) ___________ 'give!' **F** √*dhā-* :: 2. sg. imp. **dha-d-dhí* > (2.4) ___________ > (6.5) ___________ > (c23) ___________ > (27.1) ___________ > (29.1) ___________ 'put!'

G **másdi̯éti* > (22.2) ___________ > (10) ___________ > (c23) ___________ 'is/becomes fat'

H AV *mııazda-* :: **mii̯ázdʰa-* > (c23) ___________ 'sacrificial meal'

E2 Cerebralization of *z > *ẓ with subsequent loss of *ẓ and compensatory lengthening

A **dus-dāśa-* > (22.2) ___________ > (c25) ___________ > (17.2) ___________ > (20.3) ___________ 'impious' **B** **dus-dhī-* > (22.2) ___________ > (c25) ___________ > (17.3) ___________ > (20.3) ___________ 'evil minded' **C** **dus-nā́śa-* > (22.2) ___________ > (c25) ___________ > (17.2) ___________ > (20.3) ___________ 'hard to reach'

E3 Loss of retroflex *ẓ with compensatory lengthening

A LAT *nīdus* :: **nisdo-* > (22.2) ___________ > (10.3) ___________ > (c25) ___________ > (17.2) ___________ > (20.3) ___________ 'nest' **B** GR *misthós* :: **misdʰo-* > (22.2) ___________ > (10.3) ___________ > (c25) ___________ > (17.3) ___________ > (20.3) ___________ 'reward' **C** GOT *aistan* 'to pay attention' :: **h_2i-$h_2$isd-$h_2$éi̯* > (22.2) ___________ > (c3) ___________ > (1.5) ___________ > (13.1) ___________ > (26.2) ___________ > (c25) ___________ > (11.1) ___________ > (17.2) ___________ > (20.3) ___________ 'I worship'

D √*stu-* 'to praise' :: 2. pl. aor. **á-stau̯-s-dhvam* > (22.2) ___________ > (c25) ___________ > (17.3) ___________ > (20.1) ___________ > (11.2) ___________ 'you praised'

13 Primary Palatalization

Development of the PIE palatals _*ḱ, *ǵ, *ǵ^{h}_ to Sanskrit _ś, j, h_

An important criterion for subdividing the Indo-European Languages is the so-called centum-satem isogloss, referring to the development of the PIE palatal stop _*ḱ_ in the word _*ḱm̥tóm_ 'hundred' which remained a dorsal stop in LAT _centum_ but became a sibilant in AV _satəm_. The SKR result of PIE _*ḱ_ was _ś_, as it can be seen from _*ḱm̥tóm_ > _śatám_ 'hundred' and from _*ḱlutó-_ > _śrutá-_ 'famous', which is related to GR _klutós_, as well as from _*déḱm̥_ > _dáśa_ 'ten', which is related to GR _déka_.
This development also affected the PIE palatal consonants _*ǵ_ and _*ǵ^{h}_, which became _j_ and _h_. Examples for _*ǵ_ > _j_ are _jánas-_ 'race' < _*ǵénh$_1$os-_, which is related to GR _génos_ and LAT _genus_, as well as _jā́nu-_ 'knee' < _*ǵónu-_ which is related to GR _gónu_ and LAT _genu_. Examples for the development of _*ǵ^{h}_ > _h_ are _*u̯éǵ^{h}eti_ > _váhati_ 'he drives, rides' as well as _*ǵ^{h}u̯éretoi̯_ > _hvárate_ 'he diverges from the right line' or _*ǵ^{h}r̥s-i̯é-ti_ > _hr̥syáti_ 'he is happy'.

Lit.: Lipp 2009.

Development of the PIE palatals with intermediate steps

The PIE palatals _*ḱ, *ǵ, *ǵ^{h}_ on their way to SKR _ś_ [š], _j_ [d̲ž], _h_ [h] were first affricated to their IIR intermediate steps _*ć_ [t̲š], _*ȷ́_ [d̲ž], _*ȷ́^{h}_ [d̲žh]. Voiceless _*ć_ [t̲š] was subsequently deaffricated to _ś_ [š] by losing its initial stop consonant. Voiced _*ȷ́_ [d̲ž] remained as _j_. Voiced aspirated _*ȷ́^{h}_ [d̲žh] was first deaffricated to [žh] before the voiced sibilant [ž] was lost, which led to _h_. Therefore, the representation of PIE palatals in Sanskrit is not straightforward and consistent because _ś_ is a sibilant, _j_ is an affricate and _h_ a glottal fricative. It is an interesting and noteworthy feature that the development of _*ǵ_ > _j_ [d̲ž] stopped with _j_ as a result being an affricate, whereas both _*ḱ_ and _*ǵ^{h}_ were deaffricated after having become IIR affricates.

PIE		**Palatalization / Affrication**		**Deaffrication**		**Loss of Sibilant**
_*ḱ_	>	_*ć_ [t̲š]	>	_ś_ [š]		
_*ǵ_	>	_*ȷ́_ [d̲ž] = _j_				
_*ǵ^{h}_	>	_*ȷ́^{h}_ [d̲žh]	>	[žh]	>	_h_

Development of the PIE sound cluster _*ḱt_

The sound cluster _*ḱt_ first developed to IIR _*ćt_ [t̲št]. Then, initial [t̲] was lost in the Indo-Iranian period. Through this loss of initial [t̲], the sound cluster [t̲št] became [št] which developed further to retroflex _ṣṭ_ due to reciprocal assimilation.

PIE		**Palatization / Affrication**		**Simplification**		**Assimilation**
_*ḱt_	>	_*ćt_ [_t̲št_]	>	_*št_	>	_ṣṭ_

The sound change PIE _*ḱt_ > SKR _ṣṭ_ can be derived from the comparison of _aṣṭā́_ 'eight' with LAT _octō_ and AV _ašta_ which all go back to a preform _*oḱtṓ_. While PIE _*ḱ_ regularly became SKR _ś_ [š] and PIE _*ḱt_ regularly became SKR _ṣṭ_ via IIR [t̲št], we see a different development in the Avestan cognates where PIE _*ḱ_ is regularly represented as AV _s_ (_*ḱm̥tóm_ > AV _satəm_). In the sound cluster PIE _*ḱt_, however, PIE _*ḱ_ is continued as AV _š_ (_*oḱtṓ_ > AV _ašta_) just like in SKR _aṣṭā́_. This enables us to define the loss of the initial stop in this sound change IIR _*ćt_ [t̲št] > IIR [št] as belonging to the Indo-Iranian period because both Sanskrit and Avestan share this development.
The sound cluster _ṣṭ_ may also go back to _*ǵt_ via assimilation of the feature voice. This can be seen in examples like _*sl̥ǵ-tó-_ > (22.1) _*sl̥ḱtó-_ > (c13) _sr̥ṣṭá-_ 'emitted' from the verb _sr̥játi_ 'he emits' as well as in _*h$_2$mr̥ǵ-tó-_ > (22.1) _*mr̥ḱtó-_ > (c13) _mr̥ṣṭá-_ 'cleaned' of the verb _mr̥jánti_ 'they clean'. In both examples, the sound cluster _*ǵt_ was devoiced to _*ḱt_ before it developed to _ṣṭ_.

Exercises

E1 Development of PIE *ḱ, *ǵ, and *ǵʰ

A LAT *cadō* :: Fut. **ḱad-si̯e-ti* > (22.1) __________ > (c7) __________ > (10) __________ 'he will fall' **B** O-LAT *deicō* :: **dí-dei̯ḱ-e-ti* > (c7) __________ > (10) __________ > (11.1) __________ 'he shows' **C** GR *kónkhos* :: **ḱonkʰó-* > (c7) __________ > (10) __________ 'shell' **D** LAT *equus* :: **eḱu̯o-* > (c7) __________ > (10) __________ 'horse' **E** LAT *cēnseō* :: **ḱenseti* > (c7) __________ > (10.1) __________ > (s14.1) __________ 'he proclaims' **F** LAT *angus-tus* :: *h_2*énǵʰos-* > (c3) __________ > (c12) __________ > (10) __________ > (s14.1) __________ 'narrowness' **G** GR *geúō* :: **ǵéu̯sos-* > (c11) __________ > (10) __________ > (c24) __________ > (11.2) __________ 'pleasure, liking' **H** LAT *vīcus* :: **u̯oi̯ḱó-* > (c7) __________ > (10.3) __________ > (11.1) __________ 'dwelling'

E2 Emergence of the sound cluster ṣṭ

A √*darś-* (c7) < __________ 'to see' :: **dr̥ḱtó-* > (c13) __________ > (10) __________ 'seen' **B** √*piś-* (c7) < __________ 'to shape' :: **piḱto-* > (c13) __________ > (10) __________ 'tormented' **C** √*deś-* (c7) < __________ 'to show' :: **dídei̯ḱti* > (c13) __________ > (10) __________ > (11.1) __________ 'he shows' **D** **déi̯-diḱtoi̯* > (c13) __________ > (10) __________ > (11.1) __________ 'it proves itself to be' **E** √*vaś-* (c7) < __________ 'to wish' :: **u̯éḱti* > (c13) __________ > (10) __________ 'he wishes' **F** √*naś-* (c7) < __________ 'to vanish' :: **neḱtó-* > (c13) __________ > (10) __________ 'lost'

10: **e/o* > *a* and **ē/ō* > *ā*	**22.1:** *G* > *K* / _*K*	**c13:** **ḱt* > *ṣṭ*
10.1: **e* > *a*	**c3:** *h_2e* > **Ha* > *a*	**c24:** **s* > *ṣ* / *r,r̥,ŭ,k,ĭ* _
10.3: **o* > *a*	**c7:** **ḱ* > *ś*	**s14.1:** *m* +*C* > *m̥*_*C*
11.1: **ai̯* > *e*	**c11:** **g* > *j* / _(*ĕ, ĭ, i̯*)	
11.2: **au̯* > *o*	**c12:** **gʰ* > *h* / _(*ĕ, ĭ, i̯*)	

14 Secondary Palatalization

The PIE labiovelars *k^w, *g^w, *g^{wh} lost their labial element in the satem languages and merged with the plain velars **k*, **g*, *g^h which remained velars before the non-palatal vowels **o* and **u* and before consonants. Before the palatal vowels **e* and **i*, they palatalized to *c* [t̲š], *j* [d̲ž], *h*. Analogous to the development of **k* > *c* and **g* > *j*, also *g^h was palatalized and affricated to [d̲žh]. After that, [d̲žh] was further deaffricated to [žh] before the voiced sibilant [ž] was lost, thus producing the result [h].

Delabialization		Palatalization/Affrication		Deaffrication		Loss of Sibilant	
**k*, *k^w >	**k*	>	*č* [t̲š] = *c*				
**g*, *g^w >	**g*	>	*ǰ* [d̲ž] = *j*				
*g^h, *g^{wh} >	*g^h	>	$ǰ^h$ [d̲žh]	>	[žh]	>	*h* [h]

Correlation of palatal and velar consonants

We can see a correlation between the palatal consonants *c, j* and the velar consonants *k, g* when we compare the initial consonant of the reduplication morpheme with the initial consonant of the roots in the following words. The initial consonants *k, g* of the Sanskrit roots √*kar*-, √*gam*- appear as the palatal consonants *c, j* in the reduplication morpheme because they were subject to palatalization before the palatal vowel **e* which was present in the PIE reduplication morpheme whereas the same consonant remained unchanged before the vowel **o* which was present in the PIE root.

Sanskrit	Intermediate step	PIE
ca-kā́r-a 'he did'	< **ke-kór-e*	< *k^we-k^wór-e*
ja-gā́m-a 'he went'	< **ge-góm-e*	< *g^we-g^wóm-e*

The velar or labiovelar sounds *k/k^w, *g/g^w, *g^h/g^{wh} became Sanskrit *k, g, gh* before PIE **o* and were palatalized to *c, j, h* before PIE **e*. Both PIE **o* and **e* later became SKR *a*: *arká*- 'sunbeam' < *h_1erk^wó- vs. *árcati* 'he shines' < *$h_1érk^weti$, *pakvá*- 'cooked, ripe' < *pek^w-u̯ó- vs. *pácati* 'he cooks' < *$pék^weti$, *bhága*- 'wealth' < *b^hágo- vs. *bhájati* 'he distributes' < *b^hágeti and *arghá*- 'value' < *h_2elg^{wh}ó- and *árhati* 'he earns' < *$h_2élg^{wh}eti$.

Palatalization and relative chronology

The sound change **e* > (10) *a* must have occured after the secondary palatalization **k* > *c*, **g* > *j*, **gh* > *h* because this palatalization presupposes the existence of the vowel **e*. In the development of the word *ca* < *k^we 'and', labiovelar *k^w was delabialized to *k* and palatalized to *c* before **e* became *a*: *k^we > (4.1) **ke* > (c10) **ce* > (10) *ca*. This explanation disproves hypotheses of early Indo-European scholars who believed Sanskrit *a* to be original and a preform of the Latin and Greek vowel correspondence *e*.

Analogical generalization of palatal variants in the paradigm

The above mentioned example *arká*- 'sunbeam' < *h_1erk^wó- vs. *árcati* 'he shines' < *$h_1érk^weti$ shows the coexistence of non-palatalized *k* as well as its palatalized variant *c*. The verb *árcati* has the present tense forms *arcāmi* < *h_1erk^w-ō-mi, *arcasi* < *h_1erk^w-e-si, *arcati* < *h_1erk^w-e-ti but the preform of the 1. person singular *h_1erk^w-ō-mi should have become ^{x}*arkāmi* because *k^w was regularly not palatalized to *c* before **ō* according to sound rules. In this example as well as in many others, the palatalized variant *c* was generalized in the whole paradigm in order to level out differences between the forms within the paradigm. That is the reason why we mostly find palatalized consonants in the roots whereas we find non-palatalized consonants in corresponding verbal forms: √*nij*- 'to wash' ~ *nénekti* 'he washes (himself)', √*bhaj*- 'to distribute' ~ *bhaktá*- 'something distributed', √*bhuj*- 'to bend' ~ *bhugná*- 'something bent', √*bhuj*- 'to eat' ~ *bhuktá*- 'something eaten'.

Lit.: Lipp 2009; Thumb 1905:97ff; Wackernagel 1896:138ff.

Exercises

E1 Delabialization without palatalization

A LAT *iecur* :: **i̯ek^{w}r̥t* > (4.1) __________ > (10.1) __________ 'liver' **B** LAT *coctus* :: **pek^{w}-u̯ó-* > (4.1) __________ > (10) __________ 'cooked, ripe' **C** LAT *nūdus* :: **neg^{w}-nó-* > (4.2) __________ > (10) __________ 'naked'

E2 Examples of palatalizations

A GR *pénte* :: **pénk^{w}e* > (4.1) __________ > (c10) __________ > (10.1) __________ 'five' **B** LAT *vīvus* :: **g^{w}ī-u̯ós* > (4.2) __________ > (c11) __________ > (10.3) __________ 'alive' **C** GR *érebos* :: gen. sg. **h$_{1}$rég^{w}es-es* > (13.2) __________ > (4.2) __________ > (c11) __________ > (10.1) __________ 'darkness' **D** GR *delphús* :: **g^{w}ólb^{h}o-* > (4.2) __________ > (9) __________ > (10) __________ 'fruit of the womb' **E** GR *sébomai* :: **ti̯eg^{w}eti* > (4.2) __________ > (c11) __________ > (10.1) __________ 'he leaves' **F** OHG *quena* 'woman' :: **g^{w}énH-* > (4.2) __________ > (c11) __________ > (1.7) __________ > (10.1) __________ 'woman' **G** **sék^{w}-mon-* > *sákman-* 'fellowship' :: **sék^{w}-e-ti* > (4.1) __________ > (c10) __________ > (10.1) __________ 'he follows' **H** 3. pl. *ghnánti* 'they slay' :: 3. sg. **g^{wh}én-ti* > (4.3) __________ > (c12) __________ > (10) __________ 'he slays' **I** LAT *ninguit* 'it snows' :: **snig^{wh}-e-ti* > (4.3) __________ > (c12) __________ > (10.1) __________ 'he loves' **J** LAT *foveō* :: **d^{h}ég^{wh}eti* > (4.3 __________ > (c12) __________ > (27.1) __________ > (10.1) __________ 'he/it burns' **K** LAT *vovēre* :: **h$_{1}$éu̯g^{wh}-e-toi̯* > (c1) __________ > (4.3) __________ > (c12) __________ > (10) __________ > (11.2) __________ 'he speaks solemnly' **L** GR *óphis* :: **h$_{3}$ég^{wh}i-* > (c5) __________ > (4.3) __________ > (c12) __________ > (10.3) __________ 'snake' **M** LAT *augēre* 'to increase' :: gen. sg. **h$_{2}$éu̯geses* > (c3) __________ > (c11) __________ > (10.1) __________ > (11.2) __________ 'vigor' **N** LAT *lūcēre* :: **lou̯kéi̯eti* > (c10) __________ > (9) __________ > (10) __________ > (11.1/2) __________ 'he shines'

1.7: $*H > i\ /\ \_\#\#$	**9:** **l/l̥ > r/r̥*	**11.1:** **ai̯ > e*	**c5:** **h$_{3}$e > *Ho > o*
4.1: $*k^{w} > *k$	**10:** **e/o > a* and **ē/ō > ā*	**13.2:** **H > Ø / #_C*	**c10:** **k > c / _(ĕ, ĭ, i̯)*
4.2: $*g^{w} > *g$	**10.1:** **e > a*	**27.1:** $C^{h}...C^{h} > C...C^{h}$	**c11:** **g > j / _(ĕ, ĭ, i̯)*
4.3: $*g^{wh} > *g^{h}$	**10.3:** **o > a*	**c1:** **h$_{1}$e > *He > e*	**c12:** **g^{h} > h / _(ĕ, ĭ, i̯)*

15 Consonant Clusters with Palatal Consonants

Development of the consonant clusters *_tḱ_ > _kṣ_ and *_ḱs_ > _kṣ_

The combination of palatal and dental consonants yielded a retroflex consonant cluster due to reciprocal assimilation. This can be seen in the development of PIE *_ḱt_ > _ṣṭ_ in *_oḱtṓ_ > IIR *_aštā́_ > _aṣṭā́_ which is described in chapter 13. The reverse combination of sounds *_tḱ_ first yielded IIR *_tć_ [tt̠š] and then retroflex *_ṭṣ_: *_tḱéi̯-ti_ > (5.1) *_tćéi̯ti_ [tt̠šéi̯ti] > (18.4) *_ṭṣéi̯ti_ > (10) *_ṭṣái̯ti_. But this sequence *_ṭṣ_ was not stable in Sanskrit and therefore transformed into _kṣ_ due to phonotactic reasons: *_ṭṣái̯ti_ > (19.1) *_kṣái̯ti_ > (11.1) _kṣéti_ 'he lives' (GR _ktízein_ 'to inhabit', LAT _situs_ 'position, site'). The sequence PIE *_ḱs_ likewise first yielded IIR *_ćs_ [t̠šs] and was then transformed into retroflex *_ṭṣ_ before it joined the above mentioned development to _kṣ_. This accounts for the etymology of _ákṣa-_ 'axis' (GR _áksōn_, LAT _axis_) which developed as follows: PIE *_h$_2$éḱso-_ > IIR *_áćsa-_ [át̠šsa] > (18.6) *_áṭṣa-_ > (19.1) _ákṣa-_. Another example is PIE *_réḱs-es-_ > IIR *_raćsas-_ > (c14) _rákṣas-_ 'damage' which is related to GR _erékhthō_ 'I tear apart'.
The similarity between PIE *_ḱs_ and SKR _kṣ_ therefore only exists at the surface level. During the development of *_ṭṣ_ > _kṣ_, sound change 28.1 started to be active which caused final consonant clusters to be reduced to their first element. Sound changes are usually active over a long period of time so that both *_ṭṣ_ as well as _kṣ_ were affected by SC 28.1. The consequence was that we find the divergent outputs _ṭ_ < *_ṭṣ_ and _k_ < *_kṣ_ for the same PIE input *_ḱs_. This accounts for the divergent final consonants in *_rēǵs_ > *_rēḱs_ > IIR *_rāćs_ > (18.6) *_rāṭṣ_ > (28.1) _rāṭ_ 'king' and *_diḱs_ > IIR *_dićs_ > (18.6) *_diṭṣ_ > (19.1) *_dikṣ_ > (28.1) _dik_ 'direction'.

Lit.: Lipp 2009 volume I:210; Thumb 1905:117ff.

Development of the consonant clusters *_d^{h}ǵ^h_ > _kṣ_ and *_d^{h}g^{wh}_ > _kṣ_

The consonant cluster *_d^{h}ǵ^h_ in *_d^{h}ǵ^{h}ém-_ > _kṣám-_ 'earth' first became *_d^{h}j́^{h}_ and then *_dj́^{h}_, before the sequence of dental _d_ plus palatal _j́^{h}_ became retroflex *_ḍẓ_: *_d^{h}ǵ^{h}ém-_ > (5.3) *_d^{h}j́^{h}ém-_ > (22.4) *_dj́^{h}ém-_ [dd̠žhém] > (18.5) *_ḍẓhém-_ > (10) *_ḍẓhám-_. Then, the consonant cluster *_ḍẓh_ became *_gẓh_ analogous to the development of *_ṭṣ_ > _kṣ_ mentioned above: *_ḍẓhám-_ > (19.2) *_gẓhám-_. As the consonant cluster [gẓh] was regarded as the phonological surface of an underlying /g^{h}ṣ/ (cf. Bartholomae's law), it was devoiced and deaspirated and became _kṣ_: *_gẓhám-_ /*_g^{h}sám-_/ > (19.3) _kṣám-_. This is also the explanation of the development of *_d^{h}g^{wh}_ in *_d^{h}g^{wh}íti-_ > _kṣíti-_ 'extinction'. First, *_d^{h}g^{wh}_ became *_d^{h}g^h_ and then *_dg^h_, before *_g^h_ was palatalized to *_j́^{h}_ before *_i_: *_d^{h}g^{wh}íti-_ > (4.3) *_d^{h}g^{h}íti-_ > (22.4) *_dg^{h}íti-_ > (5.6) *_dj́^{h}íti-_ [dd̠žhíti]. The resulting consonant cluster *_dj́^{h}_ is similar to the cluster *_d^{h}ǵ^h_ > *_dj́^{h}_ and shared the same further development: *_dj́^{h}íti-_ [dd̠žhíti] > (18.5) *_ḍẓhíti_ > (19.2) *_gẓhíti_ = */g^{h}síti/ > (22.5) _kṣíti-_.

Development of the consonant clusters *_sḱ_ > _ch_ and *_sg(h)_ > _jj_

Some words like *_sḱeh$_1$-i̯éh$_2$_ > _chāyā́-_ 'shade' (GR _skiā́_ 'shade', TOCH B _skiyo_ 'shade') exhibit the development *_sḱ_ > _ch_ in the initial position. But in the medial position, we contrarily find the development *_sḱ_ > _cch_ like in *_g^{w}m̥-sḱé-ti_ > (c20) _gaccháti_ 'he walks' and *_i̯m̥-sḱé-ti_ > (c20) _yaccháti_ 'he stretches out'. The difference between geminated medial _cch_ in contrast to non-geminated initial _ch_ is due to the PIE sound cluster *_sḱ_ which consisted of two consonants which closed a preceding syllable. But the Sanskrit result _ch_ counted as a single consonant and did therefore not close a preceding syllable. In order to keep up the original syllabification, _ch_ was geminated to _cch_ which counted as two consonants.
Another development is seen in the voiced consonant cluster *_zg^h_ before palatal *_e_ like in *_mazg^h-én-_ > (16.4) *_mozj́^{h}-én-_ > (22.11) _majján-_ 'marrow' as well as in *_rézge/o-_ > _rájju-_ 'rope' (~LAT _restis_ 'rope, cord'). In these cases, the sequences *_zj́_ and *_zg(e)_ > *_zj(e)_ were assimilated to _-jj-_. The _u_-stem of _rájju-_ must furthermore be an innovation because *_g_ would not have been palatalized before _u_.

Lit.: Allen 1972:47; Thumb 1905:113.

Exercises

E1 Developments with intermediate steps

A GR *téktōn* :: **tétḱon-* > (5.1) __________ [__________] > (18.4) __________ > (19.1) __________ > (10) *tákṣan-* 'carpenter' **B** GR *phthísis* :: **d^hg^{wh}íti-* > (4.3) __________ > (22.4) __________ > (5.6) __________ > (18.5) __________ > (19.2) __________ = /*g^hṣíti/ > (19.3) __________ 'destruction' **C** LAT *ursus* :: **Hr̥ḱtḱo-* > (13.1) __________ > (5.1) __________ [__________] > (18.4) __________ > (19.1) __________ > (10) __________ 'bear' **D** LAT *hum-us* :: **$d^h\acute{g}^h$ém-* > (22.4) __________ > (5.3) __________ [__________] > (18.5) __________ > (19.2) __________ = /*g^hṣém-/ > (19.3) __________ > (10) __________ 'earth' **E** AV *cašte* :: **k^wéḱs-toi̯* > (4.1) __________ > (5.1) __________ [__________] > (6.3) __________ > (c10) __________ > (10) __________ > (18.1) __________ > (11.1) __________ 'he proclaims' **F** LAT *rēx* :: **rēǵs* > (22.1) __________ > (5.1) __________ [__________] > (18.4) __________ > (10) __________ > (28.1) __________ 'king' **G** GR *kteínō* :: **tḱn̥-néu̯-ti* > (5.1) __________ [__________] > (18.4) __________ > (19.1) __________ > (15.1) __________ > (10) __________ > (11.2) __________ 'he hurts/damages'

E2 Exercises for the sound cluster *sḱ

A AV *saδaiieiti* :: **sḱn̥d-éi̯e-ti* > (c19) __________ > (15.1) __________ > (10) __________ 'he/it shines/pleases' **B** LAT *pōscō* :: **pr̥ḱ-sḱé-ti* > (6.2) __________ > (c20) __________ > (10) __________ 'he asks' **C** *vāsáyati* 'he illuminates' < **h_2u̯os-éi̯e-ti* :: **$h_2$us-sḱé-ti* > (3.1) __________ > (13.1) __________ > (c20) __________ > (10) __________ 'it dawns (in the morning)' **D** AV *isaiti* :: **$h_2$is-sḱé-ti* > (3.1) __________ > (13.1) __________ > (c20) __________ > (10) __________ 'he searches, strives for' **E** GR *érkhomai* 'I come, go' :: **h_1r̥-sḱé-ti* > (13.1) __________ > (c20) __________ > (10) __________ 'he reaches'

3.1: **ss > s*	**5.2:** **ǵ > *ǰ* [d̲ž]	**11.1:** **ai̯ > e*	**18.4:** **tt̲š* /tć/ > **ṭṣ*	**22.1:** *G > K / _K*
4.1: **k^w > *k*	**5.3:** **$\acute{g}^h$ > *$\check{j}^h$* [d̲žh]	**11.2:** **au̯ > o*	**18.5:**	**22.4:** *D^H > D / _D^H*
4.2: **g^w > *g*	**5.6:**	**13.1:** *H > Ø / _V*	**d$\underline{d}\check{z}^{(h)}$* /dǰ/ > **ḍẓ*	**28.1:**
4.3: **g^{wh} > *g^h*	**g^h > *$\check{j}^h$ / _(ĕ, ŏ, i̯)*	**15.1:** **n̥ > a*	**19.1:** **ṭṣ > kṣ*	**$C_1C_2(C_3)$ > C_1 / _##*
5.1: **ḱ > *ć* [t̲š]	**6.3:** **ćt* [t̲št] > *[št]	**18.1:** **št > ṣṭ*	**19.2:** **$ḍẓ^{(h)}$ > *$gẓ^{(h)}$*	**c10:** **k > c / _(ĕ, ĭ, i̯)*
	10:		**19.3:** **$gẓ^{(h)}$ > kṣ*	**c19:** **sḱ > ch / #_*
	**e/o > a; *ē/ō > ā*			**c20:** **sḱ > cch /* V_V

16 Consonant Clusters with the Structures *CsC* and *ss

Development of the consonant cluster *ḱsd(ʰ)

The development *ḱsdʰ > *ẓḍ is the voiced counterpart to the development *ḱt > ṣṭ, which is presented in chapter 13, with the only difference that voiced *ẓ was lost afterwards. The formation of the imp. 2. sg. *tāḍhi* < **taḱ-s-dhi* 'fashion, make!', which is related to 3. pl. *tákṣati* 'they fashion' < **taḱ-s-n̥ti* can be explained by assuming that **ḱsdh* first became IIR **ćsdh* [t̠šsdh] before the two adjacent sibilants merged to *š* which produced a structure *Cs(s)C*. Then, the initial [t̠] was lost and *dh* voiced the preceding *š* regressively to *ž*: **t̠šsdh* > **t̠šdh* > **šdh* > **ždh*. Finally, the combination of the palatal and dental consonants **ždh* yielded retroflex **ẓḍh* before **ẓ* was lost with compensatory lengthening: **taḱsdhi* > (5.1) **taćsdhi* [tat̠šsdhi] > (6.7) **tat̠šdhi* > (6.4) **tašdhi* > (22.2) **taždhi* > (18.3) **taẓḍhi* > (20.3) *tāḍhi*.

Insertion and ejection of *s* between dental stops

Data from the PIE languages suggest that already in PIE times an insertion of **s* must have taken place between two dental stops *(*t/d/dʰ-*t/d/dʰ-)* which came into contact. This **s* was still preserved in IIR but was ejected in Sanskrit. Furthermore, we find in Sanskrit the ejection of every morphologically conditioned *s* between stops which can be seen particularly in the athematic *s*-aorist if the verbal root ended in a stop consonant and the personal ending that followed the aorist morpheme *s* began with a stop consonant. Therefore, in the development of 3. sg. aor. mid. **á-rudh-s-ta* > *árutta* 'he obstructed' from the root √*rudh-* 'to obstruct', the first step was devoicing and deaspiration of *dh* before *s*, and then *s* was ejected between two stops: **á-rudh-s-ta* > (22.5) **á-rut-s-ta* > (6.1) *árutta*. The ejection of *s* had not yet taken place in IIR as we find different results from equal preforms in Sanskrit and Avestan. The past participle **bʰn̥dʰ-tó-* 'bound' from the root √*bhand-* < **bʰendʰ-* first yielded IIR **badzdhá-* via the stages **bʰn̥dʰ-tó-* > (2.3) **bʰn̥dʰztó-* > (7.3) **bʰn̥dzdʰó-* > (15.1) **bhadzdhó-* > (10) **bhadzdhá-* > (27.1) **badzdhá-* before **z* was ejected in Sanskrit which led to *baddhá-*. In the Avestan language **dzdh* was simplified via **zdh* to **zd* according to SC 6.5 which can be seen from AV *basta-* < **bazda-*. In this example, however, the voiceless cluster *st* cannot go back directly to **zd* but must have been analogically influenced by other *ta*-participles.

Simplification of PIE *ss > *s and the development *ss > ts

The sequence **ss* was simplified to **s* in PIE times already as we find SKR *asi* and GR *eĩ* which both go back to a preform **esi* 'you are' with single *s* although morphologically this form goes back to **h₁és-si* which is an athematic root present from the root **h₁es-* 'to be'. However, we find an exception to this rule in 2. sg. *śā́s-si* < **ḱeHs-si* 'you command' in which the sequence *ss* was remodelled analogically in order to make the morpheme boundaries clearer.

In some roots with final *s* (e.g. √*vas-* 'to dwell' and √*ghas-* 'to eat'), we find the strengthening of *s* > *t* when speakers added a morpheme that started with *s* which means that in this case double *ss* was not simplified to single *s*. From the root √*vas-*, we find the prs. *vásati* 'he dwells' and the fut. **vas-sya-ti* > (25.2) *vatsyati* 'he will dwell', and from √*ghas-* we find the prs. *ghasati* 'he eats' and the des. **ji-ghas-sa-ti* > (25.2) *jighatsati* 'he wants to eat'. This development can be interpreted as the attempt to mark the morpheme boundaries clearer. If **vassyati* had been simplified to ˣ*vasyati*, the speakers would have probably thought this form to be something like **vas-ya-ti* and not the future tense form.

This sound change also affected retroflex **ṣṣ* in the 2. sg. ipf. *adveṭ* 'you hated' < **a-dvai̯ṣ-s* from √*dviṣ-* 'to hate' in which case root final *ṣ* caused the assimilation of the morpheme *-s* > *-ṣ* of the 2. sg.: **a-dvai̯ṣ-s* > **a-dvai̯ṣ-ṣ*. Then, **ṣṣ* became **ṭṣ* before the simplification of the final double consonant and monophthongization of **ai̯* > *e* created the form *adveṭ*: **a-dvai̯ṣ-ṣ* > (25.3) **a-dvai̯t-ṣ* > (28.1) **a-dvai̯ṭ* > (11.1) *adveṭ*. Alternatively, the development **ss* > *ts* can also be classified as a dissimilation process.

Exercises

E1 Changes in consonant clusters

A *vásati* 'he dwells' :: aor. **e-u̯ēs-sīt* > (10) ____________ > (25.2) ____________ 'he dwelled' **B** *bhájati* 'he distributes' :: aor. **e-*b^h*ag-s-to* > (22.1) ____________ > (10) ____________ > (6.1) ____________ 'he distributed' **C** *ghasati* 'he eats' :: **e-*g^h*s-to-* > (10) ____________ > (6.1) ____________ > (7.4) ____________ 'uneaten' **D** *jíghatsati* 'he wants to eat' :: 2. sg. imp. **jaghsdhi* > (6.1) ____________ > (22.4) ____________ 'eat!' **E** √*lep-* 'to smear' :: 3. sg. aor. mid. **a-lip-s-ta* > (6.1) ____________ 'he smeared' **F** *sthitá-* 'standing' :: **ud-sth*$_2$*-to-* > (1.8) ____________ > (1.6) ____________ > (10) ____________ > (22.1) ____________ > (6.1) ____________ 'risen' **G** *stambha-* 'supporting pillar' :: **ud-stémb*^{h}*Heno-* > (22.1) ____________ > (13.1) ____________ > (10) ____________ > (6.1) ____________ 'supporting beam' **H** *sthāpáyati* 'he puts' :: **úd-sthāpayati* > (22.1) ____________ > (6.1) ____________ 'he puts up' **I** *stabhitá-* 'underpinned' :: **úd-stm̥b*^{h}*H-to-* > (22.1) ____________ > (1.6) ____________ > (15.2) ____________ > (10) ____________ > (6.1) ____________ 'erected' **J** HIT *kappilalli-* 'cursed' :: aor. 2. pl. **ḱēp-s-to* > (c7) ____________ > (10) ____________ > (6.1) ____________ 'you curse' **K** *tápati* 'is hot' :: aor. 2. du. **a-tāp-s-tam* > (6.1) ____________ 'you two burned'

1.6: **H* > *i* / *C*_*C*	**10:** **e/o* > *a* and **ē/ō* > *ā*	**22.4:** D^{II} > *D* / _D^{II}
1.8: *T* > T^h / _h_2	**13.1:** **H* > Ø / _*V*	**25.2:** **s̤s̤* > *ts̤*
6.1: **CsC* > *CC*	**15.2:** **m̥* > *a*	**c7:** **ḱ* > *ś*
7.4: *g^h*t* > *gdh*	**22.1:** *G* > *K* / _*K*	

INFORMATION REGARDING SC 1.8: The laryngeal caused the aspiration of the preceding stop consonant. After the aspiration had been put into effect, the laryngeal remained as *H* which became *i* according to SC 1.6/1.7.

17 Consonant Simplification / Transition Sounds / Distant Assimilation

Consonant clusters were sometimes simplified if the speakers found them too difficult to pronounce. We can therefore trace SKR stána- 'female breast' back to IIR *pstana- by comparing it to AV fštā-na-. Also the initial consonant of turī́ya- 'the fourth' is a simplification from *kturī́ya- < *k^{w}tur-ii̯ó-, which is a zero grade formation of *k^{w}etu̯er- > catvar- 'four'. The initial consonant k which was lost in Sanskrit can be found as x in AV ā-xtūirīm 'four'. The initial consonant of PIE *ḱm̥tóm > SKR śatám 'hundred' goes back to **dḱm̥tóm if it is really a derivation from *deḱm̥ > daśa 'ten'. The stem nápāt- 'offspring, grandchild' had a dat. pl. *nápt-bhyas > nádbhyas which shows the simplification of *ptbh to dbh in which case p was lost, before t became d before bh: *ptbh > *tbh > dbh. Vedic manuscripts sometimes show the loss of a stop between a nasal and a stop e.g. paṅti < paṅkti 'number 5'. More examples are the instr. sg. forms bhūnā́ < *bhūmnā́ and mahinā́ < *mahimnā́ from the man-stems bhūmán- 'multitude, wealth' and mahimán- 'magnitude, size' which display the simplification of two adjacent nasals *mn > n. As these forms are built from the suffix -mn- plus the ending ā we can derive them from *bhū-mn-ā́ and *mahi-mn-ā́.
We find another simplification in VED loc. jmán < *d^{h}ǵ^{h}m-én, gen. jmás < *d^{h}ǵ^{h}m-és from kṣám- < *d^{h}ǵ^{h}om- 'earth' which happened because three consonants clashed in the initial position of PIE *d^{h}ǵ^{h}m-és/én. Therefore, the first consonant was lost, before *ǵ^h lost its aspiration before m and became j: *d^{h}ǵ^{h}m-én > *ǵ^{h}m-én > jmán (for more information on kṣám- cf. SC c17 and chapter 15).
At first glance, the initial variation of nom. ātmā́ and dat. tmáne from ātmán- 'breath, soul' also hints at a simplification process. But in this case the reason was probably an original PIE apophonic paradigm with the case forms nom. sg. *éh_1-t-mō(n) > *ā́tmā(n) > ātmā́ (with further change of accent) and dat. sg. *h_1t-mén-ei̯ > tmáne. The initial variation was therefore due to morphological and not to phonological reasons.

Distant assimilation

Assimilation frequently occurs when two sounds are located directly next to each other but it is also possible that two sounds exert an assimilatory influence onto each other when they are not directly next to each other which is called distant assimilation. SKR śmáśru- 'beard' can therefore be traced back to *smáśru- and further to *sméḱru- by comparing it to LIT smakras 'chin'. After PIE *ḱ had become ś in *smeḱru- > *smaśru-, the sequence s…ś became ś…ś.
The reverse sequence ś...s became ś... ś in SKR śaśa- < *śasa- 'rabbit' which is related to MHG Hase 'rabbit'. After PIE *ḱaso- had become *śasa-, it further became śaśa- whereby in both cases the exact choronological rule ordering is unclear.

Insertion of homorganic stops in the sandhi of nasal plus sibilant

In the case of a final nasal before an initial sibilant in sandhi, we sometimes find the insertion of a homorganic stop between the two sounds e.g. prāṅ śete > (s14.6) prāṅk_śete 'he lies towards the East' and tān sahate > (s14.7) tānt_sahate 'he overcomes them'. The first example displays the preservation of the original final consonant of the stem prāṅk- / prāñc- and the second example displays the development *ss > ts because tān goes back to *tāns (cf. the previous chapter).
The sandhi of tān śaśān > (s14.5) tāñ_chaśān 'these rabbits' probably preserves an earlier language state, too. If we start from the IIR preform *tāns_ćasān, we find at the word boundaries the sound cluster *s_ć [s_t̠š] which is comparable to the phonological context of *g^{w}m̥-sḱe-ti > IIR *gasćati > gacchati 'he walks' in which case medial sć became cch. Initial ch of the sandhi form tāñ_chaśān could therefore be evidence for an IIR initial *ć [t̠š].

Lit.: Lipp 2009 volume I:173ff.

Exercises

E1 Distant assimilation and simplification of consonant clusters

A AV *saŋuhaṇt-* :: *śasvant- > (27.3) __________ 'frequent' **B** LATV *sàuss* 'dry' :: *seu̯sei̯eti > (c24) __________ > (10) __________ > (11.2) __________ > (s...ṣ > ś...ṣ) __________ 'he dries' **C** *bhūmán-* 'multitude, wealth' :: instr. sg. *bhūmnā́ > (27.2) __________ **D** *mahimán-* 'size' :: instr. sg. *mahimnā́ > (27.2) __________ **E** *drāghimán-* 'length' :: instr. sg. *drāghmnā́ > (27.2) __________ **F** *raśmán-* 'rein' :: instr. sg. *raśmnā́ > (27.2) __________ **G** *yunákti* 'he yokes' :: 2. pl. imp. *yuṅgdhi > (27.3) __________ 'yoke!'

E2 Exercises regarding chapter 18 and 19

A *séǵ^{h}tr̥- > (5.3) __________ > (7.6) __________ > (6.6) __________ > (10) __________ > (18.2) __________ > (20.3) __________ 'winner' **B** AV *dərəz-* 'fetter' :: *d^{h}r̥ǵ^{h}-tó- > (5.3) __________ > (7.6) __________ > (6.6) __________ > (27.1) __________ > (10) __________ > (18.2) __________ > (20.1) __________ 'determined' **C** *br̥háti* 'he rips out' :: *br̥ǵ^{h}tó- > (5.2) __________ > (7.6) __________ [__________] > (6.6) __________ > (10) __________ > (18.3) __________ > (20.1) __________ 'ripped out' **D** AV *dißžaidiiāi* :: *d^{h}í-d^{h}b^{h}-sati > (22.4) __________ > (7.2b) __________ > (simplification *dbz* >*bz*) __________ > (27.1) __________ > (19.4) __________ 'he wants to hurt' **E** *bábhasti* < *b^{h}e-b^{h}osti 'he chews' :: 3. pl. *b^{h}é-b^{h}s-ati > (7.2b) __________ > (27.1) __________ > (19.4) __________ 'they chew' **F** *dáhati* < *d^{h}éǵ^{wh}eti 'he/it burns' :: *d^{h}éǵ^{wh}-s-n̥t- > (4.3) __________ > (15.1) __________ > (7.5b) __________ > (8.2) __________ > (10.1) __________ > (27.1) __________ > (23.2) __________ > (19.3) __________ 'burning' **G** AV *pasča* :: *po-sk^{w}-éh$_{1}$ > (c2) __________ > (4.1) __________ > (5.4) __________ > (10) __________ > (22.10) __________ 'behind, after' **H** LAT *mergit* :: *mézgeti > (5.5) __________ > (10) __________ > (22.11) __________ 'he sinks'

4.3: *g^{wh} > *g^{h}	**8.2:** *z > *ž / r,r̥,ŭ̄,k,ī̆ _	**20.1:** *z / ẓ > Ø without CL	**27.2:** *mn > n
5.3: *ǵ^{h} > *ȷ́^{h} [d̲žh]	**10:** *e/o > a and *ē/ō > ā	**20.3:** *ẓ > Ø / _G + CL	**27.3:** $NC_1C_2 > NC_2$
5.5: *g > *ǰ [dj] / _(ĕ̄, ī̆, i̯)	**11.2:** *au̯ > o	**22.10:** *sč > *šč > śc	**27.4:** $C_1...C_2 > C_1...C_1$
6.6: *ȷ́d^{h} [d̲ždh] > *ždh	**18.2:** *žd > *ẓḍ	**22.11:** *zǰ > *žǰ > *ǰǰ > jj	**c24:** *s > ṣ / r,r̥,ŭ̄,k,ī̆ _
7.6: *ȷ́^{h}t [džht] > *ȷ́d^{h} [d̲ždh]	**19.3:** *gẓ$^{(h)}$ /g^{h}s/ = kṣ	**23.2:** *ž > ẓ / r,r̥,ŭ̄,k,ī̆ _	
7.2b: *b^{h}s > *bz^{h}	**19.4:** *bz^{h} / b^{h}s/ = ps	**27.1:** $C^{h}...C^{h} > C...C^{h}$	

CONSONANTS

18 Dissimilation

Grassmann's law and analogical exceptions

Compare the following forms of the roots √*doh-* < **d^heu̯g^h-* 'to milk' and √*deh-* < **d^hei̯$\acute{g}^h$-* 'to smear' regarding the proportion of aspirated and non-aspirated consonants in the initial and final position of the roots. The consonant *h* counts as an aspirated consonant.

Root	1. sg. act.	2. sg. act.	3. sg. act.	2. pl. mid.
√*doh-* 'to milk'	*dohmi* 'I milk'	*dhokṣi* 'you milk'	*dogdhi* 'he milks'	*dhug-dhvam* 'you-all milk'
√*deh-* 'to smear'	*dehmi* 'I smear'	*dhekṣi* 'you smear'	*degdhi* 'he smears'	*dhig-dhvam* 'you-all smear'

The forms *dohmi* and *dehmi* display non-aspirated *d* in the initial position and *h* in the position before the ending -mi. The forms *dhokṣi* and *dhekṣi* display aspirated *dh* in the initial position and non-aspirated *k* in the position before the ending *-ṣi*. The forms *dogdhi* and *degdhi* display non-aspirated *d* in the initial position and the sound cluster *gdh* < **gh-t* which goes back to the combination of aspirated *gh* plus the ending *-ti* (cf. chapter 19). The forms *dhugdhvam* and *dhigdhvam* display aspirated *dh* in the initial position and aspirated *dh* in the ending.
The reason for this change of aspirated and non-aspirated consonants in √*doh-* < **d^heu̯g^h-* and √*deh-* < **d^hei̯$\acute{g}^h$-* is that there were originally two aspirated consonants in the PIE roots. But the phonological structure of Sanskrit allowed only one aspirated consonant in the root so that the first one was changed into its non-aspirated counterpart.
Therefore, we can trace the development of **d^heu̯g^h-mi* > **dhaugh-mi* > *dohmi* and **d^hei̯$\acute{g}^h$-mi* > **dhaigh-mi* > *dehmi* with monophthongization of **au* > *o* and **ai* > *e* and the development *$\acute{g}^h$ > *h* which had its starting point before palatal vowels and then spread analogically within the whole paradigm. The aspiration of initial *dh* was lost because root final *h* was an aspirated consonant. The same is true for **d^heu̯g^h-ti* > *dogdhi* and **d^hei̯$\acute{g}^h$-ti* > *degdhi* in which the aspiration was preserved between the morpheme boundary and the ending **-ti* as *gdh* which itself caused the deaspiration of initial *dh*. Furthermore, the form *degdhi* is an analogical formation because **d^hei̯$\acute{g}^h$ti* should have regularly developed to ^{x}*deḍhi* which did not happen because the phonological similarity to the other forms within the paradigm would have been lost. When the second aspirated consonant lost its aspiration through the addition of an attached ending e.g. **d^heu̯g^h-si* > *dhokṣi* or **d^hei̯$\acute{g}^h$-si* > *dhekṣi*, the initial aspiration remained. This gives the impression that the aspiration jumps around in the different words of the paradigm.
In the 2. pl. mid. *dhugdhvam* and *dhigdhvam* we find two aspirated consonants in the same word which contradicts the rule introduced above that in a sequence of two aspirated consonants the first one loses its aspiration. These words can be classified as analogical formations in which the speakers wanted to express unambiguously both the structure of the root and the structure of the morpheme *-dhvam*. Changes like these often occur when the content of the lexeme or the ending is in danger of not being understood correctly.

Lit.: Thumb 1905:102ff; Mayrhofer 1978:25.

Dissimilation

The sequence of the two labial sounds *p...m* could be changed by dissimilatory effects which can be seen in *klomán-* 'lungs' < **ploman-* < **pleu̯-mon-* in which *p...m* became *k...m*. Cognates from other languages include LAT *pulmō* and GR *pleúmōn* which retained the initial stop *p*.
Furthermore, VED *kṣumánt-* < **pḱu-mént-* 'abounding in cattle' can be traced to its preform by comparing it with AV *pasu-* < **peḱu-* and VED *paśú-* < **peḱú-* 'cattle' and by assuming the dissimilatory change of *p...m* to *t...m* before the sound cluster **tḱ* regularly became *kṣ* according to SC c15.

Exercises

E1 Loss of aspiration due to Grassmann's law

A *dáhati* 'he/it burns' < *d^hég^{wh}eti* :: **e-d^hēg^{wh}-s-t* > (4.3) ____________ > (22.5) ____________ > (10) ____________ > (8.1) ____________ > (23.1) ____________ > (17.1) ____________ > (28.1) ____________ 'he burned' **B** **di-d^heg^{wh}-s-e-ti* > (4.3) ____________ > (22.5) ____________ > (c24) ____________ > (10) ____________ 'he burns' **C** **gau̯-dhugh-s* > (11.2) ____________ > (22.5) ____________ > (c24) ____________ > (28.1) ____________ 'milker' **D** **arthabhudh-s* > (22.5) ____________ > (28.1) ____________ 'expert' **E** *dhāyā-* 'layer' :: 1. sg. mid. **d^he-$d^h$$h_1$-ói̯* > (13.1) ____________ > (10) ____________ > (11.1) ____________ > (27.1) ____________ 'I put' **F** GR *títhēmi* :: **d^hé-d^heh_1-ti* > (c2) ____________ > (27.1) ____________ > (10) ____________ 'he puts' **G** LAT *fiber* :: **b^heb^hrú-* > (27.1) ____________ > (10) ____________ 'a brown animal'

E2 Dissimilation / Simplification

A AV *taf-nah-* :: **tap-mán-* > *(p...m > k...m)* ____________ 'fever' **B** *áp-* 'water' :: dat. pl. **ap-bhis* > (22.2) ____________ > *(b...b > d...b)* ____________ > (28.3) ____________ **C** masc. sg. *tráyaḥ* :: fem. sg. **trisráḥ* > *(r...r > Ø...r)* ____________ 'three' **D** *tri-* 'three'+ *stár-* 'star' :: **tri-str-i̯i̯o-* > (8.1) ____________ > *(tr...tr > t...r)* ____________ > (23.1) ____________ > *(ṣr > ṣ)* VED ____________ name of a fixed star with the original meaning of 'belonging to a triple star' **E** LAT *sistō* :: **sth$_2$i-sth$_2$-e-ti* > (1.8) ____________ > (8.1) ____________ > (10) ____________ > (27.1) ____________ > *(st...št > t...št)* ____________ > (23.1) ____________ 'he stands'

1.8: $T > T^h$ / _h_2	**13.1:** *H* > Ø / _*V*	**28.3:** **s* > *ḥ* / _##
4.3: **g^{wh}* > **g^h*	**17.1:** **ṣt* > *ṣṭ*	**c2:** **eh$_1$* > **eH* > **ē*
8.1: **s* > **š* / *r,r̥,ŭ,k,ĭ* _	**22.2:** *K* > *G* / _*G*	**c24:** **s* > *ṣ* / *r,r̥,ŭ,k,ĭ* _
10: **e/o* > *a* and **ē/ō* > *ā*	**22.5:** $D^H > T$ / _*S*	**27.1:** $C^h...C^h > C...C^h$
11.1: **ai̯* > *e*	**23.1:** **š* > *ṣ* / *r,r̥,ŭ,k,ĭ* _	
11.2: **au̯* > *o*	**28.1:** **$C_1C_2(C_3)$* > *C_1* / _##	

19 Bartholomae's Law

Overall rule: D^{h}T > DD^h

Bartholomae's law is the name of an IIR sound change in which the sequence of media aspirata plus tenuis was substituted through a sequence of media plus media aspirata (_*b^{h}t, *d^{h}t, *g^{h}t, *ǰ^{h}t_ > _bdh, ddh, gdh, *ǰdh_) This sound change also affected words with the sound clusters _*g^{h}st_ > _*gsd^h_ and _*d^{h}st_ > _*dsd^h_ which means that a medial _s_ did not prevent the sound change from happening before it was lost afterwards (cf. chapter 16).
The sequences with the most straightforward developments were _*b^{h}t_ > _bdh_ and _*g^{h}t_ > _gdh_ in which the second consonant was voiced before the aspiration of the consonant cluster was transferred onto the cluster as a whole and noted at the end of it: _*b^{h}t_ > _*b^{h}d_ > _bdh_ as well as _*g^{h}t_ > _*g^{h}d_ > _gdh_. Therefore, we can explain the forms of the inf. _*labh-tum_ > (7.1) _labdhum_ 'to acquire' from the verb _labhate_ 'he acquires' and the PPP _*mughtá-_ > (7.4) _mugdhá-_ 'confused, foolish' with its synchronic root √_moh-_ < PIE _*meu̯gh-_ which ends in final _h_.
The explanation of the development _*d^{h}t_ > _ddh_ in _*badh-tá-_ > (7.2) _baddhá-_ 'bound' from the root √_bandh-_ is more difficult although we do not see a difference to _*b^{h}t_ > _bdh_ and _*g^{h}t_ > _gdh_ at the surface. But already in PIE, a sequence of two dental sounds was modified by inserting an _*s_ into them which led to _*t-t_ > _*tst_ or to _*d^h-t-_ > _*-d^{h}zt-_ respectively because _*s_ was pronounced as its voiced allophone _*z_ after _*d^h_. The sequence _*-d^{h}zt-_ was then subject to Bartholomae's law which led to _*-d^{h}zt-_ > _*-dzd^h-_ before the fricative _*z_ was ejected in Sanskrit. We can therefore sketch the development of _baddhá-_ as: _*b^{h}n̥d^h-tó-_ > (15.1) _*b^{h}ad^h-tó-_ > (2.3) _*b^{h}ad^{h}ztó-_ > (7.3) _*bhadzdhó-_ > (27.1) _*badzdhó-_ > (10) _*badzdhá-_ > (6.1) _baddhá-_. We can find Indo-Iranian evidence for the sound cluster _*dzdh_ in AV _basta-_ < _*bazda-_ in which case _*-dzdh-_ became _*-zd-_ which emerged as _st_ through analogical influence. This sound change also affected formations of roots like √_nah-_ < PIE _*ned^h-_ which ended in final _h_ in Sanskrit because this _h_ goes back to _dh_. The development of _*nadh-tá-_ > (7.2) _naddhá-_ 'bound' was similar to that of _baddhá-_.

The PIE sound cluster _*-ǵ^{h}t-_ which appears in PIE _*liǵ^{h}tó-_ > IIR _*liǰd^{h}á-_ > SKR _līḍhá-_ 'licked' from the root PIE _*liǵ^h-_ was subject to the palatalization _*ǵ^h_ > _*ǰ^h_ and influence of Bartholomae's law. In this case, it is difficult to determine the relative sequence of these sound changes and to say whether the palatalization _*liǵ^{h}tó-_ > _*liǰ^{h}tó-_ or Bartholomae's law _*liǵ^{h}tó-_ > _*liǵd^{h}ó-_ first influenced the PIE input form which became IIR _*liǰd^{h}á-_. The sequence [d̲ždh] in the form _*liǰd^{h}á-_ [lid̲ždhá] displays a similar sound structure compared to [dzdh] in the form _*badzdhá-_. We can therefore assume that the sequence [d̲ždh] first became _*-ždh-_ through deaffrication, then the sibilant _*ž_ became _*ẓ_ through the preceding _i_ according to the ruki rule, then retroflex _*ẓ_ assimilated _d_ to become _ḍ_, before retroflex _*ẓ_ was lost with compensatory lengthening: _*liǰd^{h}á-_ [_lid̲ždhá_] > (6.6) _*liždhá-_ > (23.2) _*liẓdhá-_ > (17.3) _*liẓḍhá-_ > (20.3) _*līḍhá-_.

Analogical and hybrid forms

Sanskrit speakers did not know the etymology of final _h_ in roots like √_nah-_ < PIE _*ned^h-_, √_muh-_ < _*meu̯g^h-_ or √_lih-_ < PIE _*lei̯ǵ^h-_ if they could not deduce it by comparing related words. Therefore, in some cases we find retroflex consonants which should not be there according to regular sound changes because in these cases final _h_ does not go back to a former palatal consonant. The verb _rohati_ 'he grows' < _*h₁leu̯d^h-e-ti_ goes back to a root with final _*d^h_ (~LAT _līberī_ < PIE _*h₁leud^h-ero-_ 'children', OHG _liut_ 'people') so that its PPP _*h₁lud^h-tó-_ should be ^{x}_ruddhá-_ but the actual form was _rūḍhá-_ as if the underlying root would have had a palatal consonant. The root √_muh-_ < _*meu̯gh-_ 'to be confused' even had the two participles _mugdhá-_ and _mūḍhá-_, the latter being either an analogical remodeling or the result of a root variant _*meu̯ǵ^h-_ with final palatal consonant.

Lit.: Mayrhofer 1978:24; Thumb 1905:107.

Exercises

E1 Bartholomae's law

A VED *bhásat* :: *ba-b^{h}s-tām > (7.2) ______ > (6.1) ______ 'shall chew' **B** *ghasati* 'he eats' < *g^{h}eseti :: *g^{h}s-to > (7.5) ______ > (8.2) ______ > (6.1) ______ > (10) ______ 'shall eat' **C** √*droh-* 'to hurt' :: *d^{h}rug^{h}tó- > (7.4) ______ > (27.1) ______ (10) ______ 'hurt' **D** *duha-* 'giving milk' :: *d^{h}ug^h-tó- > (7.4) ______ > (27.1) ______ > (10) ______ 'milked' **E** *budha-* 'intelligent' :: *b^{h}ud^h-tó- > (2.3) ______ > (7.3) ______ > (6.1) > ______ > (27.1) ______ > (10) ______ 'awakened' **F** *dáhati* 'he burns' :: *d^{h}eg^{wh}tó- > (4.3) ______ > (7.4) ______ > (27.1) ______ > (10) ______ 'burnt' **G** AV *azdā* :: *Hed^h-téh$_2$ > (c4) ______ > (13.1) ______ > (2.3) ______ > (7.3) ______ > (6.1) ______ > (10) ______ 'truly' **H** √*rodh-* 'to obstruct' :: 3. sg. aor. mid. *á-rud^h-s-ta > (7.3) ______ > (6.1) ______ 'he obstructed'

E2 Bartholomae's law with palatal *ǵ^h

A GR *leíkhō* :: 3. sg. *léi̯ǵ^{h}ti > (5.3) ______ [______] > (7.6) ______ [______] > (6.6) ______ > (9) ______ > (18.3) ______ > (10) ______ > (11.1) ______ > (20.1) ______ 'he licks' **B** *gā́hate* 'he dives into' :: *geǵ^{h}tó- > (5.3) ______ > (7.6) ______ [______] > (6.6) ______ > (18.3) ______ > (10) ______ > (20.3) ______ 'shallow, deep' **C** *vahati* 'he rides' :: *uǵ^{h}tó- > (5.3) ______ > (7.6) ______ > (6.6) ______ > (10) ______ > (18.3) ______ > (20.3) ______ 'moved' **D** *sáhate* 'he wins' :: *seǵ^{h}tó- > (5.3) ______ > (7.6) ______ > (6.6) ______ > (18.3) ______ > (10) ______ > (20.3) ______ 'defeated'

2.3: *d^{h}t > *d^{h}zt	**7.2:** *b^{h}st > bzdh	**8.2:** *z > *ž / r,r̥,ŭ̄,k,ĭ̄ _	**20.1:** *z /z̥ > Ø without CL
4.3: *g^{wh} > *g	**7.3:** *d^{h}zt > *dzd^h	**9:** *l/l̥ > r/r̥	**20.3:** *z̥ > Ø / _G + CL
5.3: *ǵ > *ǰ [d̲ž]	**7.4:** *g^{h}t > gdh	**11.1:** *ai̯ > e	**27.1:** C^h...C^h > C...C^h
6.1: *CsC > CC	**7.5:** *g^{h}st > gzd^h	**13.1:** H > Ø / _V	**c4:** *eh$_2$ > *aH > ā
6.6: *ǰd^h [d̲ždh] > *ždh	**7.6:** *ǰ^{h}t [d̲žht] > *ǰd^h [d̲ždh]	**18.3:** *žd^h > *z̥d̥^{h}	**c11:** *g > j / _(ĕ̄, ĭ̄, i̯)

20 Retroflex Consonants

Retroflex consonants as a peculiarity of Sanskrit

The retroflex consonants *ṭ, ṭh, ḍ, ḍh, ṇ* are a peculiarity of Sanskrit and cannot be found as such in other old Indo-European languages. Moreover, we can see an increase of their frequency from the oldest Vedic texts to classical Sanskrit texts. As retroflex consonants are very common in the Dravidian languages, we can suggest that their emergence can at least be partly attributed to a substrate effect of the indigenous Dravidian languages. But, as these consonants also emerge regularly from sound laws (cf. SC 18; chapter 13; further below), we must seek their origin in the interaction of substrate effects and regular sound laws. The development of a non-retroflex into a retroflex consonant is also referred to as cerebralization.

The ruki rule

A striking similarity between Baltic, Slavic, Albanian and Indo-Iranian is the retraction of dental-alveolar *s* after *r, u, k, i* which resulted in Slavic *x*, Baltic *š*, Albanian *sh* and Indo-Iranian **š* which further developed to retroflex *ṣ* in Sanskrit. Examples are **tr̥snā-* > (c24) **tr̥ṣṇā-* > (24) *tr̥ṣṇā-* 'thirst' and **ristó-* > (c24) **riṣtó-* > (17.1) *riṣṭá-* 'damaged', where we see in both cases an additional progressive assimilation of the place of articulation onto the following consonants *n* and *t* respectively which became retroflex *ṇ* and *ṭ*. An *r* following could prevent the development of retroflex *ṣ* due to dissimilatory effects which explains the absence of *ṣ* in *usra-* 'morning, bright' which did not become *ˣuṣra-*. The development of retroflex *ṣ* is also found in sandhi e.g. *abhí syāma* > *abhí_ṣyāma* 'we want to overcome' or *diví santu* > *diví_ṣantu* 'they shall be in the sky'. The ruki rule is also the reason for alternating allomorphs, e.g. the loc. pl. endings *-su* and *-ṣu* in *nāma-su* 'in the names' in contrast to *agni-ṣu* 'in the fires' as well as the 2. sg. endings *-si* and *-ṣi* in *ruṇatsi* 'you obstruct' in contrast to *bibharṣi* 'you carry'.

Development of dental *n* to retroflex *ṇ*

Medial dental *n* became retroflex *ṇ* if preceded directly by one of the retroflex consonants *r̥, r̥̄, r, ṣ,* or if between dental *n* and *r̥, r̥̄, r, ṣ* there was no dental or palatal consonant or *l, s, ś*. Furthermore, dental *n* had to be followed by a vowel. This explains the instr. sg. *kṣatreṇa-* < **kṣatrena* with retroflex *ṇ* from *kṣatra-* 'reign, sovereignty' whereas the instr. sg. *balena-* from *bala-* 'strength' does not have retroflex *ṇ*. The word *nagara-* 'city' has a nom. acc. pl. *nagarāṇi* < **nagarāni* with retroflex *ṇ* whereas the nom. acc. pl. *phalani* from *phala-* 'fruit' exhibits a dental *n*. Two retroflex *ṇ* separated only by a single vowel were prevented through dissimilation. This explains the instr. sg. *prāṇena* from *prāṇá-* 'breath' against expected *ˣprāṇeṇa*.

Lit.: Stiehl 2007:320–321.

Dental consonant plus palatal consonant yielded a retroflex consonant

Retroflex consonants also originated through a reciprocal assimilation of dental and palatal consonants which can be seen from examples like **dr̥ḱtó-* > *dr̥ṣṭá-* 'seen' from the root √*dr̥ś-*. In this case, **ḱt* first became **ćt* [t̠št] before it was simplified to [št] which became *ṣṭ*. The reverse sequence **tḱ* developed via IIR **tć* [tt̠š] to SKR retroflex **ṭṣ* before it developed further to *kṣ* due to phonotactic reasons: **tétḱon-* > (5.1+10) IIR **tátćan-* [tátt̠šan] > (18.4) **táṭṣan-* > (19.1) *tákṣan*. The sequence **ḱs* became IIR **ćs* [t̠šs] and resulted via **ṭṣ* in SKR *kṣ* as well: **h₂éḱso-* > (c3) **áḱso-* > (5.1) IIR **ácsa-* [át̠šsa] > (18.4) **áṭṣa-* > (19.1) *ákṣa-*. Only the sequence **sḱ* did not have a retroflex result but developed to *ch* in the initial position and to *cch* in the medial position: **sḱeh₁-i̯eh₂* > (c19) *chāyā́-* 'shade', **gʷm̥-sḱe-ti* > (c20) *gacchati* 'he walks'. This development can be explained by assuming that the palatal feature of **ḱ* had been lost early before *s*.

Exercises

E1 The ruki rule with Indic comparanda / Emergence of retroflex ṇ

A √*sad-* 'to sit' :: *sad-ná- > (22.3) ____________ 'sitting' :: *ni-sad-na- > (22.3) ____________ > (c24) ____________ > (24) ____________ 'leaned at' **B** *nayati* 'he leads' :: *pari-nayati > (24) ____________ 'he leads around' **C** *namati* 'he worships' :: *pra-namati > (24) ____________ 'he worships' **D** √*naś-* 'to die' :: *pra-naśyati > (24) ____________ 'he dies' **E** √*stigh-* 'to rise, to raise' :: 3. sg. des. *ti-stigh-is-ate > (c24) ____________ > (17.1) ____________ 'he wants to climb' **F** √*stubh-* 'to cheer, to praise' :: *anu-stúbh- > (c24) ____________ > (17.1) ____________ 'hymn of praise' **G** √*syand-* 'to hurry' :: *raghu-syád- > (c24) ____________ 'hurrying quickly' **H** *sarpa-* 'snake' :: instr. sg. *sarpena > (24) ____________ **I** *hari-* Epithet of Viṣṇu :: instr. *harinā > (24) ____________

E2 The ruki rule with comparanda from other languages

A GR *dís* :: *du̯is > (c24) ____________ 'two times' **B** GR *ársēn* :: *h_2u̯ŕ̥sen- > (13.2) ____________ > (c24) ____________ > (10) ____________ 'male animal' **C** LAT *iūs* :: *i̯ūs > (c24) ____________ 'broth' **D** LAT *mūs* :: *múHs > (13.4) ____________ > (c24) ____________ 'mouse' **E** LAT *coxa* :: *kokseh$_2$ > (c4) ____________ > (10) ____________ > (c24) ____________ 'curve' **F** LAT *ūvidus* :: *ug^w-sé-ti > (4.2) ____________ > (22.1) ____________ > (c24) ____________ > (10) ____________ 'he moistens' **G** LAT *perna* :: *pḗrsni- > (c24) ____________ > (10) ____________ 'heel' **H** √*vas-* 'to stay' :: *pra-ús-tha- > (c24) ____________ > (17.1) ____________ > (11.2) ____________ 'place for the night' **I** GR *ksyrón* :: *ksu-ró- > (c24) ____________ > (10) ____________ 'razor'

4.2: *g^w > *g	**13.2:** *H > Ø / #_C	**22.1:** G > K / _K	**c4:** *eh$_2$ > *aH > ā
10: *e/o > a and *ē/ō > ā	**13.4:** *VH > V̄	**22.3:** C > N / _N	**c24:** *s > ṣ / r,r̥,ŭ,k,ĭ _
11.2: *au̯ > o	**17.1:** *st > ṣṭ	**24:** *n > ṇ	

21 Final Consonants I

Reduction of final consonants to one single consonant

Consonant clusters consisting of more than one consonant were reduced to one single consonant in the absolute final position. This can be seen in the nominative singular of the present participle **bharant-s* > (28.1) *bharan* 'carrying' in contrast to its accusative singular *bharant-am* or in the nominative singular **prā́ṅkṣ* > (28.1) *prā́ṅ* 'eastward' from the stem *prā́ñc-*. If the final consonant was *k*, *ṭ*, *t*, *p* and it belonged to the root like in *ūrk* 'strength' and if this consonant stood after *r*, it was not lost in order to maintain the information content of the word. In ipf. **abibhar-t* > *abibhar* 'he carried' from the root √*bhar-* 'to carry', however, the 3. sg. ending *-t* was lost because it was a morphological ending and did not belong to the root.

Lit.: Thumb 1905:121ff.

Devoicing and deaspiration of stops in the absolute final position

In the absolute final position, Sanskrit phonology only permitted vowels, diphthongs, semivowels, nasals and visarga *ḥ* as well as voiceless non-aspirated consonants. Therefore, the labial stops *p*, *ph*, *b*, *bh* surfaced as *p*, the dental stops *t*, *th*, *d*, *dh* surfaced as *t*, the retroflex stops *ṭ*, *ṭh*, *ḍ*, *ḍh* surfaced as *ṭ* and the guttural stops *k*, *kh*, *g*, *gh* surfaced as *k*. The palatal stops *c*, *ch*, *j*, *jh* were not permitted in the final position and had either the same result as the dorsal stops, which was *k*, or the same result as the retroflex stops, which was *ṭ*. Also the consonants *h*, *ś*, *ṣ* resulted either in *k* or in *ṭ*. Furthermore, *s* and *r* became *ḥ*.

Lit.: Thumb 1905:128: Stiehl 2007:309.

Divergent results from equal preforms

In some words we find divergent results although we have the same phonological starting point, e.g. compare the final consonants in *viṭ* < **u̯iḱs* 'village' and *dik* < **diḱs* 'cardinal direction' from the stems *viś-* < **u̯iḱ-* and *diś-* < **diḱ-* with final *ś* going back to **ḱ*. The reason for the two divergent results retroflex *ṭ* and velar *k* in the final position is the overlap of two different sound changes, one of them is the above mentioned simplification of final consonants and the other one is the development of **ṭṣ* > (19.1) *kṣ* which is explained in chapter 15.
The consonant cluster **ḱs* of the preforms **u̯iḱs* and **diḱs* first became IIR **ćs* [t̠šs] through the development **ḱ* > **ć*. Then it changed to **ṭṣ* due to reciprocal assimilation: **ćš* [t̠šs] > *[t̠s] > **ṭṣ*. This consonant cluster **ṭṣ* then developed to *kṣ* due to phonotactic reasons, a process that can also be seen in **réḱses-* > IIR **rácsas-* > (18.6) **ráṭṣas-* > (19.1) *rákṣas-* 'damage'. After the preforms **u̯iḱs* and **diḱs* had become **u̯iṭṣ* and **diṭṣ*, SC 28.1 had already started being active, which caused **u̯iṭṣ* to become *viṭ*. But the word **diṭṣ* was not influenced by SC 28.1 before it had become **dikṣ*, causing it to become *dik*.

Differences between synchronic and diachronic derivation

The Indic grammarians derived the nominative form of a word from its word stem e.g. *vāk* < *vāc-* 'voice', *ásr̥k* < *ásr̥j-* 'blood', *divaspr̥k* < *divaspr̥ś-* 'touching the sky' which is historically not correct. In the case of *vāk*, stem final *c* of *vāc-* already represents the palatalized variant of velar *k* which is preserved in *vāk*. Furthermore, *vāk* goes back to PIE **u̯ōkʷs* and the development of the nom. was as follows: **u̯ōkʷs* > (4.1) **u̯ōks* > (c24) **u̯ōkṣ* > (10) **vākṣ* > (28.1) *vāk*. The nom. ending *s* first became *ṣ* after *k* before it was lost in the final position because of its reduction to a single consonant. But in several case forms within the paradigm, palatalized *c* had originated out of **kʷ* before a palatal vowel, e.g. gen. sg. **u̯ōkʷes* > (4.1) **u̯ōkes* > (c10) *vācas*, and therefore Indic grammarians regarded this sound as the word stem. In the Avestan cognate *vāxš* 'voice' we can still see final *-s* which was lost in Sanskrit.

Exercises

E1 Simplification of final consonant clusters

A LAT *nox* :: **nok*^{w}*t-s* > (4.1) ___________ > (10.3) ___________ > (28.1) ___________ 'night' **B** acc. sg. *bhavantam* :: nom. sg. **bhavants* > (28.1) ___________ 'being' **C** LAT *rēx* :: **h*$_3$*rēǵ-s* > (13.2) ___________ > (22.1) ___________ > (5.1) ___________ [___________] > (18.6) ___________ > (10) ___________ > (28.1) ___________ 'king' **D** *hanti* 'he slays' :: **h*$_1$*e-g*^{wh}*en-t* > (c1) ___________ > (4.3) ___________ > (c9) ___________ > (10.1) ___________ > (28.1) ___________ 'he slayed' **E** *santi* 'they are' :: **h*$_1$*s-ent-s* > (13.2) ___________ > (10.1) ___________ > (28.1) ___________ 'being' **F** *dhákṣu-* 'burning' :: 3. sg. aor. **a-dhāgh-s-t* > (22.5) ___________ > (c24) ___________ > (17.1) ___________ > (28.1) ___________ 'it/he burned' **G** OHG *tugan* 'to be useful, suitable' :: **h*$_1$*e-d*^{h}*eu̯g*^{h}*t* > (c1) ___________ > (22.5) ___________ > (10.1) ___________ > (11.2) ___________ > (28.1) ___________ 'he milked (an animal)' **H** LAT *māter* :: **mā́tēr* > (10) ___________ > (28.2) ___________ 'mother' **I** **chand-ti* > (22.1) ___________ 'it pleases' :: 3. sg. aor. **achānd-s-t* > (22.1) ___________ > (28.1) ___________ 'it pleased' **J** *aśnóti* 'he reaches' :: aor. **Hé-Hneḱ-t* > (13.1) ___________ > (13.4) ___________ > (5.1) ___________ [___________] > (18.6) ___________ > (10) ___________ > (28.1) ___________ 'he reached' **K** *vīrudha-* 'plant' :: **vīrudh-s* > (22.5) ___________ > (28.1) ___________ 'herb' **L** √*marj-* 'to wipe off' < **merǵ-* :: **h*$_1$*e-mērǵ-t* > (c1) ___________ > (22.1) ___________ > (5.1) ___________ [___________] > (10) ___________ > (18.6) ___________ > (28.1) ___________ 'he wiped off' **M** √*leh-* 'to lick' < **lei̯ǵ*^{h}*-* :: **med*^{h}*u-liǵ*^{h}*s* > (22.5) ___________ > (5.1) ___________ > (18.6) ___________ > (10) ___________ > (28.1) ___________ 'bee' **N** LAT *sex* :: **seḱs* > (5.1) ___________ > (18.6) ___________ > (10) ___________ > (*s*... *ṣ* > *ṣ*... *ṣ*) ___________ > (28.1) ___________ 'six' **O** *kāmaduh-* :: nom. **keh*$_2$*mo-d*^{h}*ug*^{h}*s* > (c4) ___________ > (22.5) ___________ > (10) ___________ > (28.1) ___________ 'heavenly cow'

4.1: **k*^{w} > **k*	**10.3:** **o* > *a*	**17.1:** **ṣt* > *ṣṭ*	**28.2:** **r/n* > Ø / *V̄*_##
4.3: **g*^{wh} > **g*^{h}	**11.2:** **au̯* > *o*	**18.6:** **ćs* [t̲šs] > **ṭṣ*	**c1:** **h*$_1$*e* > **He* > *e*
5.1: **ḱ* > **ć* [t̲š]	**13.1:** **H* > Ø / _*V*	**22.1:** *G* > *K* / _*K*	**c4:** **eh*$_2$ > **aH* > *ā*
10: **e/o* > *ā* and **ē/ō* > *ā*	**13.2:** **H* > Ø / #_*C*	**22.5:** *D*^{H} > *T* / _*S*	**c9:** **ǵ*^{h} > *h*
10.1: **e* > *a*	**13.4:** **VH* > *V̄*	**28.1:** **C*$_1$*C*$_2$*(C*$_3$*)* > *C*$_1$ / _##	**c24:** **s* > *ṣ* / *r,r̥,ū̆,k,ī̆* _

22 Final Consonants II

Final *-ns remains in sandhi forms

The simplification of final consonant clusters, which is described in the previous chapter, also affected the PIE acc. pl. ending **-ns*. That is why the preform of the acc. pl. **devāns* became *devān* 'gods' through the loss of final *-s*. The absolute final position, however, only occurs at the end of a sentence or in words uttered in isolation. This had the effect that the old ending **ns* was preserved in certain sandhi positions in contrast to the absolute final position where it was lost. From a synchronic standpoint, this looked like the insertion of an additional *s* which is contrary to the historical development in which *s* was lost. Therefore, we find the synchronic sandhi rule that states the insertion of a homorganic sibilant *ś*, *ṣ*, *s* between final *-n* and initial palatal *c*, *ch*, retroflex *ṭ*, *ṭh* or dental *t*, *th*. Additionally, *-n* becomes anusvāra *ṃ*. Thus, the synchronic sandhi rule was *devān ca* > (s15.1) *devāṃś_ca*, whereas diachronically we see the following process: *devāns ca* > (22.10) *devānś_ca* > (s14.1) *devāṃś_ca*. The first step describes the assimilation of final *s* to *ś* before palatal *c* and in the second step the nasal *n* is articulated as *ṃ* before a following consonant. In Vedic texts, we find this sandhi only where it has an etymological justification, which means only where there had originally been the final consonant cluster *-ns*. But the speakers of classical Sanskrit generalized a more general sandhi rule out of this special phonological context and extended its range to similar phonological contexts even if they had not originated from original **ns*.

Lit.: Thumb 1905:130.

Sandhi of final -n and -ṅ after a short vowel before an initial vowel

The simplification of final consonant clusters also affected final **-nts* and **-nt*, e.g. in the present participle **bharants* > (28.1) *bharan* 'carrying' or in the 3. ps. pl. prt. **āsant* > (28.1) *āsan* 'they were'. This simplification of word final consonants before an initial vowel had the effect that a former closed final syllable became an open syllable because final *-n* was counted with the word initial vowel as one syllable. In order to maintain the former syllabification, Sanskrit speakers doubled the sequence of final short vowel plus nasal before the initial vowel of the next word. They thus imitated the syllable-closing lost consonant in their pronunciation. Therefore, we find the sandhi of **āsant atra* > (28.1) *āsan atra* > (s16.1) *āsann_atra* 'they were here' if a word like *āsan* stood before a word like *atra* which started with an initial short vowel. This rule only concerns *-n* and *-ṅ* but not *-ñ* and *-ṇ* because they did not appear in the final position. It also did not affect final *m*. Furthermore, the rule applied to final *ṅ* only in directional adverbs like *pratyaṅ* 'westwards' e.g. in *pratyaṅ āsīnaḥ* > (s16.2) *pratyaṅṅ_āsīnaḥ* 'sitting westwards'. Similiar to the extension of phonological contexts like in the example of *devāns ca* > (s15.1) *devāṃś_ca* above, also the sandhi of doubling a final nasal before an initial vowel was generalized to all cases of final nasals, even if they did not go back to a sequence of more than one consonant like in the example of **āsant* > *āsan* 'they were'.

Sandhi of initial ch after vowel

A structurally similar sandhi phenomenon is the development of initial *ch* after a short vowel, and more seldom after a long vowel. The consonant *ch* goes back to PIE **sḱ* or **sḱʰ* which can be seen from some clear etymologies like *chāyā-* 'shade' < **sḱeh₁-i̯eh₂-* (GR *skiá*, TOCH B *skiyo*) and √*ched-* 'to split' < **sḱ⁽ʰ⁾ei̯d-* (GR *skhízō*, LAT *scindō*). Synchronically, the consonant *ch* counted as a single consonant although it had emerged from the two former consonants **sḱ⁽ʰ⁾*. Therefore, *ch* became geminated *cch* in sandhi forms in order to keep up the syllabic structure: *na chāyām vindāmi* > (s5.1) *nacchāyāṃ_vindāmi* 'I do not find shade'. This process was afterwards transferred to medial contexts like **gʷm̥-sḱe-ti* > *gacchati* 'he walks' or **i̯m̥-sḱe-ti* > *yacchati* 'he reaches'. In *ā chādayati* > *ā_cchādayati* 'he covers', this sandhi can be found also after a long vowel although a resyllabification would not have been necessary because the syllable before *ch* already counted as long due to the long vowel.

Exercises

E1 Etymological **-ns* reappears in sandhi forms

A *vṛkān ca* > (s15.1) ___________ ‘and the wolves’ **B** *abharan ca* > (s15.1) ___________ ‘and they carried’ **C** *tān ṭaṅkān* > (s15.2) ___________ ‘these hoes’ **D** *devān tatra* > (s15.3) ___________ ‘the gods over there’ **E** *śaśin tvarasva* > (s15.3) ___________ ‘oh moon, hurry up!’ **F** *hasan cakāra* > (s15.1) ___________ ‘he did it laughingly’ **G** *pāśān chettum* > (s15.1) ___________ ‘in order to loosen chains/bonds’ **H** *patan taruḥ* > (s15.3) ___________ ‘a falling tree’ **I** *hasan ṭīkate* > (s15.2) ___________ ‘he jumps laughingly’ **J** *calan ṭiṭṭibhaḥ* > (s15.2) ___________ ‘a running bird’

E2 Sandhi of final nasals after a short vowel before an initial vowel

A *tasmin adrau* > (s16.1) ___________ ‘on this mountain’ **B** *gacchan īkṣate* > (s16.1) ___________ ‘he watches while walking’ **C** *pratyaṅ āste* > (s16.2) ___________ ‘he sits westwards’ **D** *yogin āgaccha* > (s16.1) ___________ ‘oh yogi, come!’ **E** *dhāvan aśvaḥ* > (s16.1) ___________ ‘running horse’ **F** *pratyaṅ āsīnaḥ* > (s16.2) ___________ ‘sitting westwards’

E3 Initial *ch* after short vowel or after *ā* and *mā*

A *tava chāyā* > (s5.1) ___________ ‘your shadow’ **B** *taru chāyā* > (s5.1) ___________ ‘shade of a tree’ **C** *ā chādayati* > (s5.1) ___________ ‘he covers’ **D** *ā chāditaḥ* > (s5.1) ___________ ‘covered’ **E** 3. sg. prs. *mā chidat* > (s5.1) ___________ ‘he shall not cut!’ **F** 3. sg. aor. *mā chaitsīt* > (s5.1) ___________ ‘he shall not cut!’ **G** *badarī chāyā* > (s5.1) ___________ ‘shadow of the jujuba-tree’

s5.1: *V̆ + ch > V̆_cch*	**s15.2:** *n + ṭ(h) > ṃṣ_ṭ(h)*	**s16.1:** *n > nn / V̆_#V*
s15.1: *n+c(h) > ṃś_c(h)*	**s15.3:** *n + t(h) > ṃs_t(h)*	**s16.2:** *ṅ > ṅṅ / V̆_#V*

23 Syllabic Nasals and Liquids

Merger of *l/l̥ and *r/r̥ in *r/r̥

In Proto-Indo-Iranian, the phonemes *l and *r merged to *r and their syllabic allophones *r̥ and *l̥ merged to *r̥ nearly completely. However, in some words, e.g. lúbhyati 'he desires greatly' < PIE *leu̯b^h-, original *l remained as l. Examples for this regular merger are *u̯ĺ̥k^{w}o- > IIR *u̯ŕ̥ka- > vŕ̥ka- 'wolf' (~GR lúkos, LAT lupus) as well as *$h_1$élḱos- > árśas- 'wound' (~GR hélkos). From the Sanskrit point of view it was not possible to determine whether the sound r went back to *r or *l.

Lit.: Thumb 1905:62.

The syllabic nasals

The comparison of the root √nam- 'to bow' with its PPP *nm̥-tó- > natá- 'bowed' as well as of √bandh- 'to bind' with its PPP *b^{h}n̥d^{h}tó- > baddhá- 'bound' displays a regular change of related word forms with and without nasal because in these cases Sanskrit a in n**a**tá- and b**a**ddhá- goes back to the syllabic variant of the nasal which is preserved in √na**m**- and √ba**n**dh-. Past perfect participles in Proto-Indo-European were regularly built from the zero grade of the root. Bold **a** in n**a**tá- goes back to syllabic *m̥ and bold **a** in b**a**ddhá goes back to syllabic *n̥. Further examples are ś**a**tám 'hundred' < *ḱm̥tóm and s**a**ptá 'seven' < *septm̥ which correspond to LAT ce**n**tum and sept**em**. Before *i̯, *u̯, *m, the syllabic nasals *n̥ and *m̥ became an and am which can be seen from *g^{w}m̥-i̯e-toi̯ > gamyate 'he walks' and *g^{wh}n̥-i̯e-toi̯ > hanyáte 'he is killed'. The outcome -am < * m̥ in the acc. sg. of the consonant stems pā́dam < *pód-m̥ 'foot' is not a straightforward phonological rule because the uninflected dáśa 'ten' < *déḱm̥ (cf. GR déka) shows the expected development of *m̥ > a. In the case of the acc. sg. the phonological development first led to -a to which -m was added in order to remark the accusative ending. Long ā in pā́dam is caused by Brugmann's law (cf. chapter 5). Also in the cases of gamyate and hanyate, we cannot completely rule out the interference of analogy or phonological restitutions.

Lit.: Thumb 1905:65–69.

Resonant plus laryngeal before consonant

The consonant clusters consisting of a syllabic resonant plus laryngeal *r̥H, *l̥H first merged into *r̥H. Before a following consonant, this sequence then became either īr or ūr, the latter in labial environments. In this way, we can connect stīrṇá- 'spread out' < *str̥$h_3$nó- with GR strōtós built from the PIE root *sterh_3-, and pūrṇá- 'full' < *pl̥$h_1$nó- with LAT plēnus from the PIE root *pelh_1-. The sequence *m̥H became ām, which can be seen from the connection of adāmta- 'untamed' < *n̥-dm̥h_2-tó- with GR ádmētos from the PIE root *demh_2-. This also explains lengthened vowels of some Sanskrit verbs e.g. bhram- 'to wander about' > bhrāmyati 'he wanders about' as the underlying PIE root *b^{h}remH- had a laryngeal in the final position. The sequence *n̥H became ā, which can be seen from the connection of jātá- 'born' < *ǵn̥h_1-tó- with GR gnētós from the PIE root *ǵenh_1-.

Lit.: Thumb 1905:69–72; Mayrhofer 1978:19.

Resonant plus laryngeal before a vowel

The sequence of syllabic resonant plus laryngeal *r̥H, *l̥H became either ir or ur. The exact reasons for this divergent distribution is unclear but we can see a tendency for ur to occur before labial u. Therefore, in the development of gurú- < *g^{w}r̥H-ú- 'heavy', which is cognate to GR barús, labiovelar g^w became velar g before *r̥H became ur: *g^{w}r̥H-ú- > (4.2) *gr̥H-ú- > (14.4) gurú-. This also explains the long vowel in the paradigm of nom. gīr 'song of praise' in contrast to acc. giram. In the nominative case, the sequence *r̥H stands before a consonant: *g^{w}r̥H-s > (4.2) *gr̥H-s > (14.1) *gīrs > (28.1) gīr and in the accusative case the sequence *r̥H stands before a vowel *g^{w}r̥H-m̥ > (4.2) *gr̥H-m̥ > (15.4) *gr̥H-am > (14.2) giram.

Exercises

E1 Merger of *l and *r / Syllabic nasals

A LAT *pluit* 'it rains' :: 3. pl. *pleu̯onto > (9) __________ > (10) __________ 'they swim' **B** LAT *relinquō* :: *linékʷti > (4.1) *linékti > (9) __________ > (10.1) __________ > (24) __________ 'he leaves' **C** LAT *mollis* :: *ml̥dú- > (9) __________ 'soft' **D** GR *tatós* :: *tn̥tó- > (15.1) __________ > (10) __________ 'stretched' **E** GR *elakhús* :: *$h_1$ln̥gʷʰú- > (13.2) __________ > (4.3) __________ > (15.1) __________ > (9) __________ 'lightweight' **F** √*bhañj-* 'to break' :: *bhn̥gná- > (15.1) __________ 'broken' **G** LAT *mēns* 'mind' :: *mn̥tá- > (15.1) __________ 'having thought' **H** √*daṃś-* 'to bite' :: *dm̥śati > (15.2) __________ 'he bites' **I** LAT *ventus* :: *gʷm̥tó- > (4.2) __________ > (15.2) __________ > (10) __________ 'having come' **J** *nébʰos- > (10) __________ 'cloud' :: *n̥bʰ-ró- > (15.1) __________ > (10.3) __________ 'thunder-cloud' **K** LAT *nox* :: *n̥kʷtéh_2 > (c4) __________ > (4.1) __________ > (15.1) __________ 'night' **L** HIT *peru* 'rock' :: *péru̯n̥to- > (15.1) __________ > (10) __________ 'mountain(ous)'

E2 Syllabic resonant plus laryngeal before consonant and before a vowel

A √*tam-* 'to stiffen' :: *tm̥H-i̯e-ti > (14.7) __________ > (10) __________ 'he becomes immovable' **B** √*śram-* 'to tire' :: *ḱrm̥h_2-i̯e-ti > (14.7) __________ > (c7) __________ > (10) __________ 'he gets/is tired' **C** *támas-* 'darkness' :: *tm̥H-ró- > (14.7) __________ > (10.3) __________ 'dark red' **D** LAT *antae* :: *h_2n̥Ht-eh_2- > (c4) __________ > (14.6) __________ > (13.1) __________ 'doorframe' **E** lit. *ántis* :: *h_2n̥h_2-tí- > (1.5) __________ > (14.6) __________ > (13.1) __________ 'duck' **F** LAT *glōs* :: *gl̥h_2-i- > (9) __________ > (14.2) __________ 'sister-in-law' **G** GR *trõma* 'wound' :: *tr̥h_3-o- > (14.4) __________ > (10.3) __________ 'ill, wounded' **H** LAT *lātus* 'carried' :: *tl̥h_2-éh_2 > (c4) __________ > (14.5) __________ 'balance' **I** HIT *tarh-* 'to overcome' :: *tr̥Hés > (14.2) __________ > (10) __________ 'through' **J** √*kr̥̄* 'to scatter' :: *kr̥H-e-ti > (14.2) __________ > (10) __________ 'he scatters'

1.5:	*$h_{1/2/3}$ > *H	**10:**	*e/o > a and *ē/ō > ā	**14.4:**	*r̥H > ur / _V	**15.2:**	*m̥ > a
4.1:	*kʷ > *k	**10.3:**	*o > a	**14.5:**	*l̥h_2 > ul / _V	**24:**	*n > ṇ
4.2:	*gʷ > *g	**13.1:**	*H > Ø / _V	**14.6:**	*n̥H > *aH > ā	**c4:**	*eh_2 > *aH > ā
4.3:	*gʷʰ > *gʰ	**13.2:**	*H > Ø / #_C	**14.7:**	*m̥H > ām	**c7:**	*ḱ > ś
9:	*l/l̥ > r/r̥	**14.2:**	*r̥H > ir / _V	**15.1:**	*n̥ > a		

24 Laryngeal Developments I

Laryngeals next to vowels

PIE laryngeal *h$_2$ colored adjacent *e to *a and PIE laryngeal *h$_3$ colored adjacent *e to *o. Laryngeal *h$_1$ did not alter adjacent *e. After the vowel coloring, the laryngeals were lost completely **before** a vowel and with compensatory lengthening **after** a vowel. This is the reason for the initial *a* in GR *antí*, LAT *ante* and SKR *ánti* < *h$_2$énti 'in front of' which developed out of *e which had become *a* through its adjacent position to *h$_2$. The Anatolian language Hittite preserved the initial laryngeal as in *hant-* 'front'.
We do not see compensatory lengthening here because the laryngeal stood before the colored vowel in contrast to *péh$_2$ti > (1.2) *páh$_2$ti > (1.5) *páHti > (13.4) *pā́ti* 'he protects' where laryngeal *h$_2$ stood after *e. Hittite preserved the laryngeal in *pahhasmi* 'I protect'.
Another example is *ákṣi-* 'eye', the first part of which goes back to *h$_3$ék^{w}s- which is cognate to LAT *oculus*. The initial laryngeal caused the change of *e to *o which remained in Latin and became Sanskrit *a*. In this case, we can theoretically also assume a proto-form *h$_3$ók^{w}s- with apophonic *o which would have yielded the same result. Final *i* of *ákṣi-* is an innovation and cannot be traced back to PIE directly. It probably originated in analogy to other words for body parts with a similar shape e.g. *ásthi-* 'bone'.
Many long vowels in Sanskrit originated through the loss of a laryngeal with subsequent compensatory lengthening of the preceding vowel. Examples for *ū* and *ī* are *dhūmá-* 'smoke'< *d^{h}uh$_2$-mó-, which is related to LAT *fūmus*, or *krūrá-* 'meat, raw' < *kruh$_2$-ró-, which is related to LAT *cruor* 'blood', or *vīrá-* 'man, hero' < *u̯iH-ró-, which is related to LAT *vīs* 'force, violence'.

Laryngeals between consonants

Between consonants, the PIE laryngeals *h$_1$, *h$_2$, *h$_3$ are continued uniformly as *i*. An example for laryngeal *h$_1$ is the PPP *d^{h}h$_1$tó- > (1.6) *dhitó- > (10.3) *dhitá- > (29.1) *hitá-* 'placed' from PIE *d^{h}eh$_1$- 'to put, to place', which is cognate to GR *thetós*. An example for laryngeal *h$_2$ is the PPP *sth$_2$tó- > *sthitá-* 'established' from PIE *steh$_2$- 'to stand', which also displays the aspiration of *t* through *h$_2$ (cf. next chapter) and which is cognate to GR *statós* and LAT *status*. Another example is *dh$_1$tó- > *ditá-* 'bound' from PIE *deh$_1$- 'to bind'. From the PPP *dh$_3$-to 'given' (from the root *deh$_3$- 'to give') we can derive GR *dotós* and LAT *datus*. In Latin, interconsonantal laryngeals are uniformly continued as *a* and Greek displays the threefold result *e*, *a*, *o* coming from *h$_1$, *h$_2$, *h$_3$.

Laryngeals in the initial position before consonant

In the initial position before consonant, the PIE laryngeals were lost completely in Sanskrit in contrast to Greek where they are reflected as vowels. This can be seen from the comparision of GR *anḗr* < *h$_2$nér-s with the development of *h$_2$néro- > (1.5) *Hnéro- > (10) > *Hnára- > (13.2) *nára-* 'man'. The lengthening of the first element in VED *sū-nara-* 'joyous' < *su-Hnara- < *su-h$_2$nero- with *ū* for expected short *u* can be explained as the effect of a former laryngeal. Another example is revealed by the comparison of GR *ophrū̃s* < *h$_3$b^{h}ruH-s with *bhrū́-* < *h$_3$b^{h}ruH- 'eyebrow' in which case the laryngeal is reflected in Greek through the initial vowel.

Overview of laryngeal developments from PIE to Sanskrit

PIE	*h$_1$e	*eh$_1$	*h$_2$e	*eh$_2$	*h$_3$e	*eh$_3$	*Hi	*iH	*Hu	*uH	*CHC
Late-PIE	*He	*eH	*Ha	*aH	*Ho	*oH	*Hi	*iH	*Hu	*uH	*CHC
Proto-IIR	*Ha	*aH	*Ha	*aH	*Ha	*aH	*Hi	*iH	*Hu	*uH	*CHC
Sanskrit	*a*	*ā*	*a*	*ā*	*a*	*ā*	*i*	*ī*	*u*	*ū*	*CiC

Exercises

E1 Laryngeals next to vowels (A - N) and between vowels (O - Q)

A AV *sāma-* :: **ḱi̯e$h_1$mó-* > (c2) ____________ > (c7) ____________ > (10) ____________ 'black' **B** LAT *sōns* 'guilty' :: **n̥-$h_1$sn̥t-* > (14.6) ____________ > (15.1) ____________ 'not being' **C** LAT *agō* :: **h_2í-h_2ǵ-e-toi̯* > (1.5) ____________ > (13.1+13.4) ____________ > (c8) ____________ > (10) ____________ > (11.1) ____________ 'he impels' **D** *ákṣi-* 'eye' :: **h_3í-h_3k^ws-oi̯* > (1.5) ____________ > (13.1+13.4) ____________ > (4.1) ____________ > (c24) ____________ > (10) ____________ > (11.1) ____________ 'I perceive' **E** **h_2í-$h_2$sd-oi̯* > (1.5) ____________ > (13.1+13.4) ____________ > (22.2) ____________ > (c25) ____________ > (17.2) ____________ > (20) ____________ > (10) ____________ > (11.1) ____________ 'I praise' **F** **h_2í-h_2ḱ-oi̯* > (1.5) ____________ > (13.1+13.4) ____________ > (c7) ____________ > (10) ____________ > (11.1) ____________ 'I rule' **G** HIT *hi-iš-ši* 'at the drawbar' :: **h_2iHs-éh_2-* > (c4) ____________ > (1.5) ____________ > (13.1+13.4) ____________ > (c24) ____________ 'drawbar' **H** LAT *vānus* 'empty' :: **u̯$h_2$nó-* > (13.4) ____________ > (10) ____________ 'insufficient' **I** ON *vella* 'to bubble' :: **u̯l̥H-mi-* > (14.3) ____________ > (27.5) ____________ 'wave' **J** GR *orthós* :: **u̯r̥Hd^hu̯ó-* > (14.3) ____________ > (10) ____________ > (27.5) ____________ 'straight' **K** GR *orgḗ* 'passion' :: **u̯r̥Hǵ-éh_2-* > (c4) ____________ > (14.3) ____________ > (c8) ____________ > (27.5) ____________ 'strength' **L** MHG *Atem* 'breath' :: **eh_1t-men-* > (c2) ____________ > (10) ____________ 'soul' **M** *áp-* 'water' < **$h_2$ep-* :: **anu-h_2p-ó-* > (13.4) ____________ > (10) ____________ 'swamp' **N** **n̥b^hí-h_3k^wo-* > (13.4) ____________ > (4.1) ____________ > (15.1) ____________ > (10) ____________ 'encounter' **O** LAT *fānum* :: **$d^h h_1$s-n̥i̯o-* > (1.6) ____________ > (c24) ____________ > (24) ____________ > (10) ____________ 'holy' **P** GR *patḗr* :: **ph_2tḗr* > (1.6) ____________ > (10.2) ____________ > (28.2) ____________ 'father' **Q** GR *dósis* :: **d$h_3$ti-* > (1.6) ____________ 'donation'

1.5:	**h_1/h_2/h_3 > *H*	**13.1:**	**H > Ø / _V*	**20:**	**z / ẓ > Ø*	**c4:**	**eh_2 > *aH > ā*
1.6:	**H > i / C_C*	**13.4:**	**VH > V̄*		without CL	**c7:**	**ḱ > ś*
4.1:	**k^w > *k*	**14.3:**	**l̥H > ūr / _C*	**22.2:**	*C > G / _G*	**c8:**	**ǵ > j*
9:	**l/l̥ > r/r̥*	**14.6:**	**n̥H > *aH > ā*	**24:**	**n > ṇ*	**c24:**	**s > ṣ / r,r̥,ŭ̄,k,ī̆_*
10:	**e/o > a*	**15.1:**	**n̥ > a*	**27.5:**	**u̯ > Ø / #_ū*	**c25:**	**z > ẓ / r,r̥,ŭ̄,k,ī̆_*
	and **ē/ō > ā*	**17.2:**	**ẓd > *ẓḍ*	**28.2:**	**r/n > Ø / V̄_##*		
11.1:	**ai̯ > e*			**c2:**	**eh_1 > *eH > *ē*		

25 Laryngeal Developments II

Aspiration through laryngeals

The Sanskrit word _pánthā-_ 'path', which is cognate to LAT _pōns_ 'bridge' and GR _póntos_ 'sea', has the Vedic forms nom.sg. _pánthās_, acc.sg. _pánthām_, gen.abl.sg. _pathás_, instr.pl. _pathíbhis_. It therefore displays the three different stem variants _panth-_, _path-_ and _pathi-_, all of them with aspirated _th_. This word is also cognate to AV _paṇtā̊_ with its gen. _paθō_ where we find a change between _t_ and _θ_. According to regular sound changes, we would expect SKR _t_ to match AV _t_ and SKR _th_ to match AV _θ_. As the other non-Indo-Iranian languages do not exhibit traces of a former _th_, we can expect SKR _th_ and AV _θ_ to be of secondary origin.

The development _*t_ > _th_ can in this case be explained through the influence of _*h_$_2$. When we trace _pánthā-_ back to its prehistory, we can reconstruct a paradigm with nom. sg. _*pént-oh_$_2$_-s_ and acc. sg. _*pént-oh_$_2$_-m̥_ with the strong stem _*pent-_ plus an additional stem morpheme _*-eh_$_2$_-/*-oh_$_2$_-_ plus the case endings _-s_ and _-m_. In the weak cases e.g. the gen. sg. _*pn̥t-h_$_2$_-és_ we find the zero grade _*pn̥t-_ as well as the adjacent placement of _t_ and _h_$_2$ which led to SKR _th_ and AV _θ_. This aspiration was then analogically transferred onto the other cases in the paradigm.

Hiatus after loss of laryngeals between vowels

The loss of intervocalic laryngeals _*VHV_ > _*VØV_ left a metrically relevant hiatus in the Rigveda because the acc. sg. _pánthām_ < _*pánthaHam_ < _*pént-eh_$_2$_-m̥_ must, in some cases, be analysed as consisting of the three syllables _pán.tha.am_. After the stem _th_ had spread analogically over the whole paradigm, the laryngeal of the preform _*pánthaHam_ > _*pántha.am_ was lost and left a hiatus, before the two _a_-vowels contracted to _ā_: _*pántha.am_ > _*pánthām_. A similar result can be seen in AV _vāta-_ 'wind' < _*Hu̯áHata-_, which is cognate to VED _vā́ta-_. This word must presumably be read as consisting of the three syllables _va.a.ta_ in Yasna 44,4. The comparison with LAT _ventus_ and HIT _hu̯ant-_ 'wind' enables the establishment of the preform _*h_$_2$_u̯éh_$_1$_-n̥t-o-_ for Vedic and Avestan, which is an _nt_-participle from the PIE root _*h_$_2$_u̯eh_$_1$_-_ 'to blow'. The nasal _*n_ was articulated as syllabic _*n̥_ between the consonants _*h_$_1$ and _*t_ in the preform _*h_$_2$_u̯éh_$_1$_-n̥t-o-_. The merger of the laryngeals _*h_$_{1/2/3}$ into _*H_ and the development of _*n̥_, _*e_, _*o_ > _a_ led to _*h_$_2$_u̯éh_$_1$_-n̥t-o-_ > (1.5) _*Hu̯éHn̥to-_ > (15.1) _*Hu̯éHato-_ > (10) _*Hu̯áHata-_ before the laryngeals were lost which produced trisyllabic AV _va.a.ta_. The vowel contraction _a+a_ > _ā_ then led to the normal Avestan form _vāta-_. Therefore, we can also assume a similar development for VED _vā́ta-_.

The hiatus which was caused by the loss of a laryngeal could not only be resolved by vowel contraction but also by the insertion of the transitional consonant _y_ as Vedic evidence suggests. We can therefore trace VED _rayíṣ_ 'wealth, property' back to PIE _*reh_$_1$_-i-s_ which is an _i_-stem from the laryngeal final PIE root _*reh_$_1$_-_ 'to give', the Latin cognate of which is LAT _rēs_ 'issue, thing'. The development of _*reh_$_1$_-i-s_ led via _*raHis_ to _*ra.is_ with short _a_. The internal hiatus of the nom. sg. _*ra.is_ > _rayíṣ_ and the acc. sg. _*ra.im_ > _rayím_ was then resolved through the insertion of the transitional consonant _y_. In other word forms, which had an ending starting with a vowel, e.g. dat. sg. SKR _-e_ < PIE _*ei̯_, the stem-forming vocalic element _*i_ was transformed into its consonantal counterpart _*i̯_ and the loss of the laryngeal was compensated through lengthening of the preceding vowel. One example is dat. sg. _*reh_$_1$_-i̯-ei̯_ > (10.1) _*raHi̯ai̯_ > (c4) _*rāi̯ai̯_ > VED _rāyé_.

Exercises

E1 Aspiration of voiceless consonants by laryngeal *h_2

A LAT *sistō* :: **stí-sth$_2$-e-ti* > (1.8) __________ > (*st…st* > *t…st*) __________ > (13.1) __________ > (c24) __________ > (17.1) __________ > (10) __________ 'he stands, puts' **B** GR *platús* :: **pl̥th$_2$ú-* > (1.8) __________ > (13.1) __________ > (9) __________ 'broad' **C** **mn̥th$_2$tó-* > (1.8) __________ > (1.6) __________ > (15.1) __________ > (10) __________ 'dislocated' **D** GR *kléos* 'fame' :: **ḱléu̯-is-th$_2$o-* > (c7) __________ > (9) __________ > (1.8) __________ > (13.1) __________ > (c24) __________ > (17.1) __________ > (10) __________ 'the most famous' **E** LAT *rota* 'wheel' :: **roth$_2$ó-* > (1.8) __________ > (13.1) __________ > (10) __________ 'chariot' **F** *páñca* 'five' :: **pn̥k^{w}tHó-* > (1.8) __________ > (4.1) __________ > (13.1) __________ > (15.1) __________ > (10) __________ 'Quintus'

E2 Aspiration of voiced *ǵ by laryngeal *h_2

Laryngeal *h_2 also caused the aspiration of *ǵ which became *ǵ^h. The further development was identical with the development of primary *ǵ^h > *h*.

A GR *méga* :: **méǵh$_2$-* > (1.9) __________ > (1.7) __________ > (c9) __________ > (10) __________ 'big, great'

B LAT *egō* :: **eǵh$_2$óm* > (1.9) __________ > (13.1) __________ > (c9) __________ > (10) __________ 'I'

E3 Complete the paradigm of VED *pánthās*. The IIR forms are regular. Vedic generalized *th* in the complete paradigm through analogy.

	PIE		IIR		VED
nom.	**pént-oh$_2$-s*	>	__________	>	__________
acc.	**pént-oh$_2$-m̥*	>	__________	>	__________
gen.	**pn̥th$_2$-és*	>	__________	>	__________

1.6: *H > i / C_C	**1.9:** G > G^h > / _*h_2	**10:** *e/o > a and *ē/ō > ā	**c7:** *ḱ > ś
1.7: *H > i / _##	**4.1:** *k^w > *k	**15.1:** *n̥ > a	**c9:** *ǵ^h > h
1.8: T > T^h / _h_2	**9:** *l/l̥ > r/r̥	**17.1:** *st > ṣṭ	**c24:** *s > ṣ / r,r̥,ŭ,k,ĭ _

26 Proto-Indo-European, Indo-Iranian and Sanskrit

The Proto-Indo-European phoneme system

You can find the traditional reconstruction of the Proto-Indo-European phoneme system on the opposite page. The relevant word equations which have led to this reconstruction can be found in chapter 27. We can reconstruct stops with the manners of articulation *voiceless*, *voiced* and *voiced aspirated* at the places of articulation *labial*, *dental-alveolar*, *palatal*, *velar* and *labiovelar*. The PIE consonant $*b$ is placed in parentheses due to its rare occurrence. The three PIE guttural series *palatal*, *velar* and *labiovelar* are usually not continued as three different series in the Indo-European languages which have either merged the palatal and velar series by losing the palatal feature (centum languages like Latin), or the velar and labiovelar series by dropping the labial element of the *labiovelar* series (satem languages like Sanskrit). An exception could be the Anatolian language Luvian in which there might be evidence for the continuation of the three series. The exact phonetic nature of the laryngeals $*h_1$, $*h_2$, $*h_3$ is unknown. The laryngeals $*h_2$ and $*h_3$ are continued as separate phonemes in Anatolic but the other IE languages only display indirect evidence of their former existence.

It is getting clearer and clearer that although the traditionally reconstructed system works in terms of connecting the phonemes of the Indo-European daughter languages, it probably does not accurately represent the real phonetic nature of Proto-Indo-European. Even the traditional distinction between centum and satem languages will probably not last forever. The traditional reconstruction is not only challenged from internal linguistic evidence found in the Indo-European languages themselves but also from external sources like the Nostratic comparison of the Indo-European languages with non-Indo-European languages.

Changes from Proto-Indo-European to Proto-Indo-Iranian

- The stop consonants were enriched by a series of voiceless aspirated consonants which was mainly caused through the aspirating effect of laryngeal $*h_2$ as well as the devoicing in sound clusters like $*sb^h > sp^h$.
- The laryngeals $*h_1$, $*h_2$, $*h_3$ merged into $*H$.
- The PIE palatal consonants $*\acute{k}$, $*\acute{g}$, $*\acute{g}^h$ were the source of the so-called first palatal series $*\acute{c}$, $*\acute{j}$, $*\acute{j}^h$ and the palatalization of $*k/*k^w$, $*g/*g^w$, $*g^h/*g^{wh}$ before palatal vowels caused the so-called second palatal series $*\check{c}$, $*\check{j}$, $*\check{j}^h$. The exact phonetic difference between both series is unknown. At the time of the Indo-Iranian parent language, both series must still have been different because they show different results in Sanskrit $*k/*k^w > c$ and $*\acute{k} > ś$. We can phonetically posit that the first series was approximately IPA $*\acute{c}$ [tʃ], $*\acute{j}$ [dʒ], $*\acute{j}^h$ [dʒ^h] and the second was approximately IPA $*\check{c}$ [cç], $*\check{j}$ [ɟj], $*\check{j}^h$ [ɟj^h] (cf. Lipp 2009:XXX). At some point in time, IIR $*\acute{j}$ and $*\check{j}$ merged into Sanskrit *j* and IIR $*\acute{j}^h$ and $*\check{j}^h$ merged into Sanskrit *h* via [dʒ^h] because $*\acute{g}$ and $*g/*g^w$ are uniformely continued as *j* before palatal vowels, and $*\acute{g}^h$ and $*g^h/*g^{wh}$ are uniformely continued as *h* before palatal vowels. That is why both IIR series $*\acute{c}$, $*\acute{j}$, $*\acute{j}^h$ and $*\check{c}$, $*\check{j}$, $*\check{j}^h$ are transcribed as [t̠š], [d̠ž], [d̠žh] for the sake of simplicity. Indo-Iranian [t̠š] is therefore either continued as Sanskrit *ś* [š] if it goes back to $*\acute{k}$, or it remains as Sanskrit *c* [t̠š] if it goes back to $*k/*k^w$ before a palatal vowel.
- The sound **š* originated from **s*, which is called the ruki rule, or it was the result of the palatalization of $*\acute{k}$ > *[t̠š] > **š*. The sound **ž* likewise originated from the ruki rule in a voiced surrounding or it was the result of the palatalization of $*\acute{g} > *\acute{j}$ [d̠ž] and $*\acute{g}^h > *\acute{j}^h$ [d̠žh].
- The voiced sibilants **z* and **ž* are the allophones of the corresponding voiceless sibilants.

Changes from Proto-Indo-Iranian to Sanskrit

- Both Indo-Iranian palatal series were simplified into a single palatal series.
- Laryngeal $*H$ was lost after it had resulted out of the merger of PIE $*h_{1/2/3}$.
- The new retroflex sounds originated from the reciprocal assimilation of dental and palatal consonants in consonant clusters like $*\acute{k}t$ > *ṣṭ* and $*t\acute{k}$ > **ṭṣ*, from the ruki rule (c24/c25) as well as due to the substrate influcence of Dravidian languages.
- The sound [ḥ] was the voiceless allophone of the *s/r*-visarga.

Proto-Indo-European

		Labial	Dental / Alveolar	Palatal	Velar	Labio-velar	Glottal
Stop	**Voiceless**	*p	*t	*ḱ	*k	*k^{w}	? *h$_1$ = ?
	Voiced	*(b)	*d	*ǵ	*g	*g^{w}	
	Voiced asp.	*b^{h}	*d^{h}	*ǵ^{h}	*g^{h}	*g^{wh}	
Fricative			*s ~ *[z]		? *h$_2$ = χ ? *h$_3$ = γ	? *h$_3$ = γ^{w}	? *h$_1$ = h
Nasal		*m ~ *[m̥]	*n ~ *[n̥]	*[ɲ]	*[ŋ]		
Lateral			*l ~ *[l̥]				
Vibrant			*r ~ *[r̥]				
Approximant		*u̯		*i̯			

Proto-Indo-Iranian

		Labial	Dental/ Alveolar	Palatal 1	Palatal 2	Velar	Glottal
Stop	**Voiceless**	*p	*t	*ć	*č	*k	
	Voiceless asp.	*p^{h}	*t^{h}	*ć^{h} ?	*č^{h} ?	*k^{h}	
	Voiced	*b	*d	*ȷ́	*ǰ	*g	
	Voiced asp.	*b^{h}	*d^{h}	*ȷ́^{h}	*ǰ^{h}	*g^{h}	
Fricative			*s ~ *[z]	*š ~ *[ž]			*H
Nasal		*m ~ *[m̥]	*n ~ *[n̥]	*[ɲ]		*[ŋ]	
Lateral			*l ~ *[l̥]				
Vibrant			*r ~ *[r̥]				
Approximant		*u̯		*i̯			

Sanskrit

		Labial	Dental / Alveolar	Retroflex	Palatal	Velar	Glottal
Stop	**Voiceless**	p	t	ṭ	c	k	
	Voiceless asp.	p^{h}	t^{h}	ṭ^{h}	c^{h}	k^{h}	
	Voiced	b	d	ḍ	j	g	
	Voiced asp.	b^{h}	d^{h}	ḍ^{h}	j^{h}	g^{h}	
Fricative			s ~ *[z]	ṣ ~ *[ẓ]	ś		h / [ḥ]
Nasal		m	n	[ṇ]	[ɲ]	[ŋ]	
Lateral			*l ~ *[l̥]				
Vibrant				*r ~ *[r̥]			
Approximant		u̯			i̯		

From Proto-Indo-European to Proto-Indo-Iranian

Vowel coloring through larnygeals / Subsequent merger of laryngeals into *H

The PIE laryngeal *h$_2$ colored an adjacent *e to *a and the PIE laryngeal *h$_3$ colored an adjacent *e zu *o. After that, the three PIE laryngeals *h$_1$/*h$_2$/*h$_3$ merged into IIR *H.

Phoneme	**PIE**	>	**IIR**	>	**SKR**	
***h$_2$**	*péh$_2$ti*	>	**páHti*	>	*pā́ti*	‘(he) protects’
***h$_3$**	*h$_3$épos-*	>	**Hápas-*	>	*ápas-*	‘work’

Merger of labiovelars and velars

The labiovelars *k^w, *g^w, *g^{wh} and velars *k, *g, *g^h merged into velars because the labiovelars lost their labial coarticulation.

***k^w**	*sm̥-h$_3$k^w-ó-m	>	*saHkám	>	sākám	‘together’
***g^w**	*g^{w}ṓu̯s	>	*gā́u̯s	>	gáuṣ	‘cow’
***g^{wh}**	*g^{wh}ormó-	>	*gharmá-	>	gharmá-	‘heat’

Development of PIE palatals

The PIE palatals *ḱ, *ǵ, *ǵ^h became IIR *ć, *ȷ́, *ȷ́^{h}.

***ḱ**	*ḱm̥tóm	>	*ćatám	>	śatám	‘hundred’
***ǵ**	*ǵónu-	>	*ȷ́ā́nu-	>	jā́nu-	‘knee’
***ǵ^h**	*ǵ^{h}imó-	>	*ȷ́^{h}imá-	>	himá-	‘winter’

Merger of *r/r̥ and *l/l̥ into *r/r̥

The PIE resonants *r/r̥ and *l/l̥ merged into *r/r̥.

***l**	*ḱlutó-	>	*ćrutá-	>	śrutá-	‘heard’
***l̥**	*u̯ĺ̥k^{w}o-	>	*vŕ̥ka-	>	vŕ̥ka-	‘wolf’

Development of *n̥ and *m̥ into *a

The syllabic nasals *n̥ and *m̥ became *a and *n̥H became ā.

***n̥**	*mn̥tó-	>	*matá-	>	matá-	‘supposed’
***m̥**	*ḱm̥tóm	>	*ćatám	>	śatám	‘hundred’
***n̥H**	*ǵn̥h$_1$tó-	>	*ȷ́aHtá-	>	jātá-	‘born’

Affrication of dental clusters

In PIE, *s or its allophone *z was inserted into a sequence of two dental stops *d, *d^h, *t turning the first stop into an affricate. On the way from Proto-IIR to Sanskrit, this *s was ejected again.

***dt**	*u̯oi̯d-th$_2$a	>	*u̯ai̯t-s-tha	>	véttha	‘you know’
***d^{h}t**	*b^{h}n̥d^h-tó-	>	*bhadzdhá-	>	baddhá-	‘bound’
***tt**	*u̯r̥t-tó-	>	*u̯r̥tstá-	>	vr̥ttá-	‘turned’

Bartholomae's law

The sequence of a voiced aspirated stop **b*^{h}, **d*^{h}, **g*^{h}, **ǰ́*^{h} followed by a voiceless stop **t* turned into a sequence of voiced stop plus voiced aspirated stop.

b*^{h}*t	**lub*^{h}*-tó-*	>	**lubdha-*	>	*lubdhá-*	'greedy'
d*^{h}*t	**b*^{h}*n̥d*^{h}*tó-*	>	**bhadzdhá-*	>	*baddhá-*	'bound'
ǵ*^{h}*t	**liǵ*^{h}*tó-*	>	**lij́dhá-*	>	*līḍhá-*	'licked'
g*^{wh}*t	**d*^{h}*eg*^{wh}*tó-*	>	**dhagdhá-*	>	*dagdhá-*	'burnt'

The ruki rule

PIE **s* became IIR **š* after any of the sounds **r, *r̥, *u, *u̯, *ū, *k, *i, *i̯, *ī*. This sound **š* then developed to SKR *ṣ*.

r̥_	**pr̥sth*$_2$*ó-*	>	**pr̥št*^{h}*Há-*	>	*pr̥ṣṭhá-*	'back (of the body)'
u̯_	**ǵéu̯s-o-*	>	**ǰ́áu̯ša-*	>	*jóṣa-*	'pleasure'
k_	**k*^{w}*sép-*	>	**kšáp-*	>	*kṣáp-*	'night'
i_	**nizdó-*	>	**niždá-*	>	*nīḍá-*	'nest'

Palatalization before a palatal vowel

After the PIE labiovelars and velars had merged into **k*, **g*, **g*^{h}, these sounds were palatalized and affricated to IIR **č*, **ǰ*, **ǰ*^{h} in the position before the palatal vowels **e*, **ē*, **i*, **ī*. This sound change must have happened before the development of **e > a*.

***k*^{w}**	**k*^{w}*e*	>	**če*	>	*ca*	'and'
***g*^{w}**	**g*^{w}*iHu̯o-*	>	**ǰīu̯a-*	>	*jīva-*	'alive'
***g*^{wh}**	**g*^{wh}*énti*	>	**ǰ*^{h}*énti*	>	*hánti*	'he beats / he slays'

Vowel changes *e/*o > *a and *ē/ō > *ā

The two short PIE vowels **e* and **o* merged into IIR *a*. The same is true for the corresponding long vowels **ē* and **ō* which merged into *ā*.

e	**h*$_2$*néro-*	>	**Hnára-*	>	*nára-*	'man'
o	**póti-*	>	**páti-*	>	*páti-*	'lord, husband'
ē	**rēǵ-s*	>	**rā́ćs*	>	*rā́ṭ*	'king'
ō	**u̯ōk*^{w}*-s*	>	**u̯ā́kš*	>	*vā́k*	'voice'

Brugmann's law

In some cases, PIE **o* became IIR *ā* in open syllables next to a resonant.

o	**ǵónu-*	>	**ǰ́ā́nu-*	>	*jā́nu-*	'knee'
o	**dóru-*	>	**dā́ru-*	>	*dā́ru-*	'wood'

From Indo-Iranian to Sanskrit

Loss of Indo-Iranian laryngeal *H

After PIE *h_1/*h_2/*h_3 had become IIR *H, this unspecified laryngeal was lost before a vowel and in the initial position before consonant.

***h_2**	*$h_2$elg^{wh}ó-	>	*Harghá-	>	arghá-	'value'
***h_2**	*$h_2$ép-nes-	>	*Hápnas-	>	ápnas-	'possession'
***h_3**	*$h_3$épos-	>	*Hápas-	>	ápas-	'work'

The unspecified IIR laryngeal *H was lost after a vowel with compensatory lengthening.

***h_2**	*péh$_2$ti	>	*páHti	>	pā́ti	'he protects'

Resonant plus laryngeal

The IIR sequence of resonant plus laryngeal *r̥H before a consonant resulted in *īr* or *ūr*. The sequence *m̥H resulted in *ām*.

***r̥HC**	*dl̥h$_1$g^{h}ó-	>	*dr̥Hghá-	>	dīrghá-	'long'
***l̥HC**	*h$_2$u̯l̥H-neh$_2$	>	*Hu̯r̥HnaH-	>	ū́rṇā	'wool'
***r̥HV**	*g^{w}r̥H-í-	>	*gr̥H-í-	>	girí-	'mountain'
***r̥HV**	*g^{w}r̥H-ú-	>	*gr̥H-ú-	>	gurú-	'heavy'
***m̥H**	*n̥-dm̥h$_2$-tó-	>	*adm̥Htá-	>	adāmtá-	'untamed'

Deaffrication of affricated palatal consonants

PIE *ḱ, *ǵ, *ǵ^h developed to IIR *ć [t̠š], *j́* [d̠ž], *j́^{h}* [d̠žh] but it is not exactly clear at what stage of development the affrication process started. The sound *j́ [d̠ž] did not change anymore and resulted in SKR *j* [dž]. The sound *ć [t̠š] became *ś* [š] through deaffrication. The sound *j́^{h}* [d̠žh] was deaffricated to its intermediate step [žh] on its way to SKR *h* through the loss of the voiced sibilant.

***ć**	*km̥tóm	>	*ćatám	>	śatám	'hundred'
***j́**	*ǵónu-	>	*j́ā́nu-	>	jā́nu-	'knee'
***ǰ**	*g^{w}iHu̯ó-	>	*jīu̯á-	>	jīvá-	'alive'
***j́^{h}**	*ǵ^{h}imó-	>	*j́^{h}imá-	>	himá-	'winter'
j^h	*g^{wh}énti	>	*j^{h}énti	>	hánti	'he beats, he slays'

Monophthongization of *ai̯ and *au̯

The merger of PIE *e and *o also caused a merger of the former separate diphthongs *ei̯ and *oi̯ to *ai̯ as well as *eu̯ and *ou̯ to *au̯. The diphthong *ai̯ then became long *e* and the diphthong *au̯ became long *o* through monophthongization.

***ei̯**	*ǵ^{h}éi̯men-	>	*j́^{h}ái̯man-	>	héman-	'winter'
***oi̯**	*toi̯	>	*tai̯	>	te	'these'
***eu̯**	*leu̯kes-	>	*rau̯čas-	>	rocas-	'light'

Cerebralization of *š and *ž

Indo-Iranian *š and *ž, which had developed out of the ruki rule, became retroflex *ṣ* and **ẓ* in Sanskrit.

***r̥s**	*tr̥sneh$_2$-	>	*tr̥šnā-	>	tr̥ṣṇā-	'thirst'
***u̯s**	*teu̯so-	>	*tau̯ša-	>	tosa-	'satisfaction'
***ks**	*ksuró-	>	*kšurá-	>	kṣurá-	'sharp knife'
***īs**	*u̯isó-	>	*u̯išá-	>	viṣá-	'poison'

Loss of the voiced sibilants *z, *ẓ, *ž

The voiced sibilants were lost which was often accompanied by compensatory lengthening of the preceding vowel.

*z	*se-sǵʰ-u̯os-	>	*sazj́ʰu̯as-	>	*sazhvas-	>	sāhvas-	'mighty'
*ẓ	*ǵʰéi̯sd-os-	>	*j́ʰái̯ždas- [d̠žhái̯ždas]	>	*žhái̯ẓdas-	>	héḍas-	'anger'
*ž	*ǵʰimó-	>	*j́ʰimá- [d̠žhimá]	>	*žhimá-	>	himá-	'winter'

Development of consonant clusters

Consonant clusters with palatal consonants display difficult and divergent developments in Sanskrit.

ḱsV	*réḱs-es-	>	*raćsas-	>	rákṣas-	'damage'
ḱt	*oḱtṓ	>	*aćtā́	>	aṣṭā́	'eight'
tḱ	*tétḱon-	>	*táćtan-	>	tákṣan-	'carpenter'
sḱ	*gʷm̥-sḱ-e-ti	>	*gasćati	>	gacchati	'he walks'

Final position

Consonant clusters in the final position were simplified to their first consonant.

kʷts	*nókʷt-s	>	*nákts	>	nák	'night'
ǵs	*rḗǵ-s	>	*rā́ćs [rāṯšs]	>	*rā́ṭṣ > rā́ṭ	'king'

Exercises

E1 **In the following exercise you start from the PIE reconstruction and add the languages Indo-Iranian and Sanskrit. You arrive at the Indo-Iranian reconstruction by applying sound change rules 1–10 which can be found in the index.**

- **Diphthongs and PIE *e/*o**

PIE	>	IIR	>	SKR	
*ǵʰéi̯men-	>	______	>	______	'winter'
*toi̯	>	______	>	______	'these'
*leu̯kes-	>	______	>	______	'light'
*ǵʰéi̯sd-os-	>	______	>	______	'anger'
*teu̯so-	>	______	>	______	'satisfaction'
*$h_2$éi̯dʰes-	>	______	>	______	'firewood'
*u̯oi̯d-th_2a	>	______	>	______	'you know'
*se-sǵʰ-u̯os-	>	______	>	______	'mighty'
*nizdó-	>	______	>	______	'nest'
*póti-	>	______	>	______	'lord, master'
*dóru-	>	______	>	______	'wood'
*aǵó-	>	______	>	______	'he-goat'
*$h_2$néro-	>	______	>	______	'man'
*kʷe	>	______	>	______	'and'

- **Consonant clusters**

*réḱs-es-	>	______	>	______	'damage'
*oḱtṓ	>	______	>	______	'eight'
*tétḱon-	>	______	>	______	'carpenter'
*gʷm̥-sḱ-e-ti	>	______	>	______	'he walks'
*nókʷt-s	>	______	>	______	'night'
*rḗǵ-s	>	______	>	______	'king'
*u̯r̥t-tó-	>	______	>	______	'turned'

Laryngeals

*$h_2$énto-	>	________	>	________	'limit, end'
*$h_2$énd^{h}es-	>	________	>	________	'sprout'
*$h_2$épo	>	________	>	________	'away'
*$h_1$erh$_1$tér-	>	________	>	________	'rower'
*Hómso-	>	________	>	________	'shoulder'
*$h_2$onḱó-	>	________	>	________	'share, part'
*$h_2$énǵ^{h}es-	>	________	>	________	'fear'
*h_2éǵtreh$_2$-	>	________	>	________	'whip'
*$h_2$ósth$_2$-	>	________	>	________	'bone'
*$h_3$éh$_1$-s	>	________	>	________	'mouth'
*h_2n̥h$_2$tí-	>	________	>	________	'duck'
*h_2ŕ̥tḱo-	>	________	>	________	'bear'
*HúHd^h-er-	>	________	>	________	'udder'
*h_2iHs-éh$_2$-	>	________	>	________	'pole bar'
*Hói̯ko-	>	________	>	________	'one'
*h_2i-h$_2$ḱó-	>	________	>	________	'lord, master'
*Hénos-	>	________	>	________	'carriage'
*dl̥h$_1$g^{h}ó-	>	________	>	________	'long'

Labiovelars

*g^{w}r̥H-í-	>	________	>	________	'mountain'
*g^{w}r̥H-ú-	>	________	>	________	'heavy'
*g^{w}ṓu̯s	>	________	>	________	'cow'
*g^{wh}ormó-	>	________	>	________	'heat'
*u̯ĺ̥k^{w}o-	>	________	>	________	'wolf'
*g^{w}iHu̯o-	>	________	>	________	'alive'
*k^{w}sép-	>	________	>	________	'night'
*g^{wh}énti	>	________	>	________	'he beats, he slays'
*u̯ōk^w-s	>	________	>	________	'voice'
*$h_2$elg^{wh}ó-	>	________	>	________	'value'

- **Bartholomae's law**

*lub^{h}-tó-	>	____________	>	____________	'greedy'
*liǵ^{h}tó-	>	____________	>	____________	'licked'
*d^{h}eg^{wh}tó-	>	____________	>	____________	'burnt'

- **Syllabic nasals**

*b^{h}n̥d^{h}tó-	>	____________	>	____________	'bound'
*n̥-h$_{2}$ei̯g^{wh}és-	>	____________	>	____________	'impeccable'
*n̥b^{h}ró-	>	____________	>	____________	'thundercload'
*h$_{1}$r̥sn̥-b^{h}ó-	>	____________	>	____________	'bull'
*h$_{3}$r̥s-u̯ó-	>	____________	>	____________	'high'
*h$_{2}$m̥b^{h}í	>	____________	>	____________	'around'
*ǵn̥h$_{1}$tó-	>	____________	>	____________	'born'
*mn̥tó-	>	____________	>	____________	'thought'
*ḱm̥tóm	>	____________	>	____________	'hundred'
*n̥-dm̥h$_{2}$-tó-	>	____________	>	____________	'untamed'

- **Palatalizations**

*ǵ^{h}imó-	>	____________	>	____________	'winter'
*h$_{1}$élḱes-	>	____________	>	____________	'haemorrhoids'
*h$_{2}$éḱmon-	>	____________	>	____________	'stone'
*h$_{2}$éḱru-	>	____________	>	____________	'tear'
*h$_{1}$éḱu̯o-	>	____________	>	____________	'horse'
*h$_{3}$éng^{w}es-	>	____________	>	____________	'anointment'
*ḱlutó-	>	____________	>	____________	'heard'
*ǵónu-	>	____________	>	____________	'knee'

- **Ruki rule**

*h$_{2}$uksén-	>	____________	>	____________	'young bull'
*h$_{2}$us-és-	>	____________	>	____________	'dawn'
*h$_{2}$éḱso-	>	____________	>	____________	'axis'
*ksuró-	>	____________	>	____________	'sharp knife'
*u̯isó-	>	____________	>	____________	'poison'
*pr̥sth$_{2}$ó-	>	____________	>	____________	'back (of the body)'
*ǵéu̯s-o-	>	____________	>	____________	'pleasure'
*tr̥sneh$_{2}$-	>	____________	>	____________	'thirst'

27 Reconstruction of Proto-Indo-European Phonemes

Systematic correspondences in vocabulary and grammar

If different languages exhibit systematic correspondences regarding their vocabulary and grammar and the frequency of these correspondences is so high that it cannot be attributed to mere chance, it is possible to posit a genetic relationship between these languages and reconstruct a common ancestor or proto-language. LAT *tremō* and GR *trémō*, which both mean 'I shiver', enable the reconstruction of a common preform **trémō*, from which the two language forms originated. The comparison of LAT *serpō* and GR *hérpō*, which both mean 'I creep', furthermore shows that these two forms are not identical, but that LAT /s/ corresponds to GR /h/. One could thus posit **sérpō* as the preform and derive GR *hérpō* by the sound change **s > h / #_V*, or posit **hérpō* as the preform and explain the LAT form by the sound change **h > s / #_V*. If one additionally takes into account SKR *sárpā-mi* 'I creep' (*-mi* is the extended ending of the 1. ps. sg.), the first solution is corroborated because two languages have /s/ in the initial position. Nonetheless, **hérpō* could still be the preform of all the forms, in which case Latin and Sanskrit would exhibit a parallel development. But regarding the majority of IE languages, in which /s/ corresponds to LAT and Skr. /s/, as well as to GR /h/, the preform **serpō* with initial */s/ is reconstructed. This follows the linguistic principle of parsimony. The sound which is exhibited by most languages and which takes the fewest intermediate steps from the preform to the attested language form can be most often reconstructed for the preform.

Phonological correspondences between Sanskrit, Greek and Latin

The following charts are examples for etymological word correspondences between Sanskrit, Greek and Latin on the left side, the PIE preform and its meaning in the middle, and the sound correspondences illustrated by the examples on the right side. One example often yields correspondences for more than one sound. The sound which is being compared in a line is printed in bold. The following description serves as an introduction to the comparative method and does not exhaustively present and explain all the correspondences and irregularities of the given words. Usually, the meaning of the attested forms and the meaning of the preform are the same. Otherwise, it will be mentioned in the commentary. The abbreviation L stands for line. The following charts only provide an overview of the most important sound correspondences.

RECONSTRUCTION

1. Short vowels

	Compared Languages			Preform and Meaning		Sound Correspondences			
	San-skrit	Greek	Latin	PIE	Meaning	SKR	GR	LAT	PIE
1	_haṃsá-_	_k^{h}ḗn_ < *_k^{h}ans_	_ānser_	*_ǵ^{h}ans-_	'goose'	_a_	*_a_	*_a_	***a***
2	_jánas-_	_génos_	_genus_	*_ǵenos-_	'race'	_a_	_e_	_e_	***e***
3	_i-tá-_	(_i-énai_)	_i-ter_	*_h_$_1$_i-tó-_	'walking'	_i_	_i_	_i_	***i***
4	_áṃsa-_	_õmos_	_umerus_	*_(H)ómso-_	'shoulder'	_a_	_õ_	_u_	***o***
5	_nú_	_nú_	_nu-dius_	*_nú_	'now'	_u_	_y_	_u_	***u***

L1: We find different stem formations: SKR _haṃsá-_ < *_ǵ^{h}ans-ó-_, GR _khḗn_ < *_khā́n_ < *_kháns_ < *_ǵ^{h}áns-_, LAT _ānser_ < *_hanser_ < *_ǵ^{h}ans-ro-_[2] with secondary vowel lengthening of *_a_ > _ā_ before _ns_. English _goose_ is etymologically related.
L2: Exact correspondence of the compared words. LAT _-us_ < *_-os_ and SKR _j_ < *_ǵ_ and _a_ < *_e_, *_o_.
L3: We find different stem formations: SKR _itá-_ < *_i-tó-_, LAT _iter_ < *_i-ter_ 'walking, way'. The Greek form is the infinitive _iénai_ 'to go, to walk'.
L4: SKR _áṃsa-_ < *_ómso-_ through _a_ < *_o_ and the development _ṃ_ < *_m_ before consonant. GR _õmos_ < *_omsos_ with loss of _s_ before _m_ and compensatory lengthening of the preceding vowel. LAT _umer-us_ < *_omesos_ shows a different stem formation and rhotazism *_s_ > _r_.
L5: IE *_nú_ 'now' had a variant *_nū_ with long vowel in SKR _nū_, _nūnám_, GR _nũn_ and LAT _nūper_.

2. Long vowels

It is possible to reconstruct long vowels for PIE which mostly go back to the combination of a short vowel plus laryngeal. The loss of the laryngeal caused a compensatory lengthening of the preceding vowel. Original long vowels are apophonical *_ē_ and *_ō_ of the PIE ablaut vowel *_e/o_.

	Compared Languages			Preform and Meaning		Sound Correspondences			
	Sanskrit	Greek	Latin	PIE	Meaning	SKR	GR	LAT	PIE
6	_mātár-_	dor. _mā́tēr_	_māter_	*_mā́ter-_	'mother'	_ā_	_ē_	_ā_	***ā***
7	_mā́trā-_	_mētis_	_mētior_	***_meh_$_1$-**	'to measure'	_ā_	_ē_	_ē_	***ē***
8	_(viṣá-)_	_īós_	_vīrus_	*_u̯īsos_	'poison'	_(i)_	_ī_	_ī_	***ī***
9	_(udrá-)_	_húdōr_	_(unda)_	*_u̯edōr-_	'water'	-	_ō_	-	***ō***
10	_kūpa-_	_kūpē_	_cūpa_	*_kūp-ā/o-_	'curvature'	_ū_	_ū_	_ū_	***ū***

L6: Word equations for PIE *_ā_ are even rarer than for rare *_a_. In most cases *_ā_ originated anew through the loss of laryngeal *_eh_$_2$ in the sequence *_eh_$_2$ > *_aH_ > *_ā_ after it had colored *_e_ to *_a_. I do not consent to reconstruct the PIE word for 'mother' with a laryngeal as *_meh_$_2$_ter-_ because this word is a nursery word and goes back to the babbling of babies.
L7: SKR _mā́trā_ 'measure', GR _mētis_ 'prudence, plan' < *'contemplating, measuring in your mind', LAT _mētior_ 'I measure' are formations from the root *_meh_$_1$- 'to measure' which is also found as the basis of words for 'moon' and 'month': LAT _mēnsis_, GR _mḗn_, SKR _mā́s-_, ENG _moon_.
L8: LAT _vīrus_ < *_u̯īsos_ displays rhotazism and _-us_ < *_-os_. GR _īós_ < *_u̯īsos_ displays the loss of the initial *_u̯_ and medial *_s_. Both words indicate the reconstruction *_u̯īsos_ with long * _ī_. However, SKR _viṣá-_ only permits the reconstruction *_u̯isó-_ with short *_i_. Also TOCH A _wäs_ and TOCH B _wase_ indicate the reconstruction with a short vowel. It may be the case that the monosyllabic PIE stem

2 For the phonological development cf. Liesner, Malte. _Latin Historical Phonology Workbook_. 2014 Reichert Verlag.

*u̯is- was lengthened to *u̯īs in the nom. acc. sg. and this alternance was levelled differently in the individual languages.
L9: SKR *udrá-* was the designation of an aquatic animal presumably 'otter'. LAT *unda* 'wave' was metathized from **udna-* which was the *n*-stem of the originally heteroclitic PIE word nom. acc. **u̯ed-ōr*, gen. **ud-né-s* 'water' which is reflected in GR *húdōr, húdatos* and HIT *u̯ātar, u̯itenaš*. Hittite is the only Indo-European language which still preserves some kind of ablaut in this word while all other IE languages show levelling of the ablaut vowels in one or the other way e.g. GR **ud- > hud-* which is the secondarily aspirated zero grade of the word.
L10: SKR *kūpa-* 'cavity, well', GR *kūpē* 'cavity' and LAT *cūpa* 'barrel' seem so go back to a root **kūp-* with long *ū* which must be somehow related to the root complex **keu̯-p/b^h-* 'to bend'.

3. Diphthongs

The above described sound changes of PIE **e* > IIR *a* and PIE **o* > IIR *a* caused the PIE diphthongs **ei̯*, **oi̯* and **ai̯* to become **ai̯*, before this diphthong **ai̯* developed to SKR long *e* through monophthongization. Similarly, PIE **eu̯*, **ou̯* and **au̯* became **au̯* which developed to SKR long *o* through monophthongization. The vowel length of Sanskrit *e* [ē] and *o* [ō] is not denoted in traditional transcription.

	Compared Languages			Preform and Meaning		Sound Correspondences			
	Sanskrit	**Greek**	**Latin**	**PIE**	**Meaning**	**SKR**	**GR**	**LAT**	**PIE**
14	*héman-*	*kheĩma*	*(hībernus)*	**ǵ^h**éi̯**men-*	'winter'	*e*	*ei̯*	*ī*	****ei̯***
15	*éka-*	*õios*	*ūnus*	**(h)**oi̯**-ko-*	'one'	*e*	*oi̯*	*ū*	****oi̯***
16	*rocá-*	*leukós*	*lūx*	**l**eu̯**k-*	'to shine'	*o*	*eu̯*	*ū*	****eu̯***
17	*loká-*	-	*lūcus*	**l**ou̯**kó-*	'wide space'	*o*	*ou̯*	*ū*	****ou̯***

L14: SKR *héman-* < **hái̯man-* < **ǵ^{h}éi̯-men-* only in VED loc. sg. *héman* 'in the winter', otherwise extended to *hemantá-* 'winter'. GR *kheĩma* < **ǵ^{h}ei̯mn̥*. LAT *hībernus* < **ǵ^{h}ei̯brinos* 'of winter' is derived from LAT *hiems*, *hiemis* 'winter'.
L15: We find different stem formations: SKR *éka-* < **ái̯ka-* < **(h)ói̯-ko-* with monophthongization and the suffix **-ko-*. GR *oĩos* 'only' < **oi̯u̯os* < **(h)oi̯-u̯o* with the suffix **-u̯o-* and loss of medial **u̯*. LAT *ūnus* < **oi̯nos* < **(h)oi̯-no-* with the suffix **-no-* and the development **oi̯* > *ū*. All these words are ultimately derived from the deictic pronominal stem **Hi-* which can be found in LAT masc. *is* 'this' and SKR *idam* 'this'.
L16: SKR *róca-* < **léu̯ke-* with monophthongization **eu̯* > **au̯* > *o* and the development of **l* > *r*. The sound *c* is the palatalized variant of **k* before palatal vowels. It originated regularly before **e* and then spread analogically in the paradigm.
L17: This is the ablaut variant **lou̯ke-* of line 16 which can directly be seen in inscriptional Old Latin LOUCOM. Sanskrit *loká-* displays the rare preservation of **l* as well as the preservation of **k* because it did not become palatalized *c* before **o*.

4. Syllabic resonants

The PIE nasals **n*, **m* and the liquids **r*, **l* had syllabic allophones **n̥*, **m̥*, **r̥*, **l̥* when they functioned as the syllabic nucleus.

	Compared Languages			Preform and Meaning		Sound Correspondences			
	Sanskrit	Greek	Latin	PIE	Meaning	SKR	GR	LAT	PIE
18	*sa-kr̥t*	***há**paks*	***sim**-plex*	**s**m̥**-*	'one time'	*a*	*a*	*im*	****m̥***
19	***ma**tí-*	***é**mathon*	*mēns, **men**tis*	**m**n̥**-tí-*	'mind, thought'	*a*	*a*	*en*	****n̥***
20	*ś**ŕ̥**ṅga-*	*k**ár**nos*	*c**or**nu*	**k̑**ŕ̥**n-g-o-*	'horn'	*r̥*	*ar*	*or*	****r̥***
21	*v**ŕ̥**ka-*	***lú**kos*	***lu**pus*	**u̯**l̥**kʷo-*	'wolf'	*r̥*	*(lu)*	*(lu)*	****l̥***

L18: PIE **sm̥-* was the zero grade of **sem-* 'one' which is continued without extension in GR nt. **sém* > *hén*, fem. **smía* > *smía* 'one' and in the SKR preverb *sam-* 'together'. The prefixes in SKR *sa-kr̥t* 'once, suddenly, formerly' and GR *há-paks* 'once' go back to **sm̥* and the prefix of LAT *simplex* 'simple' goes back to **sem-*.
L19: SKR *matí-* < **mn̥tí-* preserves the original PIE zero grade and accent position of a *ti*-formation derived from the root √*men-* 'to think'. LAT *mēns* < **mens* displays secondary vowel lengthening before /ns/ which means that its gen. *mentis* can only be traced back to the zero grade form **mn̥-ti-s* by external comparison with other IE languages because *mēns* could also continue the full grade form **men-ti-s*. GR *émathon* 'he understood' is the aorist from the verb *manthánō* 'to understand'.
L20: SKR *śŕ̥ṅga-* 'horn' < **k̑r̥n-g-o-* displays an additional element *-g-* in contrast to GR *kárnos* 'cornigerous animal' < **k̑r̥nos* and LAT *cornu* < **k̑r̥nu-* 'horn'. PIE **r̥* remains in SKR and regularly develops to GR *ar* and LAT *or*.
L21: SKR *vŕ̥ka-* preserves the original accentuated syllabic resonant *ĺ̥* like in the preceding word *śŕ̥ṅga-*. In GR we find metathesis of initial **u̯l̥* > *lu* and delabialization of **kʷ* > *k* next to *u*. LAT *lupus* is probably a loan word from the Sabellic languages in which **kʷ* is continued as *p*.

5. Syllabic resonant plus laryngeal before a vowel

The combination of syllabic resonant plus laryngeal was also called "long sonant" in former times. In SKR we find different results before a vowel and consonant.

	Compared Languages			Preform and Meaning		Sound Correspondences			
	Sanskrit	Greek	Latin	PIE	Meaning	SKR	GR	LAT	PIE
22	*t**ur**a-*	*t**rō̃**ma*	*(terō)*	**t**r̥h**$_3$-ó-*	'wounded'	*ur*	*rō̃*	-	****r̥h**$_3$*
23	*g**ir**i-*	*g**ál**ōs*	*g**lō**s*	**g**l̥h**$_2$-i-*	'sister-in-law'	*ir*	*al*	*lō*	****l̥h**$_2$*

L22: SKR *turá-* 'ill, sore' < **tr̥h*$_3$*ó-*, GR *trō̃ma* 'wound'< **tr̥h*$_3$*mn̥*, LAT *terō* 'I rub' < **terh*$_1$*ō* from the root variant √**terh*$_1$*-* whose final laryngeal **h*$_1$ is necessary to explain the development of GR *téretron* 'drill' < **térh*$_1$*-tro-* and GR *trētós* 'worn down' < **tr̥h*$_1$*-tó-*. The root variants √**terh*$_1$*-* and √**terh*$_3$*-* must ultimately be derived from a primary root √**ter-* 'to rub, to drill'.
L23: SKR *giri-*, GR *gálōs*, LAT *glōs* 'sister-in-law'. In SKR we find the development of **l̥* > **r̥* in **gl̥h*$_2$*-i-* > **gr̥h*$_2$*-i-* and then the development of **r̥h*$_2$ > *ir* before a vowel via the intermediate step **r̥H*: **gr̥h*$_2$*-i-* > **gr̥H-i-* > *giri-*.

6. Resonant plus laryngeal before a consonant

	Compared Languages			Preform and Meaning		Sound Correspondences			
	Sanskrit	Greek	Latin	PIE	Meaning	SKR	GR	LAT	PIE
24	*śrā́**m**yati*	*(krémamai)*	-	**ḱr**m̥h$_2$**i̯eti*	'becomes tired'	*ām*	*(ām)*		***m̥h$_2$***
25	***ā**tí-*	***nē̆**tta*	*a**na**t-*	**h$_2$**n̥h$_2$**-tí-*	'duck'	*ā*	**nā*	*na*	***n̥h$_2$***
26	*p**ūr**ṇá-*	-	*p**lē**nus*	**p**l̥h$_1$**nó-*	'full'	*ūr*	-	*lē*	***l̥h$_1$***

L24: SKR *śrā́myati* from the root √*śram-* 'to get tired'. The development was **ḱrm̥h$_2$-i̯e-ti* > **ḱrā́mi̯eti* > **śrā́mi̯eti* > *śrā́myati* 'he gets tired'. For the development of the sound cluster **m̥h$_2$* there exist only very few examples. GR *krémamai* < **ḱrémh$_2$-mai* 'I hang' with the development of **h$_2$* > *a* between consonants.
L25: SKR *ātí-* 'duck' < **Hn̥Htí-* < **h$_2$n̥h$_2$-tí-*, GR *nē̆tta* < **nāti̯a*, LAT *anas*, *anat-is* < **h$_2$anh$_2$t-* < **h$_2$enh$_2$t-*. This is a designation of a water bird which was probably a duck. Etymologically related to OHG *anut* / *enita* 'duck'.
L26: PIE **l̥h$_1$* first became IIR **r̥H* before its development to Sanskrit *ūr* in a labial environment: **pl̥h$_1$nó-* > **pr̥Hnó-* > **pūrnó-*. Then, vowel change **o* > *a* and cerebralization of **n* > *ṇ* next to *r*. LAT *plēnus* was changed from regular **plānus* in order to differentiate it from LAT *plānus* 'even'.

7. Non-syllabic resonants, semivowels and the fricative *s

	Compared Languages			Preform and Meaning		Sound Correspondences			
	Sanskrit	Greek	Latin	PIE	Meaning	SKR	GR	LAT	PIE
27	*nā́**m**an-*	*óno**m**a*	*nō**m**en*	**(h$_1$)neh$_3$**m**n̥*	'name'	*m*	*m*	*m*	****m***
28	***n**á*	***n**e-*	***n**e-*	****ne***	'not'	*n*	*n*	*n*	****n***
29	*ant**á**r*	*énte**r**on*	*inte**r***	**n̥te**r** / *ente**r***	'inside'	*r*	*r*	*r*	****r***
30	*tu**l**ā-*	*tá**l**anton*	*to**ll**ō*	√**te**l**h$_2$-*	'to lift'	*l*	*l*	*l*	****l***
31	*ha**r**i-*	*khó**l**os*	*he**l**vus*	**ǵ^{h}e**l**-*	'bright, yellow'	*r*	*l*	*l*	****l***
32	***y**ā́tar-*	*enáter*	***i**anitrīx*	**H**i̯**n̥h$_2$-tér-*	'sister-in-law'	*i̯*	*Ø*	*i̯*	****Hi̯***
33	***v**amiti*	*eméō*	***v**omō*	√*****u̯**emh$_1$-*	'to vomit'	*u̯*	*Ø*	*u̯*	****u̯***
34	***s**i-**s**ar-**ṣ**i*	***h**állomai*	***s**aliō*	√*****s**el- /* √*****s**al-*	'to jump'	*s*	*h*	*s*	****s***

L27/28: PIE **m* and **n* are sounds which are very resistent to sound changes in the IE languages. Sanskrit displays the loss of the initial laryngeal and the further development of **eh$_3$* > **oh$_3$* > **oH* > **ō* > *ā*. The Greek word goes back to a preform **h$_1$nh$_3$mn̥*, which had a different ablaut grade compared to the Sanskrit word, and developed first to **enoma* before it became *ónoma* by regressive vowel assimilation.
L29: GR *énteron* 'gut, intestine' < *'the interior'. Latin displays fronting of **e* > *i* before nasal.
L30: SKR *tulā́* 'scales, weight' < **tl̥h$_2$-éh$_2$* with the rare preservation of the sound **l* as *l* and the development of the sound cluster **l̥H* > *ul* before a vowel: **tl̥h$_2$éh$_2$* > **tl̥HáH* > **tl̥Hā́* > *tulā́*. GR *tálanton* < **tl̥h$_2$-nt-* 'scales' is the origin of the English word *talented*. LAT *tollō* < **tol-nō* 'I raise'.
L31: SKR *hari-* < IIR **ǰ^{h}ali-* < **ǵ^{h}eli-*. GR *khólos* 'gall' is etymologically related to English *gall* and is cognate to OHG *galla* 'gall' and MHG *gelb* 'yellow'. The gall was named after its yellow secrete. LAT *helvus* 'yellow' < **ǵ^{h}el-u̯o-s*.
L32: SKR *yā́tar-* < **Hi̯n̥h$_2$-tér-* with the development **n̥H* > *ā* and secondary accentuation. GR *enátēr* is derived from the ablaut variant *Hi̯énh$_2$ter-*.
L33: SKR *vamiti* < **u̯emh$_1$ti* with the PIE laryngeal resulting in *i* between consonants. LAT *vomō* < **u̯emō*. GR *eméō* < **u̯eméō* < **u̯emh$_1$i̯ō*.
L34: SKR *sisarṣi* < **si-sel-si* or **si-sal-si* 'you run'. GR *hállomai* < **sal-i̯o-*, LAT *saliō* < **sel-i̯ō*. The root vowel of PIE **sel/sal-* is not clear.

RECONSTRUCTION

8. Labial and dental stops

We find exact correspondences for labial and dental stops.

	Compared Languages			Preform and Meaning		Sound Correspondences			
	Sanskrit	Greek	Latin	PIE	Meaning	SKR	GR	LAT	PIE
36	*bála-*	*beltíōn*	*dē-bilis*	**bel-*	'strong'	*b*	*b*	*b*	**b*
37	*prá-*	*pró*	*prō*	**prŏ̄-*	'before, forward'	*p*	*p*	*p*	**p*
38	*sádas-*	*hédos*	*sēdēs*	**sédos-*	'seat'	*d*	*d*	*d*	**d*
39	*tanú-*	*tanu-*	*tenuis*	**ten-ú-*	'thin'	*t*	*t*	*t*	**t*

9. Voiced aspirated stops (mediae aspiratae)

	Compared Languages			Preform and Meaning		Sound Correspondences			
	Sanskrit	Greek	Latin	PIE	Meaning	SKR	GR	LAT	PIE
40	*bhū-*	*phū-*	*fū-*	√*b^huH-	'to be / become'	b^h	p^h	*f*	*b^h
41	*dhā-*	*thē-*	*fē-*	√*d^heh_1-	'to put'	d^h	t^h	*f*	*d^h
42	*áṃhas-*	*ánkhō*	*angor*	*h_2éN$\acute{g}^h$es-	'anxiety'	*h*	k^h	*g*	*$\acute{g}^h$

L40: SKR √*bhū-* 'to become, to be' e.g. in *bhūtá-* 'being', *bhū́ti-* 'strength', *bhū́mi-* 'earth', *bhūmán-* 'abundance'. GR *phū-* e.g. in *phúō* 'I become' < **phū́-ō*, *phúsis* < **phū́-ti-* < *b^h*ū-ti-* 'creation, nature'. LAT *fū-* in the perfect form *fūī* 'I was' from *sum* 'I am' as well as in the inf. fut. *fore* 'will be' < **fū-se*.
L41: SKR √*dhā-* 'to place, to put' e.g. in *dá-dhā-ti* 'he puts', *dhātu-* 'layer', *dhātár-* 'founder', *dhā́man-* 'dwelling place'. GR *tí-thē-mi* 'I put', *thémis* 'natural right' < *$d^h h_1$*-mi-s*, *thésis* < *$d^h h_1$*-ti-s* 'placement'. LAT pfc. *fē-cī* < *$d^h e h_1$*-k-* 'I did' from *faciō* < *$d^h h_1$*-k-i̯ō* with unexplained *k*.
L42: The nasal of the preform *h_2*éN*$\acute{g}^h$*es-* cannot be determined with precision. We therefore reconstruct the cover symbol *N*. If HIT /hamenk-/ 'to bind' belongs to this word, the root can be reconstructed as *h_2*ém*$\acute{g}^h$-. In all languages, *h_2*e* became **Ha* which created **Háń*$\acute{g}^h$*es-*. Then, **e* became SKR *a*, *$\acute{g}^h$ became SKR *h* and **m* became SKR *ṃ* before a consonant: **Háń*$\acute{g}^h$*es-* > *áṃhas-*. In Latin, the sound *$\acute{g}^h$ remained as *g* after a nasal consonant. Final *r* of the nom. *angor*, *angōris* has been introduced into the nom. from other cases where it developed regularly through rhotazism, eg. in the gen. **angōsis* > *angōris*.

10.1 Dorsal stops

	Compared Languages			Preform and Meaning		Sound Correspondences			
	Sanskrit	Greek	Latin	PIE	Meaning	SKR	GR	LAT	PIE
43	*áṅká-*	*ónkos*	*uncus*	**(H)ónko-*	'hook'	*k*	*k*	*k*	**k*
44	*gárgara-*	*gargarízdō*	*gurguliō*	**gar-gar-*	'sound of water'	*g*	*g*	*g*	**g*
45	*śván-*	*kúōn*	*canis*	**ḱ(u)u̯ōn-*	'dog'	*ś*	*k*	*k*	**ḱ*
46	*yájati*	*hágios*	*iaiiūnus*	√**Hi̯aǵ-*	'to worship'	*j*	*g*	*i̯*	**ǵ*

L43: Exact correspondence in all three languages. **k* remains and the nasal **n* surfaces as [ŋ]. In SKR we find **o* > *a*. PIE **o* is preserved in Greek and becomes *u* in Latin.
L44: Onomatopoetic words often develop similarities independently and are therefore only of limited suitability for etymological comparisions but in this case, the formal identity of the comparanda cannot be dismissed. SKR *gárgara-* and LAT *gurgēs* are designations for the sound of flowing wa-

ter, GR _gargarízdō_ imitates the sound of gargling and LAT _gurguliō_ 'throat' finds a perfect match in its connection to MHG _gurgeln_ 'to gargle' and _Gurgel_ 'throat'.

L45: LAT _canis_ shows an unexpected _a_. Sometimes, PIE _*ḱ(u)u̯ōn-_ is analyzed as etymological _**pḱuu̯ōn_ 'belonging to the cattle' and therefore a derivation of _*péḱu-_ 'cattle'. However, we can find Hamito-Semitic reconstructions like _*kun-_ and _*küHen-_ (cf. the entries 1498 and 1511 in the _Hamito-Semitic Etymological Dictionary_ from Vladimir Orel and Olga Stolbova) which can be loan words from or even the origin of the PIE word.

L46: SKR _yájati_ < _*Hi̯aǵ-e-ti_ 'he worships', GR _hágios_ < _*Hi̯aǵ-i̯o-s_, O-LAT _iaiiūnus_ 'to have breakfast' < _*Hi̯áǵ-i̯u-_ in the sense of 'practising a ritual in the early morning' (cf. Forssman, Bernhard: "Lateinisch ieiunus und ieientare", in Gerhard Meiser (ed.): Indogermanica et Italica. Innsbruck. 1993). Later on, this form became LAT _ieiiūnus_ through the assimilation _a_ > _e_ between palatal vowels.

10.2 Labiovelars

PIE had velar stops which were co-articulated with additional rounding of the lips. These sounds are called labiovelars. The following tables have been taken from Liesner 2015:86–87.

	Compared Languages			**Preform and Meaning**		**Sound Correspondences**			
	Sanskrit	**Greek**	**Latin**	**PIE**	**Meaning**	**SKR**	**GR**	**LAT**	**PIE**
47	_riṇá**k**ti_	_leí**p**ō_	_re-lin**qu**ō_	~ _*li-n-**k^{w}**-_	'to leave'	_k_	_p_	_ku̯_	**_*k^{w}_**
48	_pa**k**vás_	_pe**p**tós_	_co**c**tus_	_*pe**k^{w}**-u̯o-_	'cooked, ripe'	_k_	_t_	_k_	**_*k^{w}_**
49	_pá**ñc**a_	_pé**n**te_	_quī**nque**_	_*pén**k^{w}**e_	'five'	_c_	_t_	_ku̯_	**_*k^{w}_**
50	_**g**atá-_	_**b**atós_	_**v**entus_	_***g^{w}**m̥tó-_	'having come'	_g_	_b_	_u̯_	**_*g^{w}_**
51	_**j**īvás_	_**b**íos_	_**v**īvus_	_***g^{w}**ih$_3$u̯ós_	'alive'	_j_	_b_	_u̯_	**_*g^{w}_**
52	_tyá**j**ati_	_sé**b**omai_	-	√_*ti̯e**g^{w}**-_	'he leaves'	_j_	_b_	-	**_*g^{w}_**
53	_u**k**ṣáti_	_hu**g**rós_	_ū**v**idus_	√_*u̯e**g^{w}**-_	'he moistens'	_k_	_g_	_u̯_	**_*g^{w}_**
54	_ó**h**ate_	_eú**kh**omai_	_vo**v**ēre_	√_*h$_1$u̯e**g^{wh}**-_	'to speak solemnly'	_h_	_k^{h}_	_gu_	**_*g^{wh}_**
55	_á**h**i-_	_ó**ph**is_	_an**gu**is_	_*h$_3$e**g^{wh}**i-_	'snake'	_h_	_p^{h}_	_gu_	**_*g^{wh}_**
56	_ra**gh**ú-_	_ela**kh**ús_	_le**v**is_	_*h$_1$l̥n**g^{wh}**u-_	'lightweight'	_gh_	_k^{h}_	_u̯_	**_*g^{wh}_**

L47: SKR _riṇákti_ < _*linék^{w}ti_. Retroflex _ṇ_ due to preceding _r_. The labial element of _*k^{w}_ was lost. The Indic result was therefore plain _k_. GR _leípō_ < _*lei̯k^{w}ō_. The Latin and Sanskrit verbs are nasal infix present formations. The labiovelar remained in Latin after a nasal consonant.

L48: SKR _pakvá-_ < _*pek^{w}-u̯ó-_ with delabialization of _*k^{w}_ and vowel change _*e/o_ > _a_. GR _peptós_ < _*pek^{w}-tó-s_ from the verbal root PIE _*pek^{w}-_ 'to cook, to ripen' with analogical _e_-grade because the past participle is regularly built from the zero grade. But PIE _*pk^{w}tós_ was probably too difficult to pronounce because of the initial consonant cluster. The Latin form displays delabialization of _*k^{w}_ and analogical influence from the related verb _coquō_ 'I cook' in which the sequence _*p…k^{w}_ became _*k^{w}…k^{w}_ through assimilation.

L49: SKR _páñca_ with delabialization of PIE _*k^{w}_ > _k_ with subsequent palatalization _*k_ > _c_ and allophonic realization _ñ_ [ñ] of the phoneme /n/ before palatal _c_. In GR _pénte_, the PIE labiovelar became a dental stop before palatal vowel. LAT _quīnque_ displays the same assimilation as in L48 _*peŋk^{w}e_ > _*k^{w}eŋk^{w}e_ and subsequent closing _e_ > _i_ before [ŋ] _*k^{w}eŋk^{w}e_ > _*k^{w}iŋk^{w}e_ as well as lengthening of _i_ > _ī_ before [ŋ].

L50: Exact correspondence of the perfect participles. Sanskrit displays delabialization _*g^{w}_ > _g_ and change of _*m̥_ > _a_ between consonants. Greek displays the development _*g^{w}_ > _b_ and aligns with Sanskrit in the change of _*m̥_ > _a_. The initial labiovelar was simplified in Latin: _*g^{w}_ > _u̯_.

L51: PIE *g^{w} first became **g* and then *j* through secondary palatalization. PIE *g^{w} developed to GR *b* before *i* and to LAT *v* in the initial position. The sequence **iH* became *ī* which remained in Sanskrit and Latin but was shortened in Greek before a vowel following.
L52: PIE *g^{w} first became **g* and then *j* through secondary palatalization. PIE *g^{w} became GR *b* before *o*. Initial **ti̯* is continued as *s* in GR *sébomai* 'I am afraid'. No corresponding Latin form.
L53: PIE *g^{w} first became SKR *g* and then *k* through devoicing. PIE *g^{w} resulted in GR *g* next to *u*. The Latin result was *v* between vowels. SKR *ukṣáti* 'he moistens' < **ug*^{w}*séti* comes from the root **u̯eg*^{w}-. Retroflex *ṣ* according to the ruki rule. GR *hygrós* 'wet' < **ug*^{w}*rós* with secondary initial aspiration.
L54: PIE *g^{wh} first became **gh* and then *h* through secondary palatalization. The preform of *óhate* was **áu̯hate* which goes back to PIE **Héu̯g*^{wh}*-e-toi* > IIR **Háu̯ǰ*^{h}*atai̯* > **áu̯ǰatai̯* > **áu̯hate* > *óhate*. LAT *vovēre* < *h_1*u̯og*^{wh}*-éi̯e-* exhibits intervocalic simplification of *g^{wh} > *v*. PIE *g^{wh} became Proto-Greek *k^{wh} and then GR k^{h} next to *u*.
L55: PIE *g^{wh} first became IIR **gh* and then *h* through secondary palatalization before *i*. PIE *g^{wh} became GR p^{h} before *i* and LAT *gu̯* after nasal. LAT *anguis* < *h_2*eng*^{wh}*is* probably comes from a phonetically similar but different root. GR *o* is due to laryngeal "coloring" from *h_3*o*.
L56: PIE *g^{wh} resulted in SKR *gh*, as well as GR k^{h} next to *u*, as well as LAT *v* between vowels. The initial vowel in Greek is either due to the former laryngeal or vowel prothesis. If LAT *levis* etymologically belongs here, the medial nasal is absent.

10.3 The traditional categorization of IE languages in Centum-languages and Satem-languages

Due to the word correspondences of L43, L45 and L47, three series of dorsal stops must be reconstructed for PIE: velar, palatal and labiovelar stops. Otherwise, it is not possible to connect all the correspondences.

	Compared Languages			**Preform and Meaning**		**Sound Correspondences**			
	Sanskrit	**Greek**	**Latin**	**PIE**	**Meaning**	**SKR**	**GR**	**LAT**	**PIE**
~43	*kaví-*	*koéō*	*caueō*	**(s)keu̯h₁-*	'to see, to look'	*k*	*k*	*k*	***k***
~45	*árśas-*	*hélkos*	*ulcus*	**h₁élḱos*	'wound'	*ś*	*k*	*k*	***ḱ***
47	*riṇákti*	*leípō*	*re-linquō*	**lei̯kʷ-*	'to leave'	*k*	*p*	*ku̯*	***kʷ***

The individual IE languages, however, always have only two series of dorsal stops. The so-called centum-languages share the same reflex of the velar and palatal series due to the loss of the palatal feature, whereas the so-called satem-languages share the same reflex of the velar and labiovelar series, due to the loss of the labial element of the labiovelars. In the satem-languages, the palatal series develops further to *s*-like sibilants or affricates although divergences to this pattern are found in Slavic and Baltic. The Anatolian language Luwian, which normally would be expected to be classified as a centum-language, even seems to have reflexes of all three series of stops. The examples used for the argumentation are, however, disputed because of alternative etymologies or scant attestation of the words.

11. Laryngeals

The Anatolian language Hittite is attested from 1700 BC on and is therefore the oldest attested IE language. In some positions, Hittite has an aspirated sound /h/ which the other IE languages do not have anymore. Therefore, one can assume at least one phoneme in an older state of language, which was lost on the way to the other languages Sanskrit, Greek and Latin. Due to different structural arguments, historical linguistics nowadays normally assumes three of those phonemes, which are called laryngeals and reconstructed for PIE. The exact phonetic value of these laryngeals is unknown. The next two tables present the correspondences, which are most relevant for this issue.

	Compared Languages				Preform and Meaning		Sound Correspondences				
	HIT	SKR	GR	LAT	PIE	Meaning	HIT	SKR	GR	LAT	PIE
57	**hant-**	anti	antí	ante	*$h_2$énti	'in front of'	ha	a	a	a	*h_2e
58	pahs-	pā-	-	pāstor	*peh_2-(s)-	'to protect'	ah	ā	-	ā	*eh_2
59	**hau̯i**	ávi-	ói̯s	ovis	*$h_2$óu̯is	'sheep'	ha	a	o	o	*h_2o

L57: The Hittite word signifies 'front' and tells us that the other languages continue an old locative form 'at the front' out of which developed the meaning 'in front of'. PIE *h_2 caused the change of PIE **e* to **a* before the laryngeal was lost which is still attested in the Hittite form. Final LAT *e* originated from **i*.
L58: Laryngeal *h_2 caused the change of **e* to **a* before it was lost with compensatory lengthening of the preceding vowel.
L59: Laryngeal *h_2 did not change the vowel color because PIE **o* was not subject to vowel coloring.

	Compared Languages			Preform and Meaning		Sound Correspondences			
	Sanskrit	Greek	Latin	PIE	Meaning	LAT	SKR	GR	PIE
60	hitá-	thetós	factus	*$d^h h_1$tó-	'put'	i	e	a	*h_1
61	~ aniti	ánemos	animus	*$h_2$én$h_1$mo-	'wind'	i	e	i	*h_1
62	sthitá-	statós	status	*st$h_2$tó-	'established'	i	a	a	*h_2
63	ditá-	dotós	datus	*d$h_3$to-	'given'	i	o	a	*h_3

L60: All laryngeals yielded SKR *i* and LAT *a* between consonants. The Greek vowel color depended on the laryngeal which was placed between the consonants. SKR sometimes continues PIE *d^h as *h*. The PPP *$d^h h_1$tós from the verb *d^heh_1- 'to put' is not continued in Latin as regular ^{x}*fatus* but it was replaced by *factus* which is built from the verb *facere* with a *k*-extension.
L61: The verbal form SKR *aniti* 'he breathes' goes back to *$h_2$en$h_1$ti. LAT *animus* < **anamos* with vowel weakening **a* > *i* in medial syllables. Proto-Italic **a* of the preform **anamos* is continued as *a* in Oscan *anams*.
L62: The Sanskrit word displays aspiration of **t* through the influence of *h_2.
L63: The Latin result of intervocalic laryngeals is always *a* if not modified by vowel weakening in medial syllables, the Sanskrit result is always *i*.

RECONSTRUCTION

Key to Exercises

Vowel Changes

The development of PIE **ĕ and *ŏ*

A LAT *novus* :: **néu̯o-* > (10.1) **náu̯o-* > (10.3) *náva-* 'new' **B** LAT *lubet* :: **lubʰeti* > (10.3) *lubhati* 'he longs for' **C** GR *treĩs* :: **tréi̯es* > (10.1) *tráyas* 'three' **D** GR *beltíōn* :: **bélo-* > (10.1) **balo-* > (10.3) *bála-* 'strong' **E** AV *x*^{u}*afna-* :: **su̯épno-* > (10) *svápna-* 'sleep' **F** LAT *fert* :: **bʰéreti* > (10.1) *bhárati* 'he carries' **G** LAT *iugum* :: **i̯ugóm* > (10.3) *yugám* 'yoke' **H** GR *nephélē* :: **nébhos-* > (10.1) **nábhos-* > (10.3) *nábhas-* 'mist, fog' **I** GR *thūmós* :: **dhū́mo-* > (10.3) *dhū́ma-* 'smoke' **J** LAT *medius* :: **médhi̯o-* > (10.1) **mádhyo-* > (10.3) *mádhya-* 'middle' **K** GR *eruthrós* :: **rudhiró-* > (10.3) *rudhirá-* 'red' **L** LAT *augēre* 'to increase' :: **ugró-* > (10.3) *ugrá-* ' big' **M** GR *hēdús* :: **su̯ēdú-* > (10.2) *svādú-* 'sweet' **N** GR *títhēmi* :: **dhé-dhē-mi* > (10) **dhádhāmi* > (27.1) *dádhāmi* 'I put' **O** LAT *serpō* :: **serpō-mi* > (10.1) **sarpōmi* > (10.4) *sarpāmi* 'I crawl' **P** GR *phérō* :: **bʰérō-mi* > (10.1) **bhárōmi* > (10.4) *bhárāmi* 'I carry' **Q** LAT *monēre* :: **monéi̯eti* > (10.1+10.5) *mānáyati* 'he values higly' **R** GR *nõton* 'back (of the body)' :: **sónu-* > (10.5) *sā́nu-* 'mountain's crest'

Monophthongization and shortening of long diphthongs

A O-LAT *loucos* :: **lou̯ko-* > (10.3) **láu̯ka-* > (11.2) *lóka-* 'clearing' **B** dat. pl. GR *lukois* :: instr. pl. **u̥lkʷōi̯s* > (4.1) **u̥lkōi̯s* > (9) **u̥rkōi̯s* > (10.4) **u̥rkāi̯s* > (12.1) **vr̥kais* > (28.3) *vr̥kaiḥ* 'wolves' **C** LAT *ūrō* :: **h₁éu̯s-e-ti* > (c1) **éu̯seti* > (10.1) **áu̯sati* > (c24) **áu̯ṣati* > (11.2) *óṣati* '(it) burns' **D** *sūnú-* 'son' :: Loc. sg. **sūnḗu̯* > (10.2) **sūnā́u* > (11.2) *sūnau* **E** GR *Zeús* :: **di̯ēu̯s* > (10.2) **di̯āu̯s* > (c24) **di̯āu̯ṣ* > (12.2) *dyaúṣ* 'sky' **F** LAT *octō* :: **óktōu̯* > (c13) **oṣṭōu̯* > (10) **aṣṭāu̯* > (12.2) *aṣṭaú* 'eight' **G** *leípō* 'I leave' :: **é-lēi̯kʷ-s-m̥* > (4.1) **élēi̯ksm̥* > (9) **érēi̯ksm̥* > (15.4) **érēi̯ksam* > (c24) **érēi̯kṣam* > (10.2) **árāi̯kṣam* > (12.1) *áraikṣam* 'I let (past tense)'

Sandhi of Vowels I - Vowel plus Vowel

Insert the sandhi results

A *kā iyam* > (s2.1) *keyam* 'Who is this woman?' **B** *tasya auṣadham* > (s2.7) *tasyauṣadham* 'his medicine' **C** *trīṇi etāni* > (s3.1) *trīṇy_etāni* 'these three' **D** *na aikṣata* > (s2.5) *naikṣata* 'he didn't see' **E** *vinā īrṣyayā* > (s2.1) *vinerṣyayā* 'without jealousy' **F** *astu etat* > (s3.2) *astv_etat* 'this shall be' **G** *asti iha* > (s1.2) *astīha* 'is here' **H** *devī iva* > (1.2) *devīva* 'like a goddess' **I** *adya eva* > (s2.4) *adyaiva* 'still today' **J** *bahūni ahāni* > (s3.1) *bahūny_ahāni* 'many days' **K** *na īkṣe* > (s2.1) *nekṣe* 'I don't see' **L** *tasya autsukyam* > (s2.7) *taysautsukyam* 'his desire' **M** *narī īkṣate* > (s1.2) *narīkṣate* 'the woman sees' **N** *madhu iva* > (s3.2) *madhv_iva* 'like honey' **O** *sā r̥ddhiḥ* > (s2.3) *sarddhiḥ* 'this miraculous power' **P** *sā oṣadhiḥ* > (s2.6) *sauṣadhiḥ* 'this medicinal herb' **Q** *yadi icchet* > (s1.2) *yadīcchet* 'if he could wish' **R** *yathā aiśvaryam* > (s2.5) *yathaiśvaryam* 'like the supremacy' **S** *sā uktvā* > (s2.2) *soktvā* 'after she had spoken' **T** *pitr̥ anuvartanāt* > (s3.3) *pitr_anuvartanāt* 'out of obedience to the father' **U** *tena uktam* > (s2.2) *tenoktam* 'is was said by him' **V** *sahasā utthāya* > (s2.2) *sahasotthāya* 'standing up suddenly'

Insert the historical development of the sandhi forms

A *adya eva* > (s2.4) *adyaiva* 'still today'

**adya_aiva* > (26.1) **adyāiva* > (12.1) **adyaiva*

We start from the preform **adya_aiva* in which the vowels *a* and *a* contracted to long *ā* which created *adya_aiva* > **adyāiva*. After that the long diphthong **āi* was shortened to *ai*.

B *na auñchat* > (s2.7) *nauñchat* 'he didn't gather'

**na_āuñchat* > (26.1) *nāuñchat* > (12.2) *nauñchat*

We start from the preform **na_āuñchat* in which the vowels *a* and *ā* contracted to *ā* which created **na_āuñchat* > *nāuñchat*. After that the long diphthong **āu* was shortened to *au*.

C *yathā r̥ṣiḥ* > (s2.3) *yatharṣiḥ* 'like a seer'

yathā r̥ṣiḥ > (12.3) *yathārṣiḥ* > (12.3) *yatharṣiḥ*

Long *ā* and *r̥* contracted to the long diphthong *ār* which was then shortened to *ar*.

D *sā uktvā* > (s2.2) *soktvā* 'after she had spoken'

sā uktvā > (shortening of final *ā*) **sa_uktvā* > (11.2) *soktvā*

The final vowel *ā* was shortened to *a* before *a_v* monophthongized to *o*.

Vowel Sandhi II - Diphthong before a Vowel

Insert the sandhi forms

A *mriyante iti* > (s4.1) *mriyanta_iti* 'they said so' **B** *dyotate avati ca* > (s4.3) *dyotate 'vati* ca '(the sun) shines and refreshes' **C** *nagare iha* > (s4.1) *nagara_iha* 'here in the city' **D** *te api* > (s4.3) *te 'pi* 'even these' **E** *vane āste* > (s4.1) *vana_āste* 'he sits in the forest' **F** *guro īkṣasva* > (s4.4) *gura_īkṣasva* 'Teacher, look!' **G** *tau ubhau* > (s4.9) *tāv_ubhau* 'these two' **H** *īkṣāvahai indum* > (s4.7) *īkṣāvahā_indum* 'we two want to see the moon' **I** *gr̥he agaccham* > (s4.3) *gr̥he 'gaccham* 'I went into the house'

Explain the historic development of the following sandhi forms

***A mriyante iti* > (s4.1) *mriyanta_iti* 'they said so'**

In the preform **mriyantay_iti*, the semivowel *y* was lost between between vowels which led to *mriyanta_iti* according to SC 21.1. The word *mriyante* is the result of the monophthongization **ai̯* > *e* in the pausa form of the **mriyantay* and not the starting point of the sound change.

***B tau ubhau* > (s4.9) *tāv_ubhau* 'these two'**

In the preform **tāu_ubhau*, the first element **tāu* remained in sandhi whereas *tau* is the result of the shortening of the long diphthong **āu̯* > (12.2) *au̯*.

***C īkṣāvahai indum* > (s4.7) *īkṣāvahā_indum* 'we two want to see the moon'**

In the preform **īkṣāvahāy indum*, the semivowel **y* was lost between two vowels according to SC 21.1. There was no sound change *ai̯* > *ā* because the diphthong *ai̯* itself was the result of the shortening of **āi̯* > (12.1) *ai̯*.

***D vane āste* > (s4.2) *vanay_āste* 'he sits in the forest'**

The sandhi form *vanay* displays the diphthong **ai̯* before its further development to *e* which means that there was no sound change. The sandhi form preserved the original sounds.

***E gr̥he agaccham* > (s4.3) *gr̥he 'gaccham* 'I went into the house'**

In the preform **gr̥hay_agaccham*, the sequence **aya* became Middle-Indo-Aryan *e* according to SC 21.5. There was no elision of the initial *a*.

Derive the sandhi forms historically

A Synchronic Sandhi: *āgatāḥ r̥śayaḥ* > (s6.4) *āgatā_r̥śayaḥ* 'the seers have come'
Historic Explanation: *āgatās r̥śayaḥ* > (22.2) **āgatāz_r̥śayaḥ* > (20.1) *āgatā_r̥śayaḥ*

B Synchronic Sandhi: *gīḥ rocate* > (s6.6) *gī_rocate* 'the voice pleases (someone)'
Historic Explanation: *gīs rocate* > (22.2) **gīz rocate* > (c26) **gīẓ_ rocate* > (20.1) *gī_rocate*

C Synchronic Sandhi: *gataḥ araṇye* > (s6.3) *gato 'araṇye* 'gone to the woods'
Historic Explanation: *gatas araṇye* > (22.2) **gataz_ araṇye* > (20.1) **gata_araṇye* > (21.3) **gatau̯_araṇye* > (11.2) *gato 'raṇye*

Visarga-Sandhi before Voiced Sounds

Insert the synchronic sandhi forms. Remember that *punaḥ* goes back to **punar* with *r*.

A *āgatāḥ r̥śayaḥ* > (s6.4) *āgatā_r̥śayaḥ* 'the seers have come' **B** *gīḥ rocate* > (s6.6) *gī_rocate* 'the voice pleases (someone)' **C** *śiśuḥ roditi* > (s6.6) *śiśū_roditi* 'the child cries' **D** *punaḥ rohati* > (s6.6) *punā_rohati* 'he grows again' **E** *kaḥ api* > (s6.3) *ko 'pi* 'someone' **F** *gataḥ araṇye* > (s6.3) *gato 'araṇye* 'gone to the woods' **G** *ānītaḥ dīpaḥ* > (s6.2) *ānīto_dīpaḥ* 'the lamp which has been brought' **H** *nr̥paḥ ādiśat* > (s6.1) *nr̥pa_ādiśat* 'the king commanded' **I** *naraḥ ayam* > (s6.3) *naro 'yam* 'this man' **J** *devaḥ api* > (s6.3) *devo 'pi* 'even the god' **K** *nr̥paḥ uvāca* > (s6.1) *nr̥pa_uvāca* 'the king said' **L** *devāḥ ūcuḥ* > (s6.4) *devā_ūcuḥ* 'the gods spoke' **M** *vidhuḥ rājate* > (s6.6) *vidhū_rājate* 'the moon shines' **N** *dāsāḥ gacchanti* > (s6.4) *dāśā_gacchanti* 'the slaves go' **O** *vr̥kṣāḥ rohanti* > (s6.4) *vr̥kṣā_rohanti* 'the trees grow' **P** *punaḥ rogī* > (s6.6) *punā_rogī* 'ill again' **Q** *kaḥ r̥ṣiḥ* > (s6.1) *ka_r̥ṣiḥ* 'who is the seer?' **R** *bālaiḥ rūpavadbhiḥ* > (s6.6) *bālai_rūpavadbhiḥ* 'with beautiful children' **S** *vr̥kṣaḥ rohati* > (s6.2) *vr̥kṣo_rohati* 'the tree grows' **T** *nr̥pāḥ jayanti* > (s6.4) *nr̥pā_jayanti* 'the kings overcome'

KEY

Visarga Sandhi before Voiceless Sounds

Insert the sandhi forms

Preform	Vedic Sandhi	Classical Sandhi	Translation
puruṣas khanati	*puruṣax_khanati*	*puruṣaḥ_khanati*	'the man digs'
kapis pibati	*kapiφ_pibati*	*kapiḥ_pibati*	'the monkey drinks'
prathamas sargaḥ	*prathamas_sargaḥ*	*prathamaḥ_sargaḥ*	'the first chant'
gurus śapate	*guruś_śapate*	*guruḥ_śapate*	'the teacher swears'
naras ṣṭhīvati	*naraṣ_ṣṭhīvati*	*naraḥ_ ṣṭhīvati*	'the man spits'

Visarga-developments before voiced initial position (additional exercise to next chapter)

A *āgatāḥ ṛṣayaḥ* > (s6.4) *āgatā_ṛśayaḥ* 'the seers have come' **B** *nṛpaḥ uvāca* > (s6.1) *nṛpa_uvāca* 'the king spoke' **C** *ānītaḥ dīpaḥ* > (s6.2) *ānīto_dīpaḥ* 'the lamp which has been brought' **D** *nadyaḥ avahan* > (s6.3) *nadyo 'vahan* 'the rivers flew' **E** *vidhuḥ rājate* > (s6.6) *vidhū_rājate* 'the moon shines' **F** *guruḥ īkṣate* > (s6.5) *gurur_īkṣate* 'the guru sees'

Assimilation I

Assimilations of stops in sandhi forms and before the ending *-bhiḥ*

A *apatat bhuvi* > (s11.2) *apatad_bhuvi* 'he fell to the ground' **B** *vaṇik bhāṣate* > (s11.1) *vaṇig_bhāṣate* 'the merchand speaks' **C** *mahat dhanuḥ* > (s11.2) *mahad_dhanuḥ* 'big bow' **D** nom. sg. *marut* :: instr. pl. **marutbhiḥ* > (22.2) *marudbhiḥ* **E** *kakup atra* > (s11.4) *kakub_atra* 'this area here' **F** *ap jaḥ* > (s11.4) *ab_jaḥ* 'water-born' **G** *nagarāt girim* > (s11.2) *nagarād_girim* 'from the city to the mountain' **H** *parivrāṭ ayam* > (s11.3) *parivrāḍ_ayam* 'he is a liar' **I** *suhṛt dhāvati* > (s11.2) *suhṛd_dhāvati* 'the friend runs' **J** *suhṛt ahasat* > (s11.2) *suhṛd_ahasat* 'the friend laughed' **K** *parivrāṭ gacchati* > (s11.3) *parivrāḍ_gacchati* 'the liar walks' **L** *abharat annam* > (s11.1) *abharad_annam* 'he brought the food' **M** *sarit atra* > (s11.2) *sarid_atra* 'the river here' **N** *samyak uktam* > (s11.1) *samyag_uktam* 'well said' **O** *tat hi* > (s13.2) *tad_dhi* 'this indeed' **P** *āsīt hanuḥ* > (s13.2) *āsīd_dhanuḥ* 'it was the chin' **Q** *tat hetuḥ* > (s13.2) *tad_dhetuḥ* 'the reason thereof' **R** *vāk hi* > (s13.1) *vāg_ghi* 'the speech indeed' **S** *samyak hutaḥ* > (s13.1) *samyag_ghutaḥ* 'correctly immolated' **T** *kakup hi* > (s13.4) *kakub_bhi* 'the direction indeed'

Devoicing and deaspiration in morphological formations

A √*pad-* 'to fall' :: 3. sg. des. **pid-s-a-ti* > (22.1) *pitsati* 'he wants to fall' **B** √*dā-* 'to give' :: 3. sg. des. **dí-d-s-a-ti* > (22.1) *dítsati* 'he wants to give' **C** 3. sg. mid. **dá-d-te* > (22.1) *dátte* 'he gives' **D** **da-d-tá-* > (22.1) *dattá-* 'given' **E** √*nod-* 'to push' :: **nudtá-* > (22.1) *nuttá-* 'pushed' **F** √*syand-* 'flowing swiftly':: **syand-tṛ-* > (22.1) *syánttṛ* 'moving' **G** √*bhed-* 'to split' :: 3. sg. **bhinád-ti* > (22.1) *bhinátti* 'he splits' **H** √*mad-* 'to be happy' :: PPP **madtá-* > (22.1) *mattá-* 'drunk' **I** √*bādh-* 'to vex' :: 3. sg. des. **bī-bhadh-s-a-te* > (22.5) *bībhatsate* 'he finds disgusting' **J** √*labh-* 'to take':: 1. sg. fut. **labh-sye* > (22.5) *lapsye* 'I will take'

Assimilation II

Stop consonant plus nasal

A *manāk magnaḥ* > (s12.1) *manāṅ_magnaḥ* 'a little immersed' **B** *dik nāgaḥ* > (s12.1) *diṅ_nāgaḥ* 'world elephant' **C** *tat mama* > (s12.3) *tan_mama* 'this is mine' **D** *vāk muñcati* > (s12.1) *vāṅ_muñcati* 'language liberates' **E** *kīdṛk naraḥ* > (s12.1) *kīdṛṅ_naraḥ* 'what kind of person?' **F** *prāk mukhaḥ* > (s12.1) *prāṅ_mukhaḥ* 'eastwards' **G** *nagarāt nagaram* > (s12.3) *nagarān_nagaram* 'from city to city' **H** *jagat nāthaḥ* > (s12.3) *jagan_nāthaḥ* 'ruler of the world' **I** *yāvat na* > (s12.3) *yāvan_na* 'as long as not' **J** *ṣaṭ māsaḥ* > (s12.2) *ṣaṇ_māsaḥ* 'period of six months' **K** √*pad-* 'fallen' :: PPP **padná-* > (22.3) *panná-* 'to fall' **L** √*bhed-* 'to split':: **bhidná-* > (22.3) *bhinná-* 'split'

Assimilations of final dental consonants

A *mahat cāpam* > (s10.1) *mahac_cāpam* 'big bow' **B** *aharat śiraḥ* > (s10.6) *aharac_chiraḥ* 'he decapitated' **C** *mṛt chādayati* > (s10.2) *mṛc_chādayati* 'the clay covers' **D** *tat chinatti* > (s10.2) *tac_chinatti* 'he cuts this' **E** *etat ṭhakkuraḥ* > (s10.4a) *etaṭ_ṭhakkuraḥ* 'this idol' **F** *tat jāyate* > (s10.3) *taj_jāyate* 'this is born' **G** *tat ślokena* > (s10.6) *tac_chlokena* ‘through this verse’ **H** *tat ca* > (s10.1) *tac_ca* ‘and this’ **I** *abhavat jaḍaḥ* > (s10.3) *abhavaj_jaḍaḥ* ‘it became stiff’ **J** *suhr̥t ṭīkate* > (s10.4a) *suhr̥ṭ_ṭīkate* ‘the friend jumps’ **K** *tat labdham* > (s10.5) *tal_labdham* ‘having taken this’ **L** *tat ḍhaukate* > (s10.4b) *taḍ_ḍhaukate* ‘it approaches’ **M** *vidyut-latā* > (22.6) *vidyullatā* ‘flash of lightning’ **N** *mr̥d-* ‘clay’ :: **mr̥d-loṣṭa-* > (22.6) *mr̥lloṣṭa-* ‘clod of earth’

Sandhi of final nasals

A *arīn jayati* > (s14.3) *arīñ_jayati* ‘he overcomes the enemies’ **B** *bhadram te* > (s14.1) *bhadraṃ_te* ‘Hail thee!’ **C** *tān jayati* > (s14.3) *tāñ_jayati* ‘he overcomes them’ **D** *yān jantūn* > (s14.3) *yāñ_jantūn* ‘which beeings’ **E** *svargam jagāma* > (s14.1) *svargaṃ_jagāma* ‘he went to the sky’ **F** *kim karomi* > (s14.1) *kiṃ_karomi* ‘what shall I do?’ **G** *pakṣin ḍīyasva* > (s14.2) *pakṣiṇ_ḍīyasva* ‘fly, bird!’ **H** *mahān ḍamaraḥ* > (s14.2) *mahāṇ_ḍamaraḥ* ‘great turmoil’ **I** *yachhan śrāddham* > (s14.5) *yacchañ_chrāddam* ‘handing out in the ceremony in honour of dead relatives’ **J** *tān śasāpa* > (s14.5) *tāñ_chaśāpa* ‘he cursed them’ **K** *paśyan lokān* > (s14.5) *paśyaṃl_lokān* ‘seeing the people’

Loss of Voiced Sibilants

The development *az > e

A AV *nazdišta-* :: **nn̥sd-istho-* > (22.2) **nn̥zdistho-* > (15.1) **názdistho-* > (c24) **názdiṣṭho-* > (10) **názdiṣṭha-* > (c23) *néd-iṣṭha-* ‘the next one’ **B** GR *mastós* ‘breast, nipple’:: **másdes-* > (22.2) **mázdes-* > (10) **mázdas-* > (c23) *médas-* ‘fat’ **C** AV *mazdā-* :: **mn̥s-d^héh_1-* > (c2) **mn̥sd^hḗ-* > (22.2) **mn̥zd^hḗ-* > (15.1) **mazdhá-* > (c23) *medhā́-* ‘wisdom’ **D** AV *pazdu-* ‘beatle’:: **pasdú-* > (22.2) **pazdú-* > (c23) *pedú-* name of a person **E** AV *dazdi* :: **da-d-dhí* > (2.4) **dadzdhí* > (6.5) **dazdhi* > (c23) **dedhí* > (29.1) *dehí* ‘give!’ **F** √*dhā-* :: 2. sg. imp. **dha-d-dhí* > (2.4) **dhadzdhí* > (6.5) **dhazdhí* > (c23) **dhedhí* > (27.1) **dedhí* > (29.1) *dehí* ‘put!’ **G** **másdi̯éti* > (22.2) **mázdi̯éti* > (10) **mázdi̯áti* > (c23) *médyati* ‘is/becomes fat’ **H** AV *miiazda-* :: **mii̯ázd^ha-* > (c23) *miyédha-* ‘sacrificial meal’

Cerebralization of *z > *ẓ with subsequent loss of *ẓ and compensatory lengthening

A **dus-dāśa-* > (22.2) **duz-dāśa-* > (c25) **duẓdāśa-* > (17.2) **duẓḍāśa-* > (20.3) *dū-ḍāśa-* ‘impious’ **B** **dus-dhī-* > (22.2) **duzdhī-* > (c25) **duẓdhī-* > (17.3) **duẓḍhī-* > (20.3) *dūḍhī-* ‘evil minded’ **C** **dus-nā́śa-* > (22.2) **duz-nā́śa-* > (c25) **duẓnā́śa-* > (17.2) **duẓṇā́śa-* > (20.3) *dū-ṇā́śa-* ‘hard to reach’

Loss of retroflex *ẓ with compensatory lengthening

A LAT *nīdus* :: **nisdo-* > (22.2) **nizdo-* > (10.3) **nizda-* > (c25) **niẓda-* > (17.2) **niẓḍa-* > (20.3) *nīḍa-* ‘nest’ **B** GR *misthós* :: **misd^ho-* > (22.2) **mizd^ho-* > (10.3) **mizd^ha-* > (c25) **miẓdha-* > (17.3) **miẓḍha-* > (20.3) *mīḍha-* ‘reward’ **C** GOT *aistan* ‘to pay attention to’ :: **h_1-$h_1$sd-$h_2$éi̯* > (22.2) **h_1-$h_1$zd-$h_2$éi̯* > (c3) **h_1i$h_1$izdHái̯* > (1.5) **Hi-Hizd-ái̯* > (13.4) **iizd-ái̯* > (26.2) **īzdái̯* > (c25) **īẓdái̯* > (11.1) **īẓdé* > (17.2) **īẓḍé* > (20.3) *īḍé* ‘he honors’ **D** √*stu-* ‘to praise’:: 2. pl. aor. **á-stau̯-s-dhvam* > (22.2) **ástau̯zdhvam* > (c25) **á-stau̯ẓdhvam* > (17.3) **á-stau̯ẓḍhvam* > (20.1) **á-stau̯ḍhvam* > (11.2) *ástoḍhvam* ‘you praised’

The Primary Palatalization

Development of PIE *ḱ, *ǵ, and *$ǵ^h$

A LAT *cadō* :: Fut. **ḱad-si̯e-ti* > (22.1) **ḱat-si̯e-ti* > (c7) **śat-si̯e-ti* > (10) *śatsyati* ‘he will fall’ **B** O-LAT *deicō* :: **dí-dei̯ḱ-e-ti* > (c7) **dídei̯śeti* > (10) **dídai̯śati* > (11.1) *dídeśati* ‘he shows’ **C** GR *kónkhos* :: **ḱonk^{h}ó-* > (c7) **śonk^{h}ó-* > (10) *śaṅkhá-* ‘shell’ **D** LAT *equus* :: **éḱu̯o-* > (c7) **éśu̯o-* > (10) *áśva-* ‘horse’ **E** LAT *cēnseō* :: **ḱenseti* > (c7) **śenseti* > (10.1) **śansati* > (s14.1) *śaṃsati* ‘he proclaims’ **F** LAT *angus-tus* :: **$h_2$éng^{h}es-* > (c3) **ánǵ^{h}es-* > (c12) **ánhes-* > (10) **ánhas-* > (s14.1) *áṃhas-* ‘narrowness’ **G** GR *geúō* :: **ǵéu̯sos-* > (c11) **jéu̯sos-* > (10) **jáu̯sas-* > (c24) **jáu̯ṣas-* > (11.2) *jóṣas-* ‘pleasure, liking’ **H** LAT *vīcus* :: **u̯oi̯ḱó-* > (c7) **u̯oi̯śó-* > (10.3) **u̯ai̯śá-* > (11.1) *veśá-* ‘dwelling’

Emergence of the sound cluster *ṣṭ*

A √*darś-* (c7) < **derḱ-* ‘to see’:: **dr̥ḱtó-* > (c13) **dr̥ṣṭó-* > (10) *dr̥ṣṭá-* ‘seen’ **B** √*piś-* (c7) < **piḱ-* ‘to shape’:: **piḱto-* > (c13) **piṣṭó-* > (10) *piṣṭá-* ‘tormented’ **C** √*deś-* (c7) < **dei̯ḱ-* ‘to show’:: **dídei̯ḱti* > (c13) **dídei̯ṣṭi* > (10) **dídai̯ṣṭi* > (11.1) *dídeṣṭi* ‘he shows’ **D** **déi̯-diḱtoi̯* > (c13) **déi̯diṣṭoi̯* > (10) **dái̯diṣṭai̯* > (11.1) *dédiṣṭe* ‘it proves

KEY

itself to be' **E** √*vaś-* (c7) < **u̯eḱ-* 'to wish':: **u̯éḱti* > (c13) **u̯éṣṭi* > (10) *váṣṭi* 'he wishes' **F** √*naś-* (c7) < **neḱ-* 'to vanish' :: **neḱtó-* > (c13) **neṣṭó-* > (10) **naṣṭá-* 'lost'

The Secondary Palatalization

Delabialization without palatalization

A LAT *iecur* :: **i̯ekʷr̥t* > (4.1) **i̯ekr̥t* > (10.1) *yakr̥t* 'liver' **B** LAT *coctus* :: **pekʷ-u̯ó-* > (4.1) **peku̯ó-* > (10) *pakvá-* 'cooked, ripe' **C** LAT *nūdus* :: **negʷ-nó-* > (4.2) **negnó-* > (10) *nagná-* 'naked'

Further examples of palatalization

A GR *pénte* :: **pénkʷe* > (4.1) **pénke* > (c10) **pénce* > (10.1) *páñca* 'five' **B** LAT *vīvus* :: **gʷīu̯ós* > (4.2) **gīu̯ós* > (c11) **jīu̯ós* > (10.3) *jīvás* 'alive' **C** GR *érebos* :: gen. sg. **$h_1$regʷes-es* > (13.2) **regʷeses* > (4.2) **regeses* > (c11) **rejeses* > (10.1) *rajasas* 'darkness' **D** GR *delphús* :: **gʷólbʰo-* > (4.2) **gólbho-* > (9) **górbho-* > (10) *gárbha-* 'the womb' **E** GR *sébomai* :: **t̯iegʷeti* > (4.2) **t̯iegeti* > (c11) **t̯iejeti* > (10.1) *tyájati* 'he leaves' **F** OHG *quena* :: **gʷénH-* > (4.2) **génH-* > (c11) **jénH-* > (1.7) **jéni-* > (10.1) *jáni-* 'woman' **G** **sékʷ-mon-* > *sákman-* 'fellowship' :: **sékʷ-e-ti* > (4.1) **séketi* > (c10) **séceti* > (10.1) *sácati* 'he follows' **H** 3. pl. *ghnánti* 'they kill' :: 3. sg. **gʷʰén-ti* > (4.3) **gʰénti* > (c12) **hénti* > (10) *hánti* 'he slays' **I** LAT *ninguit* 'it snows':: **snigʷʰ-ye-ti* > (4.3) **snigʰyeti* > (c12) **snihyeti* > (10.1) *snihyati* 'he loves' **J** LAT *foveō* :: **dʰégʷʰeti* > (4.3)**dʰégʰeti* > (c12) **dʰéheti* > (27.1) **déheti* > (10.1) *dáhati* 'he/it burns' **K** LAT *vovēre* :: **$h_1$éu̯gʷʰ-e-to̯i* > (c1) **éu̯gʷʰ-e-to̯i* > (4.3) **éu̯gʰ-e-to̯i* > (c12) **éu̯heto̯i* > (10) **áuhata̯i* > (11.1/2) *óhate* 'he speaks solemnly' **L** GR *óphis* :: **$h_3$égʷʰi-* > (c5) **ógʷʰi-* > (4.3) **ógʰi-* > (c12) **óhi-* > (10.3) *áhi-* 'snake' **M** LAT *augēre* 'to increase' :: gen. sg. **$h_2$éu̯geses* > (c3) **au̯geses* > (c11) **au̯jeses* > (10.1) **au̯jasas* > (11.2) *ójasas* 'vigor' **N** LAT *lūcēre* :: **lou̯kéi̯eti* > (c10) **lou̯céi̯eti* > (9) **rou̯céi̯eti* > (10) **rau̯cái̯ati* > (11.2) *rocáyati* 'he shines'

Consonant Clusters with Palatal Consonants

Developments with intermediate steps

A GR *téktōn* :: **tétḱon-* > (5.1) **tétćon-* [téttšon] > (18.4) **tétṣon-* > (19.1) **tékṣon-* > (10) *tákṣan-* 'carpenter' **B** GR *phthísis* :: **dʰgʷʰíti-* > (4.3) **dʰgʰíti-* > (22.4) **dgʰíti-* > (5.6) **dj́ʰíti-* > (18.5) **d̯zhíti-* > (19.2) **gẓhíti-* = /*gʰṣíti/ > (19.3) *kṣíti-* 'destruction' **C** LAT *ursus* :: **Hr̥tḱo-* > (13.1) **ŕ̥tḱo-* > (5.1) **ŕ̥tćo-* [ŕ̥ttšo] > (18.4) **ŕ̥tṣo-* > (19.1) **ŕ̥kṣo-* > (10) *ŕ̥kṣa-* 'bear' **D** LAT *hum-us* :: **dʰǵʰém-* > (22.4) **dǵʰém-* > (5.3) **dj́ʰém-* [ddžhém] > (18.5) **d̯zhém-* > (19.2) **gẓʰém-* = /*gʰṣém-/ > (19.3) **kṣém-* > (10) *kṣám-* 'earth' **E** AV *caŝte* :: **kʷéḱs-to̯i* > (4.1) **kéḱsto̯i* > (5.1) **kéćsto̯i* [kétšto̯i] > (6.3) **kéšto̯i* > (c10) **céšto̯i* > (10) **cášta̯i* > (18.1) **cáṣṭa̯i* > (11.1) *cáṣṭe* 'he proclaims' **F** LAT *rēx* :: **rēǵs* > (22.1) **rēḱs* > (5.1) **rēćs* [rētšs] > (18.4) **rēṭṣ* > (10) **rāṭṣ* > (28.1) *rāṭ* 'king' **G** GR *kteínō* :: **tḱn̥-néu̯-ti* > (5.1) **tćn̥-néu̯-ti* [ttšn̥néu̯ti] > (18.4) **ṭṣn̥néu̯ti* > (19.1) **kṣn̥néu̯ti* > (15.1) **kṣanéu̯ti* > (10) **kṣanáu̯ti* > (11.2) *kṣanóti* 'he hurts/damages'

Exercises for the sequence **sḱ*

A AV *saδaiieiti* :: **sḱn̥d-éi̯e-ti* > (c19) **chn̥déi̯eti* > (15.1) **chadéi̯eti* > (10) *chadáyati* 'he/it shines/pleases' **B** LAT *pōscō* :: **pr̥ḱ-sḱé-ti* > (6.2) **pr̥sḱéti* > (c20) **pr̥cchéti* > (10) *pr̥ccháti* 'he asks' **C** *vāsáyati* 'he illuminates' < **h_2u̯os-éi̯e-ti* :: **$h_2$us-sḱé-ti* > (3.1) **$h_2$usḱéti* > (13.1) **usḱéti* > (c20) **ucchéti* > (10) *uccháti* 'it dawns (in the morning)' **D** AV *isaiti* :: **$h_2$is-sḱé-ti* > (3.1) **$h_2$isḱéti* > (13.1) **isḱéti* > (c20) **icchéti* > (10) *iccháti* 'he searches, strives for' **E** GR *érkhomai* 'I come, go' :: **h_1r̥-sḱé-ti* > (13.1) **r̥sḱéti* > (c20) **r̥cchéti* > (10) *r̥ccháti* 'he reaches'

Consonant Clusters with the Structures *CsC* and **ss*

Changes in consonant clusters

A *vásati* 'he dwells':: aor. **e-u̯ēs-sīt* > (10) **a-vās-sīt* > (25.2) *avātsīt* 'he dwelled' **B** *bhájati* 'he distributes' :: aor. **e-bʰag-s-to* > (22.1) **e-bʰak-s-to* > (10) **a-bhak-s-ta* > (6.1) *abhakta* 'he distributed' **C** *ghasati* 'he eats' :: **e-gʰs-to-* > (10) **a-ghs-ta-* > (6.1) **a-gh-ta-* > (7.4) *a-gdha-* 'uneaten' **D** *jíghatsati* 'he wants to eat' :: 2. sg. imp. **jaghsdhi* > (6.1) **jaghdhi* > (22.4) *jagdhi* 'eat!' **E** √*lep-* 'to smear' :: 3. sg. aor. mid. **a-lip-s-ta* > (6.1) *alipta* 'he smeared' **F** *sthitá-* 'standing' :: **ud-sth$_2$-to-* > (1.8) **ud-sthH-to-* > (1.6) **ud-sthi-to-* > (10) **ud-sthita-* > (22.1) **ut-sthita-* > (6.1) *utthita-* 'risen' **G** *stambha-* 'supporting pillar' :: **ud-stémbʰHeno-* > (22.1) **ut-stémbʰHeno-* >

(13.1) *ut-stémbʰeno- > (10) *ut-stámbhana- > (6.1) *uttámbhana-* 'supporting beam' **H** *sthāpáyati* 'he puts' :: *úd-sthāpayati > (22.1) *út-sthāpayati > (6.1) *útthāpayati* 'he puts up' **I** *stabhitá-* 'underpinned' :: *úd-stm̥bʰH-to- > (22.1) *út-stm̥bʰH-to- > (1.6) *út-stm̥bhito- > (15.2) *útstabhito- > (10) *útstabhita- > (6.1) *úttabhita-* 'erected' **J** HIT *kappilalli-* 'cursed' :: aor. 2. pl. *ḱēp-s-to > (c7) *śēpsto > (10) *śāpsta > (6.1) *śāpta* 'you curse' **K** *tápati* 'is hot' :: 2. du. aor. *a-tāp-s-tam > (6.1) *atāptam* 'you two burned'

Simplification / Transition Sounds / Distant Assimilation

Distant assimilation and simplification of consonant clusters

A AV *saŋuhaṇt-* :: *śasvant- > (27.3) *śáśvant-* 'frequent' **B** LATV *sàuss* 'dry' :: *seu̯sei̯eti > (c24) *seu̯ṣei̯eti > (10) *sau̯ṣai̯ati > (11.2) *soṣayati > (s...ṣ > ś...ṣ) *śoṣáyati* 'he dries' **C** *bhūmán-* 'multitude, wealth' :: instr. sg. *bhūmnā́ > (27.2) *bhūnā́* **D** *mahimán-* 'size' :: instr. sg. *mahimnā́ > (27.2) *mahinā́* **E** *drāghimán-* 'length' :: instr. sg. *drāghmnā́ > (27.2) *drāghmā́* **F** *raśmán-* 'rein' :: instr. sg. *raśmnā́ > (27.2) *raśmā́* **G** *yunákti* 'he yokes' :: 2. pl. imp. *yuṅgdhi > (27.3) *yuṅdhi* 'yoke!'

Exercises regarding chapter 18 and 19 (attention: these are difficult exercises!)

A *séǵʰtr̥- > (5.3) *séj́ʰtr̥- > (7.6) *séj́dʰr̥- > (6.6) *séždhr̥- > (10) *sáždhr̥- > (18.2) *sáẓḍhr̥- > (20.3) *sā́ḍhr̥-* 'winner' **B** AV *dərəz-* 'fetter' :: *dʰr̥ǵʰ-tó- > (5.3) *dʰr̥j́ʰtó- > (7.6) *dʰr̥j́dʰó- > (6.6) *dʰr̥ždʰó- > (27.1) *dr̥ždʰó- > (10) *dr̥ždhá- > (18.2) *dr̥ẓḍhá- > (20.1) *dr̥ḍhá-* 'determined' **C** *br̥háti* 'he rips out' :: *br̥ǵʰtó- > (5.2) *br̥j́ʰtó- > (7.6) *br̥j́dʰó- [br̥d̠ždhó] > (6.6) *br̥ždhó- > (10) *br̥ždhá- > (18.3) *br̥ẓḍhá- > (20.1) *br̥ḍhá-* 'ripped out' **D** AV *dißžaidiiāi* :: *dʰi-dʰbʰ-sati > (22.4) *dʰídbʰsati > (7.2b) *dʰídbzʰati > (simplification *dbz > bz*) *dʰíbzʰati > (27.1) *díbzʰati > (19.4) *dípsati* 'he wants to hurt' **E** *bábhasti* < *bʰe-bʰosti 'he chews' :: 3. pl. *bʰé-bʰs-ati > (7.2b) *bʰábzʰati > (27.1) *bábzʰati > (19.4) *bápsati* 'they chew' **F** *dáhati* < *dʰégʷʰeti 'he/it burns' :: *dʰégʷʰ-s-n̥t- > (4.3) *dʰégʰ-s-n̥t- > (15.1) *dʰégʰ-s-at- > (7.5b) *dʰégzʰat- > (8.2) *dʰégžʰat- > (10.1) *dʰágžʰat- > (27.1) *dágžʰat- > (23.2) *dágẓʰat- > (19.3) *dákṣat-* 'burning' **G** AV *pasča* :: *po-skʷ-éh$_1$ > (c2) *poskʷḗ > (4.1) *poskḗ > (5.4) *posčḗ > (10) *pasčā́ > (20.10) *paścā́* 'behind, after' **H** LAT *mergit* :: *mézgeti > (5.5) *mézǰeti > (10) *mázǰati > (20.11) *májjati* 'he sinks'

Dissimilations

Loss of aspiration according to Grassmann's law

A *dáhati* 'he/it burns' < *dʰégʷʰeti :: *e-dʰēgʷʰ-s-t > (4.3) *edʰēgʰst > (22.5) *edʰēkst > (10) *adhākst > (8.1) *adhākšt > (23.1) *adhākṣt > (17.1) *adhākṣṭ > (28.1) *adhāk* 'he/it burned' **B** *di-dʰegʷʰ-s-e-ti > (4.3) *didʰegʰseti > (22.5) *didʰekseti > (c24) *didhekṣeti > (10) *didhakṣati* 'he wants to burn' **C** *gau̯-dhugh-s > (11.2) *go-dhughs > (22.5) *go-dhuks > (c24)*go-dhukṣ > (28.1) *godhuk* 'milker' **D** *arthabhudh-s > (22.5) *arthabhut-s > (28.1) *arthabhut* 'expert' **E** *dhāya-* 'layer' :: *dʰe-dʰh$_1$-ói̯ > (13.1)*dʰe-dʰ-ói̯ > (10) *dha-dh-ái̯ > (11.1) *dhadhé > (27.1) 3. sg. mid. *dadhé* 'I put' **F** GR *títhēmi* :: *dʰé-dʰeh$_1$-ti > (c2) *dʰédʰēti > (27.1) *dédhēti > (10) *dádhāti* 'he puts' **G** LAT *fiber* :: *bʰebʰrú- > (27.1) *bebʰrú- > (10) *babhrú-* 'a brown animal'

Dissimilation / Simplification

A AV *taf-nah-* :: *tap-mán- > (*p...m > k...m*) *tak-mán-* 'fever' **B** *áp-* 'water' :: dat. pl. *ap-bhis > (22.2) *ab-bhis > (*b...b > d...b*) *adbhis > (28.3) *adbhiḥ* **C** masc. sg. *tráyaḥ* :: fem. sg. *trisráḥ > (*r...r > Ø...r*) *tisráḥ* 'three' **D** *tri-* 'three'+ *stár-* 'star' :: *tri-str-ii̯o- > (8.1) *trištrii̯o- > (*tr...tr > t...r*) *tišrii̯a- > (23.1)*tiṣrii̯a- > (*ṣr > ṣ*) VED *tiṣíya-* name of a fixed star with the original meaning of 'belonging to a triple star' **E** LAT *sistō* :: *sth$_2$i-sth$_2$-e-ti > (1.8) *sthi-sth-e-ti > (8.1) *sthi-šth-e-ti > (10) *sthi-šth-a-ti > (27.1) *sti-šth-a-ti > (*st...št > t...št*) *ti-šth-a-ti > (23.1) *tiṣṭhati* 'he stands'

Bartholomae's Law

Bartholomae's law

A VED *bhásat* :: *ba-bʰs-tām > (7.2) *babzdhām > (6.1) *babdhām* 'shall chew' **B** *ghasati* 'he eats' < *gʰeseti :: *gʰs-to > (7.5) *gzdʰo > (8.2) *gždho > (6.1) *gdho > (10) *gdha* 'shall eat' **C** √*droh-* 'to hurt' :: *dʰrugʰtó- > (7.4) *dhrugdhó- > (27.1) *drugdhó- (10) *drugdhá-* 'hurt' **D** *duha-* 'giving milk' :: *dʰugʰ-tó- > (7.4) *dhugdhó- >

KEY

(27.1) *dugdhó- (10) dugdhá- ‘milked’ **E** budha- ‘intelligent’ :: *bʰudʰ-tó- > (2.3) *bhudʰztó- > (7.3) *bhudzdʰó- > (6.1) *bhuddhó- > (27.1) *buddhó- > (10) buddhá- ‘awakened’ **F** dáhati ‘he burns’ :: *dʰegʷʰtó- > (4.3) *dʰegʰtó- > (7.4) *dhegdhó- > (27.1) *degdhó- > (10) dagdhá- ‘burnt’ **G** AV azdā :: *Hedʰ-téh$_2$ > (c4) *Hedʰtā́ > (13.1) *edʰtā́ > (2.3) *edʰztā́ > (7.3) *edzdhā́ > (6.1) *eddhā́ > (10) addhā́ ‘truly’ **H** √rodh- ‘to obstruct’ :: 3. sg. aor. mid. *á-rudʰ-s-ta > (7.3) *árudzdʰa > (6.1) áruddha ‘he obstructed’

Bartholomae’s law with palatal *ǵʰ

A GR leíkhō :: 3. sg. *léi̯ǵʰti > (5.3) *léi̯ȷ́ʰti [léi̯d̠žhti] > (7.6) *léi̯ȷ́dʰi [léi̯d̠ždhi]> (6.6) *léi̯ždʰi > (9) *réi̯ždʰi > (18.3) *réi̯ẓḍʰi > (10) *rái̯ẓḍʰi > (11.1) *réẓḍʰi > (20.1) réḍhi ‘he licks’ **B** gā́hate ‘he dives into’ :: *geǵʰtó- > (5.3) *geȷ́ʰtó- > (7.6) *geȷ́dhó- [ged̠ždhó] > (6.6) *geždhó- > (18.3) *geẓḍhó- > (10) *gaẓḍhá- > (20.3) gāḍhá- ‘shallow, deep’ **C** vahati ‘he rides’ :: *uǵʰtó- > (5.3) *uȷ́ʰtós > (7.6) *uȷ́dʰós > (6.6) *uždʰó- > (10) *uždhá- > (18.3) *uẓḍhá- > (20.3) ūḍhá- ‘moved’ **D** sáhate ‘he wins’ :: *seǵʰtó- > (5.3) *seȷ́ʰtó- > (7.6) *seȷ́dʰó- > (6.6) *seždhó- > (18.3) *seẓḍhó- > (10) *saẓḍhá- > (20.3) *sāḍhá- ‘defeated’

Retroflex Consonants

The ruki rule with Indic comparanda / Emergence of retroflex ṇ

A √sad- ‘to sit’ :: *sad-ná- > (22.3) sanná- ‘sitting’ :: *ni-sad-na- > (22.3) *nisanna- > (c24) *niṣanna- > (24) *niṣaṇṇa- ‘leaned at’ **B** nayati ‘he leads’ :: *pari-nayati > (24) pariṇayati ‘he leads around’ **C** namati ‘he worships’ :: *pra-namati > (24) praṇamati ‘he worships’ **D** √naś- ‘to die’ :: *pra-naśyati > (24) praṇaśyati ‘he dies’ **E** √stigh- ‘to rise, to raise’ :: 3. sg. des. *ti-stigh-is-ate > (c24) *tiṣtighiṣate > (17.1) tiṣṭighiṣate ‘he wants to climb’ **F** √stubh- ‘to cheer, to praise’ :: *anu-stúbh- > (c24) *anuṣtúbh- > (17.1) anuṣṭúbh- ‘hymn of praise’ **G** √syand- ‘to hurry’ :: *raghu-syád- > (c24) raghu-ṣyád- ‘hurrying quickly’ **H** sarpa- ‘snake’ :: instr. sg. *sarpena > (24) sarpeṇa **I** hari- epithet of Viṣṇu :: instr. sg. *harinā > (24) hariṇā

The ruki rule with comparanda from other languages

A GR dís :: *du̯is > (c24) dviṣ ‘two times’ **B** GR ársēn :: *h$_2$u̯r̥sen- > (13.2) *u̯r̥sen- > (c24) *u̯r̥ṣen- > (10) vr̥ṣan- ‘male animal’ **C** LAT iūs :: *i̯ūs > (c24) yūṣ́- ‘broth’ **D** LAT mūs :: *múHs > (13.4) *mū́s- > (c24) mū́ṣ- ‘mouse’ **E** LAT coxa :: *kokseh$_2$ > (c4) *koksā > (10) *kaksā > (c24) kákṣā ‘curve’ **F** LAT ūvidus :: *ugʷ-sé-ti > (4.2) *ugséti > (22.1) *ukséti > (c24)*ukṣéti > (10.1) ukṣáti ‘he moistens’ **G** LAT perna :: *pḗrsni- > (c24) *pḗrṣni- > (10) pā́rṣṇi- ‘heel’ **H** √vas- ‘to stay’ :: *pra-ús-tha- > (c24) *pra-úṣ-tha- > (17.1) *pra-úṣ-ṭha- > (11.2) próṣṭha- ‘place for the night’ **I** GR ksyrón :: *ksu-ró- > (c24) *kṣuró- > (10) kṣurá- ‘razor’

Final Consonants I

Simplification of final consonant clusters

A LAT nox :: *nokʷt-s > (4.1) *nokts > (10.3) *nakts > (28.1) nak ‘night’ **B** acc. sg. bhavantam :: nom. sg. *bhavants > (28.1) bhavan ‘being’ **C** LAT rēx :: *h$_3$rēǵ-s > (13.2) *rēǵ-s > (22.1) *rēḱ-s > (5.1) *rēćs [rēt̠šs] > (18.6) *rēṭṣ > (10) *rāṭṣ > (28.1) rāṭ ‘king’ **D** hanti ‘he slays’ :: *h$_1$e-gʷʰen-t > (c1) *e-gʷʰen-t > (4.3) *e-gʰen-t > (c9) *ehent > (10.1) *ahant > (28.1) ahan ‘he slayed’ **E** santi ‘they are’ :: *h$_1$s-ent-s > (13.2) *sents > (10.1) *sants > (28.1) san ‘being’ **F** dhákṣu- ‘burning’ :: 3. sg. aor. *a-dhāgh-s-t > (22.5) *adhākst > (c24) *adhākṣt > (17.1) *adhākṣṭ > (28.1) adhāk ‘it/he burned’ **G** MHG taugen :: *h$_1$e-dʰeu̯gʰt > (c1) *e-dʰeu̯gʰt > (22.5) *e-dʰeu̯kt > (10.1) *adhaukt > (11.2) *adhokt > (28.1) adhok ‘he milked (an animal)’ **H** LAT māter :: *mā́tēr > (10) *mā́tār > (28.2) mātā́ ‘mother’ **I** *chand-ti > (22.1) chantti ‘it/he pleases’ :: 3. sg. aor. *achānd-s-t > (22.1) *achāntst > (28.1) achān ‘it pleased’ **J** aśnóti ‘he reaches’ :: aor. *Hé-Hneḱ-t > (13.1) *éHneḱt > (13.4) *ḗneḱt > (5.1) *ḗnećt [ēnet̠št] > (18.6) *ḗneṭṣṭ > (10) *ā́naṭṣṭ > (28.1) ā́naṭ ‘he reached’ **K** vīrudha- ‘plant’:: *vīrudh-s > (22.5) *vīruts > (28.1) vīrut ‘herb’ **L** √marj- ‘to wipe off’ :: *h$_1$e-mērǵ-t > (c1) *emērǵt > (22.1) *emērḱt > (5.1) *emērćt [emērt̠št] > (10) *amārćt > (18.6) *amārṭṣṭ > (28.1) amārṭ ‘he wiped off’ **M** √leh- ‘to lick’ < *lei̯ǵʰ- :: *medʰu-liǵʰs > (22.5) *medʰu-liḱs > (5.1) *medʰu-lićs > (18.6) *medhuliṭṣ > (10) *madhuliṭṣ > (28.1) madhuliṭ ‘bee’ **N** LAT sex :: *seḱs > (5.1) *sećs > (18.6) *seṭṣ > (10) *saṭṣ > (s... ṣ > ṣ... ṣ)*ṣaṭṣ > (28.1) ṣaṭ ‘six’ **O** kāmaduh- :: nom. *keh$_2$mo-dʰugʰs > (c4) *kāmodʰugʰs > (22.5) *kāmodhuks > (10) *kāmadhuks > (28.1) kāmadhuk ‘heavenly cow’

Final Consonants II

Etymological *-ns reappears in sandhi forms

A vr̥kān ca > (s15.1) vr̥kāṃś_ca ‘and the wolves’ **B** abharan ca > (s15.1) abharaṃś_ca ‘and they carried’ **C** tān ṭaṅkān > (s15.2) tāṃṣ_ṭaṅkān ‘these hoes’ **D** devān tatra > (s15.3) devāṃs_tatra ‘the gods over there’ **E** śaśin tvarasva > (s15.3) śaśiṃs_tvarasva ‘oh moon, hurry up!’ **F** hasan cakāra > (s15.1) hasaṃś_cakāra ‘he did it laughingly’ **G** pāśān chettum > (s15.1) pāśāṃś_chettum ‘in order to loosen chains/bonds’ **H** patan taruḥ > (s15.3) pataṃs_taruḥ ‘a falling tree’ **I** hasan ṭīkate > (s15.2) hasaṃṣ_ṭīkate ‘he jumps laughingly’ **J** calan ṭiṭṭibhaḥ > (s15.2) calaṃṣ_ṭiṭṭibhaḥ ‘a running bird’

Sandhi of final nasals after a short vowel before an initial vowel

A tasmin adrau > (s16.1) tasminn_adrau ‘on this mountain’ **B** gacchan īkṣate > (s16.1) gacchann_īkṣate ‘he watches while walking’ **C** pratyaṅ āste > (s16.2) pratyaṅṅ_āste ‘he sits westwards’ **D** yogin āgaccha > (s16.1) yoginn_āgaccha ‘oh yogi, come!’ **E** dhāvan aśvaḥ > (s16.1) dhāvann_aśvaḥ ‘running horse’ **F** pratyaṅ āsīnaḥ > (s16.2) pratyaṅṅ_āsīnaḥ ‘sitting westwards’

Initial *ch* after short vowel or after *ā* and *mā*

A tava chāyā > (s5.1) tava_cchāyā ‘your shadow’ **B** taru chāyā > (s5.1) taru_cchāyā ‘shade of a tree’ **C** ā chādayati > (s5.1) ā_cchādayati ‘he covers’ **D** ā chāditaḥ > (s5.1) ā_cchāditaḥ ‘covered’ **E** mā chidat > (s5.1) mā_cchidat ‘he shall not cut!’ **F** mā chaitsīt > (s5.1) mā_cchaitsīt ‘he shall not cut!’ **G** badarī chāyā > (s5.1) badarī_cchāyā ‘shadow of the jujuba-tree’

Syllabic Nasals and Liquids

Merger of *l and *r / Syllabic nasals

A LAT pluit ‘it rains’ :: 3. pl. *pleu̯onto > (9) *preu̯onto > (10) pravanta ‘they swim’ **B** LAT relinquō :: *linékʷti > (4.1) *linékti > (9) *rinékti > (10.1) *rinákti > (24) riṇákti ‘he leaves’ **C** LAT mollis :: *ml̥dú- > (9) mr̥dú- ‘soft’ **D** GR tatós :: *tn̥tó- > (15.1) *tató- > (10) tatá- ‘stretched’ **E** GR elakhús :: *$h_1$ln̥gʷʰú- > (13.2) *ln̥gʷʰú- > (4.3) *ln̥gʰú- > (15.1) *lagʰú- > (9) raghú- ‘lightweight’ **F** √bhañj- ‘to break’ :: *bhn̥gná- > (15.1) bhagná- ‘broken’ **G** LAT mēns ‘mind’ :: *mn̥tá- > (15.1) matá- ‘gedacht’ **H** √daṃś- ‘to bite’ :: *dm̥śati > (15.2) daśati ‘he bites’ **I** LAT ventus :: *gʷm̥tó- > (4.2)*gm̥tó- > (15.2) *gató- > (10) gatá- ‘having come’ **J** *nebʰos > (10) nábhas- ‘cloud’ :: *n̥bʰ-ró- > (15.1) *abhró- > (10.3) abhrá ‘thunder-cloud’ **K** LAT nox :: *n̥kʷtéh₂ > (c4) *n̥kʷtā́ > (4.1) *n̥ktā́ > (15.1) aktā́ ‘night’ **L** HIT peru ‘rock’ :: *pérun̥to- > (15.1) *péru̯ato- > (10) párvata- ‘mountain(ous)’

Syllabic resonant plus laryngeal before consonant and before a vowel

A √tam- ‘to stiffen’ :: *tm̥H-i̯e-ti > (14.7) *tā́mi̯eti > (10) tā́myati ‘he becomes immovable’ **B** √śram- ‘to tire’ :: *ḱrm̥h_2-i̯e-ti > (14.7) *ḱrā́mi̯eti > (c7) *śrā́mi̯eti > (10) śrā́myati ‘he gets/is tired’ **C** támas- ‘darkness’ :: *tm̥H-ró- > (14.7) *tāmró- > (10.3) tāmrá- ‘dark red’ **D** LAT antae :: *h_2n̥Ht-eh_2- > (c4) *h_2n̥Ht-ā- > (14.6) *h_2ā́tā- > (13.1) ā́tā- ‘doorframe’ **E** lit. ántis :: *h_2n̥h_2-tí- > (1.5) *Hn̥Htí- > (14.6) *Hātí- > (13.1) ātí- ‘duck’ **F** LAT glōs :: *gl̥h_2-i- > (9) *gr̥h_2-i- > (14.2) giri- ‘sister-in-law’ **G** GR trõma ‘wound’ :: *tr̥h_3-o- > (14.4) *turo- > (10.3) tura- ‘ill, wounded’ **H** LAT lātus ‘carried’ :: *tl̥h_2-éh_2 > (c4) *tl̥h_2-ā́ > (14.5) tulā́ ‘balance’ **I** HIT tarh- ‘to overcome’ :: *tr̥Hés > (14.2) *tirés > (10) tirás ‘through’ **J** √kr̥̄ ‘to scatter’ :: *kr̥H-e-ti > (14.2) *kireti > (10) kirati ‘he scatters’

Laryngeal Developments I

Laryngeals next to vowels (A-N) and between vowels (O-Q)

A AV sāma- :: *ḱi̯e$h_1$mó- > (c2) *ḱi̯ēmó- > (c7) *śyēmó- > (10) śyāmá- ‘black’ **B** LAT sōns ‘guilty’ :: *n̥-$h_1$sn̥t- > (14.6) *ā́sn̥t- > (15.1) ā́sat- ‘not being’ **C** LAT agō :: *h_2í-h_2ǵ-e-toi̯ > (1.5) *HíHǵetoi̯ > (13.1+13.4) *ī́ǵetoi̯ > (c8) *ī́jetoi̯ > (10) *ī́jatai̯ > (11.1) ī́jate ‘he impels’ **D** ákṣi- ‘eye’ :: *h_3í-h_3kʷs-oi̯ > (1.5) *Hí-Hkʷsoi̯ > (13.1+13.4) *ī́kʷsoi̯ > (4.1) *ī́ksoi̯ > (c24) *ī́kṣoi̯ > (10) *ī́kṣai̯ > (11.1) ī́kṣe ‘I perceive’ **E** *h_2í-$h_2$sd-oi̯ > (1.5) *HíHsdoi̯ > (13.1+13.4) *ī́sdoi̯ > (22.2) *ī́zdoi̯ > (c25) *ī́ẓdoi̯ > (17.2) *ī́ẓḍoi̯ > (20) *ī́ḍoi̯ > (10) *ī́ḍai̯ > (11.1) ī́ḍe ‘I praise’ **F** *h_2í-h_2ḱ-oi̯ > (1.5) *HíHḱoi̯ > (13.1+13.4) *ī́ḱoi̯ > (c7) *ī́śoi̯ > (10) *ī́śai̯ > (11.1) ī́śe ‘I rule’ **G** HIT hi-iš-ši ‘at the drawbar’ :: *h_2iHs-éh_2- > (c4) *h_2iHs-áH- > (1.5) *HiHsáH- > (13.1+13.4) *īsā́- > (c24) īṣā́- ‘drawbar’ **H** LAT vānus ‘empty’

:: *uh$_2$nó- > (13.4) *ūnó- > (10) *ūná-* 'insufficient' **I** ON *vella* 'to bubble' :: *u̯l̥H-mi- > (14.3) *u̯ūr-mi- > (27.5) *ūrmí-* 'wave' **J** GR *orthós* :: *u̯r̥Hd^{h}u̯ó- > (14.3) *u̯ūrdhu̯ó- > (10) *u̯ūrdhu̯á- > (27.5) *ūrdhvá-* 'straight' **K** GR *orgḗ* 'passion' :: *u̯r̥Hǵ-éh$_2$- > (c4) *u̯r̥Hǵ-ā́- > (14.3) *u̯ūrǵ-ā́- > (c8) *u̯ūrjā́- > (27.5) *ūrjā́-* 'strength' **L** MHG *Atem* 'breath' :: *eh$_1$t-men- > (c2) *ētmen- > (10) *ātmán-* 'soul' **M** *áp-* 'water' < *h$_2$ep- :: *anu-h$_2$p-ó- > (13.4) *anūpó- > (10) *anūpá-* 'swamp' **N** *n̥b^{h}í-h$_3$k^{w}o- > (13.4) *n̥b^{h}ī́k^{w}o- > (4.1) *n̥b^{h}ī́ko- > (15.1) *abhī́ko- > (10) *abhī́ka-* 'encounter' **O** LAT *fānum* :: *d^{h}h$_1$s-ni̯o -> (1.6) *dhisnyo- > (c24) *dhiṣnyo- > (24) *dhiṣṇyo- > (10) *dhíṣṇya-* 'holy' **P** GR *patḗr* :: *ph$_2$tḗr > (1.6) *pitḗr > (10.2) *pitā́r > (28.2) *pitā́* 'father' **Q** GR *dósis* :: *dh$_3$ti- > (1.6) *díti-* 'donation'

Laryngeal Developments II

Aspiration of voiceless consonants through laryngeal *h$_2$

A LAT *sistō* :: *stí-sth$_2$-e-ti > (1.8)*stíst^{h}Heti > (st...st > t...st) *tíst^{h}Heti > (13.1) *tístheti > (c24) *tíṣtheti > (17.1) *tíṣṭheti > (10) *tíṣṭhati* 'he stands, puts' **B** GR *platús* :: *pl̥th$_2$ú- > (1.8) *pl̥t^{h}Hú- > (13.1) *pl̥thú- > (9) *pr̥thú-* 'broad' **C** *mn̥th$_2$tó- > (1.8) *mn̥t^{h}Htó- > (1.6) *mn̥thitó- > (15.1)*mathitó- > (10) *mathitá-* 'dislocated' **D** GR *kléos* 'fame' :: *ḱléu̯-is-th$_2$o- > (c7) *śléu̯isth$_2$o- > (9) *śréu̯isth$_2$o- > (1.8) *śréu̯ist^{h}Ho- > (13.1) *śréu̯istho-> (c24) *śréu̯iṣtho- > (17.1) *śréu̯iṣṭho- > (10) *śraviṣṭha-* 'the most famous' **E** LAT *rota* 'wheel' :: *roth$_2$ó- > (1.8) *rot^{h}Hó- > (13.1) *rothó- > (10) *rathá-* 'chariot' **F** *páñca* 'five' :: *pn̥k^{w}tHó- > (1.8) *pn̥k^{w}t^{h}Hó- > (4.1) *pn̥kt^{h}Hó- > (13.1) *pn̥kt^{h}ó- > (15.1) *pakthó- > (10) *pakthá-* 'Quintus'

Aspiration of voiced *ǵ through laryngeal *h$_2$

A GR *méga* :: *méǵh$_2$- > (1.9) *méǵ^{h}H- > (1.7) *méǵ^{h}i- > (c9) *méhi- > (10) *máhi-* 'big, great'
B LAT *egō* :: *eǵh$_2$óm > (1.9) *eǵ^{h}Hóm > (13.1) *eǵ^{h}óm > (c9) *ehóm > (10) *ahám* 'I'

Complete the paradigm of VED *pánthās*

	PIE		IIR		SKR
nom.	*pént-oh$_2$-s	>	*pántaHs	>	*pánthās*
acc.	*pént-oh$_2$-m̥	>	*pántaHam	>	*pánthām*
gen.	*pn̥th$_2$és	>	*pathás	>	*pathás*

From Indo-Iranian to Sanskrit

PIE	>	IIR	>	SKR	
Diphthongs and PIE *e/*o					
*ǵ^{h}éi̯men-	>	*ȷ́^{h}ái̯man-	>	*héman-*	'winter'
*toi̯	>	*tai̯	>	*te*	'these'
*leu̯kes-	>	*rau̯čas-	>	*rocas-*	'light'
*ǵ^{h}éi̯sd-os-	>	*ȷ́^{h}ái̯ždas-	>	*héḍas-*	'anger'
*teu̯so-	>	*tau̯ša-	>	*toṣa-*	'satisfaction'
*h$_2$éi̯d^{h}es-	>	*Hái̯dhas-	>	*édhas-*	'firewood'
*u̯oi̯d-th$_2$a	>	*u̯ai̯tstha	>	*véttha*	'you know'
*se-sǵ^h-u̯os-	>	*sazȷ́^{h}u̯as-	>	*sāhvas-*	'mighty'
*nizdó-	>	*niždá-	>	*nīḍá-*	'nest'
*póti-	>	*páti-	>	*páti-*	'lord, master'
*dóru-	>	*dā́ru-	>	*dā́ru-*	'wood'
*aǵó-	>	*ajá-	>	*ajá-*	'he-goat'
*h$_2$néro-	>	*Hnára-	>	*nára-*	'man'
*k^{w}e	>	*če	>	*ca*	'and'
Consonant clusters					
*réḱs-es-	>	*rácsas-	>	*rákṣas-*	'damage'
*oḱtṓ	>	*aćtā́	>	*aṣṭā́*	'eight'
*rḗǵ-s	>	*rā́ćs	>	*rā́ṭ*	'king'

**tétḱon-*	>	**tátćan-*	>	*tákṣan-*	'carpenter'
*g^{w}*m̥-sḱ-e-ti*	>	**gasćati*	>	*gacchati*	'he walks'
**nók*^{w}*t-s*	>	**nákts*	>	*nák*	'night'
**rēǵ-s*	>	**rā́ćs*	>	*rā́ṭ*	'king'
**u̯r̥t-tó-*	>	**u̯r̥tstá-*	>	*vr̥ttá-*	'turned'

Laryngeals

*h_2*énto-*	>	**Hánta-*	>	*ánta-*	'limit, end'
*h_2*énd*^{h}*es-*	>	**Hándhas-*	>	*ándhas-*	'sprout'
*h_2*épo*	>	**Hápa*	>	*ápa*	'away'
*h_1*erh*$_1$*tér-*	>	**HarHtár-*	>	*aritár-*	'rower'
**Hómso-*	>	**Hámsa-*	>	*áṃsa-*	'shoulder'
*h_2*onḱó-*	>	**Hanćá-*	>	*aṃśá-*	'share, part'
*h_2*énǵ*^{h}*es-*	>	**Hánj́*^{h}*as-*	>	*áṃhas-*	'fear'
*h_2*éǵtreh*$_2$*-*	>	**Háćtrā-*	>	*áṣṭrā-*	'whip'
*h_2*ósth*$_2$*-*	>	**HásthH-*	>	*ásthi-*	'bone'
*h_3*éh*$_1$*-s-*	>	**HáHs-*	>	*ā́s-*	'mouth'
*h_2*n̥h*$_2$*tí-*	>	**HaHtí-*	>	*ātí-*	'duck'
*h_2*ŕ̥tḱo-*	>	**Hŕ̥tća-*	>	*ŕ̥kṣa-*	'bear'
**HúHd*^{h}*-er-*	>	**HúHdhar-*	>	*ū́dhar-*	'udder'
*h_2*iHs-éh*$_2$*-*	>	**HiHšáH-*	>	*īṣā́-*	'pole bar'
**Hói̯ko-*	>	**Hái̯ka-*	>	*éka-*	'one'
*h_2*i-h*$_2$*ḱó-*	>	**HiHćá-*	>	*īśá-*	'lord, master'
**Hénos-*	>	**Hánas-*	>	*ánas-*	'carriage'
**dl̥h*$_1$*g*^{h}*ó-*	>	**dr̥Hghá-*	>	*dīrghá-*	'long'

Labiovelars

*g^{w}*r̥H-í-*	>	**gr̥H-í-*	>	*girí-*	'mountain'
*g^{w}*r̥H-ú-*	>	**gr̥H-ú-*	>	*gurú-*	'heavy'
*g^{w}*ṓu̯s*	>	**gā́u̯š*	>	*gáuṣ*	'cow'
*g^{wh}*ormó-*	>	**gharmá-*	>	*gharmá-*	'heat'
**u̯ĺ̥k*^{w}*o-*	>	**vŕ̥ka-*	>	*vŕ̥ka-*	'wolf'
*g^{w}*iHu̯o-*	>	**jiHu̯a-*	>	*jīva-*	'alive'
*k^{w}*sép-*	>	**kšáp-*	>	*kṣáp-*	'night'
*g^{wh}*énti*	>	*j^{h}*énti*	>	*hánti*	'he beats, he slays'
**u̯ōk*^{w}*-s*	>	**u̯ākš*	>	*vā́k*	'voice'
*h_2*elg*^{wh}*ó-*	>	**Harghá-*	>	*arghá-*	'value'

Bartholomae's law

**lub*^{h}*-tó-*	>	**lubdha-*	>	*lubdhá-*	'greedy'
**liǵ*^{h}*tó-*	>	**lij́dhá-*	>	*līḍhá-*	'licked'
**d*^{h}*eg*^{wh}*tó-*	>	**dhagdhá-*	>	*dagdhá-*	'burnt'

Syllabic nasals

**b*^{h}*n̥d*^{h}*-tó-*	>	**bhadzdhá-*	>	*baddhá-*	'bound'
**n̥-h*$_2$*ei̯g*^{wh}*és-*	>	**aHai̯j́hás-*	>	*anehás-*	'impeccable'
**n̥b*^{h}*ró-*	>	**abhrá-*	>	*abhrá-*	'thundercloud'
*h_1*r̥sn̥-b*^{h}*ó-*	>	**Hr̥šabhá-*	>	*r̥ṣabhá-*	'bull'
*h_3*r̥s-u̯ó-*	>	**Hr̥šu̯á-*	>	*r̥ṣvá-*	'high'
*h_2*m̥b*^{h}*í*	>	**Habhí*	>	*abhí*	'around'
**ǵn̥h*$_1$*tó-*	>	**ǰaHtá-*	>	*jātá-*	'born'

KEY

*mn̥tó-	>	*matá-	>	matá-	'thought'
*ḱm̥tóm	>	*ćatám	>	śatám	'hundred'
*n̥-dm̥h_2-tó-	>	*adm̥Htá-	>	adā́m̩ta-	'untamed'

Palatalizations

*ǵ^{h}imó-	>	*ȷ́^{h}imá-	>	himá-	'winter'
*$h_1$élḱes-	>	*Hárćas-	>	árśas-	'haemorrhoids'
*h_2éḱmon-	>	*Háćman-	>	áśman-	'stone'
*h_2éḱru-	>	*Háćru-	>	áśru-	'tear'
*h_1éḱu̯o-	>	*Háću̯a-	>	áśva-	'horse'
*$h_3$éng^{w}es-	>	*Hánǰas-	>	áñjas-	'anointment'
*ḱlutó-	>	*ćrutá-	>	śrutá-	'heard'
*ǵónu-	>	*ȷ́ā́nu-	>	jā́nu-	'knee'

Ruki rule

*$h_2$uksén-	>	*Hukšán-	>	ukṣán-	'young bull'
*$h_2$us-és-	>	*Hušás-	>	uṣás-	'dawn'
*h_2éḱso-	>	*Háćsa-	>	ákṣa-	'axis'
*ksuró-	>	*kšurá-	>	kṣurá-	'sharp knife'
*u̯isó-	>	*u̯išá-	>	viṣá-	'poison'
*pr̥sth_2ó-	>	*pr̥šthá-	>	pr̥ṣṭhá-	'back (of the body)'
*ǵéu̯s-o-	>	*ȷ́áu̯ša-	>	jóṣa-	'pleasure'
*tr̥sneh_2-	>	*tr̥šnaH-	>	tr̥ṣṇā-	'thirst'

Sound Change Index

From Proto-Indo-European to Proto-Indo-Iranian

Laryngeals

Vowel coloring through laryngeals

SC	Rule	Example
1.1	*h_2e > *h_2a	LAT *ante* :: *h_2*énti* > *h_2*ánti* > IIR **Hánti* > *ánti* 'before'
1.2	*eh_2 > *ah_2	LAT *pāstor* :: **péh*$_2$*ti* > **páh*$_2$*ti* > IIR **páHti* > *pā́ti* 'he protects'
1.3	*h_3e > *h_3o	LAT *opus* :: *h_3*épes-* > *h_3*ópes-* > IIR **Hápas-* > *ápas-* 'work'
1.4	*eh_3 > *oh_3	LAT *pōtus* 'drunk' :: imp. **peh*$_3$*-d*^{h}*í* > **poh*$_3$*d*^{h}*í* > IIR **paHdhí* > *pāhí* 'drink!'

Merger of laryngeals

SC	Rule	Example
1.5	*$h_{1/2/3}$ > **H*	LAT *ante* :: *h_2*énti* > *h_2*ánti* > IIR **Hánti* > *ánti* 'before'

Vocalization of laryngeals between consonants and in the final position

SC	Rule	Example
1.6	**H* > *i* / *C_C*	LAT *genitor* :: **ǵenh*$_1$*tór-* > IIR **ȷ́anHtár-* > **ȷ́anitár-* > *janitár-* 'progenitor'
1.7	**H* > *i* / _##	GR *méga* :: **méǵh*$_2$*-* > **méǵ*^{h}*H-* > IIR **máȷ́*^{h}*H-* > **máȷ́*^{h}*i-* > *máhi-* 'big'

Aspiration and voicing caused by laryngeals

SC	Rule	Example
1.8	*C* > *C*^{h} / _*h_3	GR *platús* :: **pl̥th*$_2$*ú-* > **pl̥t*^{h}*Hú-* > IIR **pr̥thú-* > *pr̥thú-* 'broad'[3]
1.9	*G* > *G*^{h} / _*h_2	GR *méga* :: **méǵh*$_2$*-* > **méǵ*^{h}*h*$_2$ > IIR **máȷ́*^{h}*H-* > **máȷ́*^{h}*i-* > *máhi-* 'big'
1.10	*C* > *G* / _*h_3	LAT *bibit* :: **pi-ph*$_3$*-e-ti* > **pibeti* > *pibati* 'he drinks'[4]

Insertion of *s in dental clusters in late Proto-Indo-European

SC	Rule	Example
2.1	**tt* > **tst*[5]	LAT *vertō* 'I turn' :: **u̯r̥t-tó-* > IIR **u̯r̥tstá-* > *vr̥ttá-* 'turned'
2.2	**dt* > **dzt*	GR *oĩda* :: **u̯oi̯d-th*$_2$*e* > IIR **u̯ai̯dztha* > **u̯ai̯dtha* > *vettha* 'he knows'
2.3	**d*^{h}*t* > **d*^{h}*zt*[6]	AV *vərəzda-* :: **u̯r̥d*^{h}*-tó-* > **u̯r̥d*^{h}*ztó-* > IIR **u̯r̥dzd*^{h}*á-* > *vr̥ddhá-* 'great, big, grown'

3 SC 1.8 and 1.9 exhibit the aspiration of a beforegoing stop through the laryngeal which itself remains as *H* before it becomes *i* according to SC 1.6 or SC 1.7 respectively.

4 Unique example. We might be dealing with a simple dissimilation *p...p* > *p...b*.

5 The sound cluster *-*tst*- is preserved in Hittite while the other IE languages simplified it in some way. In Greek, Baltic, Slavic and Iranian, the sequence *-*tst*- became *-*st*- and in Latin and Germanic it was simplified to *-*ss*-.

6 Followed by Barthomolae's law SC 7.

Simplification of PIE *ss

SC	Rule	Example
3.1	**ss* > *s*	GR *eĩ* :: **h$_1$es-si* > **h$_1$esi* > IIR **Hasi* > *asi* ‘you are’

Delabialization of labiovelars[7]

SC	Rule	Example
4.1	**k^{w}* > **k*	GR *pénte* :: **pénk^{w}e* > **pénke* > IIR **pánča* > *páñca* ‘five’
4.2	**g^{w}* > **g*	LAT *vīvus* :: **g^{w}ī̯uó-* > **gī̯uó-* > IIR **ǰī̯uá-* > *jīvá-* ‘alive’
4.3	**g^{wh}* > **g^{h}*	LAT *dē-fendō* :: **g^{wh}nénti* > **g^{h}nénti* > IIR **ghnánti* > *ghnánti* ‘they hit/kill’

Primary palatalization[8]

SC	Rule	Example
5.1	**ḱ* > **ć* [t̲š]	GR *klutós* :: **ḱlutó-* > IIR **ćrutá-* > *śrutá-* ‘famous’
5.2	**ǵ* > **ǰ́* [d̲ž]	GR *gónu* :: **ǵónu* > IIR **ǰ́ā́nu-* > *jā́nu-* ‘knee’
5.3	**ǵ^{h}* > **ǰ́^{h}* [d̲žh]	LAT *vehit* :: **u̯eǵ^{h}eti* > **u̯eǰ́^{h}eti* > IIR **u̯aǰ́^{h}ati* [u̯ad̲žhati] > *vahati* ‘he rides’

Secondary palatalization[9]

SC	Rule	Example
5.4	**k* > **č* / _(ĕ̄, ĭ̄, i̯)	LAT *que* :: **k^{w}e* > **ke* > **če* > IIR **ča* > *ca* ‘and’
5.5	**g* > **ǰ* / _(ĕ̄, ĭ̄, i̯)	LAT *augēre* ‘to increase’ :: **h$_2$éu̯ges-* > IIR **Háu̯ǰas-* > *ójas-* ‘strength’
5.6	**g^{h}* > **ǰ^{h}* / _(ĕ̄, ĭ̄, i̯)	LAT *vovēre* :: **h$_1$eu̯g^{wh}-e-toi̯* > IIR **Háu̯ǰ^{h}atai̯* > *óhate* ‘he speaks solemnly’

Simplification of consonant clusters of the structure *CsC

SC	Rule	Example
6.1	**CsC* > *CC*	GR *oĩda* :: **u̯oi̯d-th$_2$e* > IIR **u̯ai̯dztha* > **u̯ai̯dtha* > *vettha* ‘he knows’
6.2	**ḱsḱ* > **sḱ*	LAT *pōscō* :: **pr̥ḱ-sḱé-ti* > **pr̥sḱéti* > IIR **pr̥sćáti* > *pr̥ccháti* ‘he asks’
6.3	**ćt* [t̲št] > **št*	**dr̥ḱtó-* > IIR **dr̥ćtá-* [dr̥t̲štá] > **dr̥štá* > *dr̥ṣṭá-* ‘seen’
6.4	**t̲šdh* > **šdh*	IIR **tatćdhí* [tatt̲šdhí] > **tat̲šdhí* > **tašdhí* > **taždhí* > **taẓḍhí* > *tāḍhí* ‘make!’
6.5	**dzd(^{h})* > **zd(^{h})*	AV *dazdi* :: IIR **dadzdhí* > **dazdhí* >**dedhí* > *dehí* ‘give!’
6.6	**ǰ́d^{h}* [d̲ždh] > **ždh*	**liǰ́d^{h}á-* [*lid̲ždhá*] > **liždhá-* >**liẓdhá-* > **liẓḍhá-* >**līḍhá-* ‘licked’

7 The velars **k*, **g*, **g^{h}*, which originated out of labiovelars, remained as *k, g, g^{h}* if not in the position before *ĕ̄, ĭ̄, i̯*.

8 The PIE palatal series **k̂*, **ǵ*, **ǵ^{h}* probably originated out of the positional allophonic variants of the velars **k*, **g*, **g^{h}* in palatal environments e.g. before **e*/**ē*/**i*/**ī*/**i̯*. Through internal paradigmatic levelling, these palatal sounds spread to non-palatal positions e.g. before *a* in examples like PIE **k̂asó-* ‘rabbit’ or **ǵ^{h}ans-* ‘goose’. **Lit.:** Lipp 2009:5–10.

9 **k* from PIE **k*/**k^{w}*, **g* from PIE **g*/*g^{w}*, **g^{h}* from PIE **g^{h}*/**g^{wh}*.

Bartholomae's law / Rule: *D^h(z)T > D(z)D^h*

SC	Rule	Example
7.1	**b^{h}t > bdh*	*labhate* 'he gets' :: Inf. **labh-tum > labdhum* '(in order) to get'
7.2	**b^{h}st > *bzdh*	VED *bhásat* :: **ba-bhs-tām > *babzdhām > babdhām* 'he shall chew'
7.2b	**b^{h}s > *bz^h*	*bábhasti* 'he chews' :: 3. pl. **b^{h}é-b^{h}s-ati > *b^{h}ábz^{h}ati > *bábz^{h}ati > bápsati* 'they chew'
7.3	**d^{h}zt > *dzd^h*	GOT *bindan* :: **b^{h}n̥d^h-tó- > *b^{h}n̥d^{h}ztó-* > IIR **bhadzdhá- > baddhá-* 'bound'
7.4	**g^{h}t > gdh*	*múhyati* 'he gets confused' :: **mughtá- > mugdhá-* 'confused'
7.5	**g^{h}st > *gzd^h*	*ghasati* 'he eats' < **g^{h}eseti* :: **g^{h}s-to > *gzd^{h}o* > IIR **gzdha > gdha* 'he shall eat'
7.5b	**g^{h}s > *gz^h*	*dáhati* 'he burns' :: **d^{h}ég^{wh}-s-n̥t- >*d^{h}ég^h-s-n̥t- > *d^{h}ég^h-s-at-* > IIR *dhágh-sat- > *dhágzhat- > dákṣat-* 'burning'
7.6	**ȷ́^{h}t* [d̠žht] > **ȷ́d^h* [d̠ždh]	GR *leík^{h}ō* :: **léi̯ǵ^{h}ti > *rái̯ȷ́^{h}ti > IIR *rái̯ȷ́dhi > réḍhi* 'he licks'

Ruki rule part 1[10]

SC	Rule	Example
8.1	**s > *š / r,r̥,ŭ,k,ĭ _*	GR *dís* :: **du̯is* > IIR **dviš > dviṣ* 'two times'
8.2	**z > *ž / r,r̥,ŭ̄,k,ĭ̄ _*	PIE **nisdó-* > IIR **niždá- > *niẓdá- > *niẓḍá- > nīḍá-* 'nest'

Merger of *l* and *r*

SC	Rule	Example
9	**l/l̥ > r/r̥*	GR *hélkos* :: **h₁élḱos-* > IIR **Hárćas- > árśas-* 'wound'

Development of **ĕ̄* and **ŏ̄*

SC	Rule	Example
10.1	**e > a*	GR *pénte* :: **pénk^{w}e > *pénke* > IIR **pánča > páñca* 'five'
10.2	**ē > ā*	GR *títhēmi* :: **d^{h}é-d^{h}eh₁-mi* > IIR **dhádhaHmi > dádhāmi* 'I put'
10.3	**o > a*	LAT *iugum :: *i̯ugóm* > IIR **i̯ugám > yugám* 'yoke'
10.4	**ō > ā*	LAT *dōnum :: *dṓnom* > IIR **dā́nam > dā́nam* 'donation, gift'

Brugmann's law

SC	Rule	Example
10.5	**ó > ā́ / _RV*	GR *dóru* :: **dóru- > dā́ru-* 'wood'

10 Followed by ruki rule 2 (SC 23), through which retroflex **š > ṣ* and **ž > ẓ* originate.

From Proto-Indo-Iranian to Sanskrit

Monophthongization[11]

SC	Rule	Example
11.1	*ai̯ > e	PIE *d^he-$d^h h_1$-ói̯ > IIR *dhadhái̯ > 3. sg. mid. *dadhé* 'he puts'
11.2	*au̯ > o	LAT *augēre* 'to increase' :: *$h_2$éu̯ges- > IIR *Háu̯ǰas- > *ójas-* 'strength'

Shortening of IIR long diphthongs before consonant or in the absolute final position[12]

SC	Rule	Example
12.1	*āi̯ > ai̯	GR *leípō* 'I leave' :: 1. sg. aor. *é-lēi̯k^w-s-m̥ > IIR *árāi̯kšam > *áraikṣam* 'I let'
12.2	*āu̯ > au̯	LAT *bōs* :: *g^wṓu̯s > IIR *gā́u̯š > *gáuḥ* 'cow'
12.3	*ār > ar[13]	*yathā r̥ṣiḥ* > (s2.3) *yatharṣiḥ* 'like a seer'

Loss of laryngeal before a vowel and in the initial position before consonant

SC	Rule	Example
13.1	*H > Ø / _V	*h_2i-$h_2$isd-$h_2$éi̯ > IIR *Hi-Hižd-Hái̯ > *īẓḍé > *īḍé* 'I worship'
13.2	*H > Ø / #_C	GR *anḗr* :: *$h_2$nér-o- > IIR *Hnára- > *nára-* 'man'

Loss of laryngeal after a vowel with compensatory lengthening

SC	Rule	Example
13.4	*VH > V̄	LAT *fūmus* :: *d^huh_2-mó- > IIR *dhuHmá- > *dhūmá-* 'smoke'

Loss of laryngeal between vowels creates internal hiatus

SC	Rule	Example
13.5	*H > Ø / V_V[14]	LAT *rēs* 'thing' :: *reh_1-i-s > IIR *raHis > *rayíṣ* 'possession, wealth'

Laryngeal plus resonant

SC	Rule	Example
14.1	*r̥H > īr / _C	AV *darəgō* :: *dl̥$h_1$$g^h$ó- > IIR *dr̥Hghá- > *dīrghá-* 'long'
14.2	*r̥H > ir / _V	OCS *gora* :: *g^wr̥H-í- > IIR *gr̥H-í- > *girí-* 'mountain'
14.3	*l̥H > ūr / _C[15]	LAT *lāna* :: *h_2u̯l̥H-neh_2- > IIR *Hu̯r̥H-naH- > *u̯ū́rnā- > *ū́rṇā-* 'wave'[16]
14.4	*r̥H > ur / _V[17]	GR *barús* :: *g^wr̥H-ú- > IIR *gr̥H-ú- > *gurú-* 'heavy'

11 Some non-monophthongized forms have been preserved in Mitanni-Aryan which are written records of Indo-Aryan loanwords in the Mitanni Empire which existed approximately around 1500–1300 BC in Northern Syria. These loanwords consist of names of people, names of gods, expressions for horse training as well as some numbers. In the Kikulli text we find the designations *aikawartanna* 'one round', in which the first element *aika-* still represents the non-monophthongized preform IIR *ai̯ka- which developed to SKR *eka-* 'one'.

12 In Middle Indic the newly formed diphthongs *ai̯* and *au̯* monophthongized to *ē* and *ō* as well.

13 This rule is needed for the historic explanation of sandhi s2.3 (cf. chapter 6).

14 *H disappeared between vowels and created a metrically relevant hiatus in the oldest texts.

15 In labial environment.

16 Plus the initial simplification of *u̯ū > ū.

17 In labial environment.

14.5	*l̥h_2 > ul / _V	LAT *lātus* :: *tl̥h_2-éh_2- > IIR *tl̥H-ā́- > *tulā́-* 'balance, scales'
14.6	*n̥H > *aH > ā[18]	GR *gnētós* :: *ǵn̥$h_1$tó- > IIR *ȷ́ātá- > *jātá-* 'born'
14.7	*m̥H > ām	GR *ádmētos* :: *n̥-dm̥h_2-tó- > IIR *a-dāmtá- > *adāṃta-* 'untamed'

The syllabic nasals[19]

SC	Rule	Example
15.1	*n̥ > a	GR *tatós* :: *tn̥tó- > IIR *tatá- > *tatá-* 'stretched'
15.2	*m̥ > a	LAT *septem* :: *septḿ̥ > IIR *saptá > *saptá* 'seven'
15.3	*n̥ > an / _(i̯, u̯, m, #)[20]	3. sg. opt. prs. *g^{wh}n̥-i̯ḗ-t > IIR *ghani̯ā́t > VED *hanyā́t* 'he shall kill'
15.4	*m̥ > am / _(i̯, u̯, m, #)	GR *baínō* :: *g^{w}m̥-i̯e-toi̯ > IIR *gamyatai > *gamyate* 'he walks'

Deaffrication of IIR palatal affricates

SC	Rule	Example
16.1	*ć [tš] > ś [š]	GR *klutós* :: *ḱlutó- > IIR *ćrutá- [t͡šrutá] > *śrutá-* 'famous'
16.2	*$ȷ́^h$ [d͡žh] > *žh	IIR *u̯a$ȷ́^h$ati [u̯ad͡žhati] > *u̯ažhati > *vahati* 'he rides'

Secondary palatalization

SC	Rule	Example
16.3	*č > c [t͡š][21]	LAT *que* :: *k^we > *ke > *če > IIR *ča > *ca* 'and'
16.4	*ǰ > j	LAT *augēre* 'to increase' :: *$h_2$éu̯ges- > IIR *Háu̯ǰas- > *ójas-* 'force'
16.4	*g^h > *h	LAT *vovēre* :: *$h_1$eu̯g^{wh}-e-toi̯ > IIR *Háu̯$ǰ^h$atai̯ > *óhate* 'he speaks solemnly'

Assimilation involving retroflex consonants

SC	Rule	Example
17.1	*ṣt > ṣṭ	*iṣa-* 'desiring' :: *iṣ-tá- > *iṣṭá-* 'desired'
17.2	*ẓd > *ẓḍ	*nisdó- > IIR *niždá- > *niẓdá- > *niẓḍá- > *nīḍá-* 'nest'[22]
17.3	*ẓdh > *ẓḍh	*misd^hó- > IIR *miždhá- > *miẓdhá- > *miẓḍhá- > *mīḍhá-* 'reward'

18 Probably already in Proto-IIR because of AV *zāta-* < *ǵn̥$h_1$tó-.
19 Probably already in Proto-IIR.
20 In my opinion, SC 14.7, 15.3 and 15.4 are not phonologically regular developments but analogical formations.
21 In contrast to [t͡š], which originated out of *k̂ > *ć, this sound [t͡š] was preserved as SKR *c*.
22 Cf. SC 18.2 and 18.3.

Reciprocal assimilation: palatal + dental > retroflex

SC	Rule	Example
18.1	*št > ṣṭ	PIE *oḱtṓ > IIR *aćtā́ [at̠štā́] > *aštā́ > aṣṭā́ ‘eight’
18.2	*žd > *ẓḍ	PIE *nisdó- > *nizo- > IIR *niždá- > *niẓḍá- > nīḍá- ‘nest’[23]
18.3	*ždʰ > *ẓḍʰ	3. pl. tákṣati ‘they produce’ :: 2. sg. imp. *taḱsdhi > (5.1) *taćsdhi [tat̠šsdhi] > (6.7) *tat̠šdhi > (6.4) *tašdhi > (22.2) *taždhi > (18.3) *taẓḍhi > (20.3) tāḍhi ‘produce!’
18.4	*tt̠š /tć/ > *ṭṣ	PIE *tétḱon- > IIR *tátćan- [tátt̠šan] > *táṭṣan- > tákṣan- ‘carpenter’
18.5	*dd̠ž(ʰ) /dǰ/ > *ḍẓ	PIE *dʰgʷʰíti- > IIR *dǰʰíti- [dd̠žhíti] > *ḍẓhíti- > *gẓʰíti- > kṣíti- ‘destruction’
18.6	*t̠šs /ćs/ > *ṭṣ	PIE *h_2éḱso- > IIR *ácsa- [át̠šsa] > *áṭṣa- > *ákṣa- ‘axis’
18.6b	*t̠št > *ṭṣṭ[24]	PIE *h_1e-mērǵ-t > *emērḱt > IIR amārćt [emērt̠št] > *amārṭṣṭ > amārṭ ‘he wiped off’
18.7	*d̠žʰ > *ḍẓʰ	PIE *dʰgʷʰíti- > IIR *dǰʰíti- [dd̠žhíti] > *ḍẓʰíti- > kṣíti- ‘destruction’

Phonotactic development of *ṭṣ > kṣ and *ḍẓʰ > *gẓʰ > kṣ and *bzʰ > ps

SC	Rule	Example
19.1	*ṭṣ > kṣ	PIE *tétḱon- > IIR *tátćan- [tátt̠šan] > *tát̠šan- > *táṭṣan- > tákṣan- ‘carpenter’
19.2	*ḍẓ(ʰ) > *gẓ(ʰ)	IIR *dǰʰíti- [dd̠žhíti] > *ḍẓʰíti- > *gẓʰíti- = *gʰṣíti- > kṣíti- ‘destruction’
19.3	*gẓ(ʰ) /gʰs/ = kṣ	IIR *dǰʰíti- [dd̠žhíti] > *ḍẓʰíti- > *gẓʰíti- = *gʰṣíti- > kṣíti- ‘destruction’
19.4	*bzʰ / bʰs/ = ps	3. pl. *bʰé-bʰs-ati > *bʰábzʰati > *bábzʰati > bápsati ‘they chew’

Loss of sibilants

SC	Rule	Example
20.1	*z /*ẓ > Ø without CL	√śās- ‘to command’ :: *śās-dhi > *śāzdhi > śādhi ‘command!’
20.2	*z > Ø / _G + CL	*séǵʰos- > sáhas- ‘power’ :: *se-sǵʰ-u̯os- > *sazǰʰu̯as- > sāhvas- ‘mighty’
20.3	*ẓ > Ø / _G + CL	ENG nest :: *nisdo- > IIR *niždá- > *niẓḍá- > nīḍa- ‘nest’
20.4	*ž > Ø / _h	IIR *u̯aǰʰati [u̯ad̠žhati] > *u̯ažhati [u̯ažhati] > vahati [u̯ahati] ‘he rides’

Loss and restitution of transition sounds

SC	Rule	Example
21.1	*i̯ > Ø	Sandhi: *yogay ālasyam > yoga_ālasyam ‘laziness in yoga’
21.2	Ø > i̯	asti ‘is’ :: imp. *as-dhi > *azdhi > *aØdhi > *ai̯dhi > edhi ‘be!’
21.3	Ø > u̯	Nalas nāma > *Nalaz_nāma > *NalaØ_ nāma > *Nalau̯_nāma > Nalo_nāma ‘called Nala’
21.4	Ø > r	agniẓ_dahati > agniØ_dahati > agnir_dahati ‘the fire burns’

23 We find a phonological overlapping with SC 17.2. In analogy to SC 18.3, the sound cluster *žd should have regularly become *ẓḍ even without the influence of the ruki rule. I did not find an example without the phonological ruki-context.

24 This derivation presents some problems. The sound cluster should have been simplified either to *ṭṣṭ > (6.1) *ṭṭ or to *ćt [t̠št] > (6.2) *št.

Middle Indic monophthongization

SC	Rule	Example
21.5	*aya > e	*tay abruvan > te 'bruvan 'they spoke'
21.6	*au̯a > o	*nadyaz_avahan > *nadyaØ_avahan > *nadyau̯_avahan > nadyo 'vahan 'rivers flew'

Assimilations[25]

SC	Rule	Example
22.1	G > K / _K	√vid- 'to know' :: *u̯oi̯d-ti > IIR *u̯ai̯dzti > *u̯aid-ti > vetti 'he knows'
22.2	K > G / _G	vāc- 'voice' :: instr. pl. *vākbhiḥ > vāgbhiḥ
22.3	C > N / _N	admi 'I eat' :: *adna- > anna- 'food'
22.4	DH > D / _DH	jíghatsati 'he wants to eat' :: 2. sg. imp. *jaghšdhi > *jaghdhi > jagdhi 'eat!'
22.5	DH > T / _S	3. sg. mid. des. *bhu-bhudh-sa-te > *bhubhutsate > bubhutsate 'he wants to get to know'
22.6	d/t/z > l / _l	mr̥d- 'clay' :: *mr̥d-loṣṭa- > mr̥lloṣṭa- 'lump of earth'
22.7	*u̯ > *m / _m[26]	PIE **di̯éu̯-m > **di̯émm > *di̯ḗm > acc. sg. dyā́m 'heaven, sky'
22.8	n > ñ / j(h), c(h)_	GR gignṓskō :: *ǵneh₃-ti > jñāti 'he knows'
22.9	m > n / _t[27]	bhrāma- 'roaming about' :: *bhrāmtá > bhrāntá- 'confused'
22.10	*sč > *šč	AV pasča :: *po-skʷ-éh₁ > *poskéH > IIR pasčáH > *paščā́ > paścā́ 'posterior'
22.11	*zǰ > *žǰ >*ǰǰ > jj[28]	LAT mergit :: *mézgeti > IIR *mázǰati > *mážǰati > *máǰǰati > májjati 'he sinks'

Ruki rule part 2

SC	Rule	Example
23.1	*š > ṣ / r,r̥,ŭ,k,ĭ _	GR dís :: *du̯is > IIR *dviš > dviṣ 'two times'
23.2	*ž > ẓ / r,r̥,ŭ,k,ĭ _	PIE *nisdó- > IIR *nižda- > *niẓdá- > *niẓḍá- > nīḍá- 'nest'

Cerebralization of *n* > *ṇ*

SC	Rule	Example
24	*n > ṇ[29]	sarpa- 'snake' :: Instr. pl. *sarpena > sarpeṇa

25 Assimilations occur at all times of language development. Therefore, these rules cannot be precisely dated.

26 This sound change is called Stang's law. It was active in PIE already and affected the acc. sg. of **gʷóu̯-m > **gʷómm > *gʷṓm > gām 'cow'. Also *h_2 is said to have affected the ending of the acc.sg. of h_2-stems: *Vh_2m > *Vmm > V̄m.

27 This is an example of a nasal assimilating to the place of articulation of the consonant following.

28 *zge > *zǰe [zd̲že] > jje [d̲dže]: In analogy to the phonetically similar development of c19-c21: *sk̂ > *sć > *šć [št̲š] > ch [t̲šh] in the initial position and cch in the medial position, we can suppose that two consonantal jj < *zg was the result of the preservation of the former medial two consonants. Therefore, we can expect that simple j would have appeared in the final position.

29 Stiehl 2007:320 in translation: "A dental n becomes retroflex ṇ in the word internal position if the following retroflex sounds r̥, r̥̄, r, ṣ (not ṭ, ṭh, ḍ, ḍh, ṇ) precede the dental n either directly or between them and the dental n there are no other sounds than vowels, gutturals (k, kh, g, gh, ṅ) or labials (p, ph, b, bh, m) or y, v, h, ṃ AND dental n is followed directly by either a vowel or by n, m, y, v. (…) That means that a dental n does not become retroflex ṇ if it stands in the word final position (e.g. brahman) or it is preceded by a dental consonant, a palatal consonant or by l, ś, s or if the dental n is preceded by a retroflex (ṭ/ṭh/ḍ/ḍh/ṇ) plus vowel."

Morphonological restitution at morpheme boundaries

SC	Rule	Example
25.1	_*ss > ts_	_vásati_ 'he lives' :: 3. sg. aor. _*e-u̯ēs-sīt_ > _*a-vās-sīt_ > _avātsīt_ 'he lived'
25.2	_*ṣṣ_ > _*ṭṣ_	√_dviṣ_- 'to hate' :: 2. sg. ipf. _*a-dvai̯ṣ-ṣ_ > _*a-dvai̯ṭ-ṣ_ > _*a-dvai̯ṭ_ > _adveṭ_ 'you hated'

Morphological vowel contractions[30]

SC	Rule	Example
26.1	_ă̄ + ă̄ > ā_	_*bhar-a-ti_ > _bharati_ 'he carries' :: _*bhára-a-ti_ > _bhárāti_ 'it is to be expected that he carries/will carry'
26.2	_ĭ̄ + ĭ̄ > ī_	GOT _aistan_ 'to honor' :: _*_h_2_i-_h_2_isd-_h_2_éi̯_ > IIR _*Hi-Hizd-Hái̯_ > _*iizdái̯_ > _*īẓḍé_ > _īḍé_ 'I worship'
26.3	_ŭ̄ + ŭ̄ > ū_	_ripu-uras_ > _ripūras_ 'chest of the enemy'

Metathesis / Dissimilation / Distant assimilation

SC	Rule	Example
27.1	$C^h...C^h > C...C^h$	LAT _fiber_ :: _*b_^{h}_eb_^{h}_rú-_ > _babhrú-_ 'a brown animal'[31]
27.2	_*mn > n_	_bhūman_ 'multitude' :: instr. sg. _*bhūmnā́_ > _bhūnā́_
27.3	$NC_1C_2 > NC_2$	_yunákti_ 'he yokes' :: imp. 2. sg. _yuṅgdhi_[32] > _yuṅdh_i 'yoke!'
27.4	$C_1...C_2 > C_1...C_1$	_*śasvant-_ > _śáśvant-_ 'frequent'
27.5	_*u̯_ > Ø / #_ _ū_	ON _vella_ 'to bubble' :: _*u̯l̥H-mi-_ > _*u̯ūr-mi-_ > _ūrmí-_ 'wave'

Final position sound changes

SC	Rule	Example
28.1	$*C_1C_2(C_3) > C_1$ / _##	LAT _nox, noctis_ :: _*nók_^{w}_t-s_ > _nák-_ 'night'
28.2	_*r/n_ > Ø / _V̄_ _##[33]	LAT _māter_ :: _*mā́tēr_ > _mātā́_ 'mother'
28.3	_*s > ḥ_ / _##	_devas_ > _devaḥ_ 'god'

Dialectal rules

SC	Rule	Example
29.1	_dh > h_	_rodhati_ > _rohati_ 'he grows'[34]
29.2	_bh > h_	_gr̥bhṇā́ti_ 'he seizes' :: _grábha-_ > _gráha-_ 'taking possession of'
29.3	_ḍh > ḷh_	LAT _vector_ :: _voḍhar-_ > VED _voḷhar-_ 'rider'

30 Cf. the sandhi rules at SÇ s1.
31 Probably already Proto-IIR accorrding to AV examples.
32 Mr Jared S. Klein knows that this form is attested several times in the Atharvaveda. He truly is a professor with a lot of knowledge.
33 This also explains the development of the nom. sg. of the _n_-stems e.g. _*rā́jān_ > _rā́jā_ 'king'.
34 Likewise: MHG _Garten_, LAT _hortus_ :: _*ǵ_^{h}_r̥d_^{h}_ó-_ > IIR _*gr̥dhá-_ > _gr̥há-_ 'house'.

Sound change cover rules

The following rules serve as a summary of related sound changes which always occur after each other.

Laryngeals[35]

SC	Rule	Example
c1	*h$_1$e > *He > *e	*h$_1$éu̯g^{wh}-e-toi > *Héu̯g^{wh}-e-toi > IIR *Háu̯ȷ́^{h}atai̯ > óhate 'he speaks solemnly'
c2	*eh$_1$ > *eH > *ē	*d^{h}e-d^{h}eh$_1$ti > *d^{h}ed^{h}ēti > IIR *dhadhāti > dadhāti 'he puts'
c3	*h$_2$e > *Ha > *a	LAT ante :: *h$_2$énti > IIR *Hánti > ánti 'before'
c4	*eh$_2$ > *aH > *ā	LAT pāstor :: *péh$_2$ti > IIR *páHti > pā́ti 'he protects'
c5	*h$_3$e > *Ho > *o	LAT opus :: *h$_3$épes- > IIR *Hápas- > ápas- 'work'
c6	*eh$_3$ > *oH > *ō	LAT pōtus 'drunk' :: imp. *peh$_3$-d^{h}í > *poHd^{h}í > IIR *paHd^{h}í > pāhí 'drink!'

Primary palatalization

SC	Rule	Example
c7	*ḱ > ś	GR klutós :: *ḱlutó- > IIR *ćrutá- > śrutá- 'famous'
c8	*ǵ > j	GR gónu :: *ǵónu > IIR *ǰā́nu- > jā́nu- 'knee'
c9	*ǵ^{h} > h	LAT vehit :: *u̯eǵ^{h}eti > IIR *u̯aȷ́^{h}ati > vahati 'he rides'

Secondary palatalization

SC	Rule	Example
c10	*k > c / _(ĕ, ĭ, i̯)	LAT que :: *k^{w}e > IIR *ča > ca 'and'
c11	*g > j / (ĕ, ĭ, i̯)	LAT augēre 'to increase' :: *h$_2$éu̯ges- > IIR *Háu̯ǰas- > ójas- 'force'
c12	*g^{h} > h / _(ĕ, ĭ, i̯)	LAT vovēre :: *h$_1$eu̯g^{wh}-e-toi̯ > IIR *Háu̯ȷ́^{h}atai̯ > óhate 'he speaks solemnly'

Development of palatal consonant clusters

SC	Rule	Example
c13	*ḱt > ṣṭ[36]	LAT octō :: *oḱtṓ > IIR *aćtā́ > aṣṭā́ 'eight'
c14	*ḱs > kṣ[37]	*réḱs-es- > IIR *raćšas- [rát̲šsas] > rákṣas- 'damage'
c15	*tḱ > kṣ[38]	GR téktōn :: *tétḱon- > IIR *tátćan- [tátt̲šan] > tákṣan- 'carpenter'
c16	*d^{h}g^{wh} > kṣ / _e,i[39]	LAT sitis 'thirst' :: *d^{h}g^{wh}íti- > IIR *dȷ́^{h}íti- > kṣíti- 'ruin'
c17	*d^{h}ǵ^{h} > kṣ[40]	HIT tekan :: *d^{h}ǵ^{h}óm- > IIR *dȷ́^{h}ám- > kṣám- 'earth'

35 These rules are historically not correct because PIE *h$_3$e did not simply become *o which became SKR a but *h$_3$e became PIE *h$_3$o and afterwards IIR *Ha which became SKR a through the loss of the initial laryngeal. These rules serve as a summary and simplification of the phonological processes.

36 Detailed development: *k̂t > (5.1) *ćt [t̲št] > (6.3) *št > (18.1) ṣṭ.

37 Detailed development: *k̂s > (5.1) *ćs [t̲šs] > (18.6) *ṭṣ > (19.1) kṣ.

38 Detailed development: *tk̂ > (5.1) *tć [tt̲š] > (18.4) *ṭṣ > (19.1) kṣ.

39 Detailed development: *d^{h}g^{wh}íti- > (4.3) *d^{h}g^{h}íti- > (22.4) *dg^{h}íti- > (5.3) *dȷ́^{h}íti- [dd̲žhíti] > (18.5) *ḍẓ^{h}íti- > (19.2) *gẓ^{h}íti- > (19.3) kṣíti- 'destruction'.

40 Detailed development: *d^{h}ǵ^{h}- > (22.4) *dǵ^{h} > (5.2) *dȷ́^{h} [dd̲žh] > (18.5) *ḍẓ^{h} > (19.2) *gẓ^{h} > (19.3) kṣ.

INDEX

c18	N/A	
c19	**sḱ > ch / #_*	GR *skiā́* :: **sḱeh$_1$-i̯éh$_2$-* > IIR **sćā̯ā́-* > *chāyā́-* 'shade'
c20	**sḱ > cch* / V_V	GR *báskō* :: **g^{w}m̥-sḱ-e-ti* > IIR **gasćati* > *gácchati* 'he goes'
c21	**sḱ^{h}- > ch / #_*	GR *skhídzō* :: **sḱ^{h}i-né-d-ti* > IIR **sć^{h}inátti* > *chinátti* 'he cuts'

SC	Rule	Example
c22	**aẓ > o*	LAT *vector* :: **u̯eǵ^{h}tor-* > IIR **u̯aj́dhar-* > **u̯aẓḍhar-* > *voḍhar-* 'rider'
c23	**az > e*	*asmi* 'I am' :: 2. sg. imp. **as-dhi* > **azdhi* > *edhi* 'be!'

The ruki rule without IIR intermediate steps

SC	Rule	Example
c24	**s > ṣ / r,r̥,ū̆,k,ī̆ _*	GR *dís* :: **du̯is* > *dviṣ* 'two times'
c25	**z > ẓ / r,r̥,ū̆,k,ī̆ _*	PIE **nizdó-* > **niẓḍá-* > *nīḍá-* 'nest'

Sandhi

Sandhi of Final Vowels

Identical vowels contract to long vowels

SC	Rule	Example
s1.1	*ā̆ + ā̆ > ā*	*mātā agacchat* > *mātāgacchat* 'the mother went'
s1.2	*ī̆ + ī̆ > ī*[41]	*narī īkṣate* > *narīkṣate* 'the woman sees'
s1.3	*ū̆ + ū̆ > ū*	*ripu uras* > *ripūras* 'chest of the enemy'
s1.4	*r̥̄̆ + r̥̄̆ > r̥̄*[42]	*kartr̥ r̥ju* > *kartr̥̄ju* 'honest author'

Long or short *ā̆* + dissimilar vowel or diphthong

SC	Rule	Example
s2.1	*ā̆ + ī̆ > e*	*vinā īrṣyayā* > *vinerṣyayā* 'without jealousy'
s2.2	*ā̆ + ū̆ > o*	*tena uktam* > *tenoktam* 'it was said by him'
s2.3	*ā̆ + r̥̄̆ > ar*	*yathā r̥ṣiḥ* > *yatharṣiḥ* 'like a seer'
s2.4	*ā̆ + e > ai*	*adya eva* > *adyaiva* 'still today'
s2.5	*ā̆ + ai > ai*	*yathā aiśvaryam* > *yathaiśvaryam* 'like the supremacy'
s2.6	*ā̆ + o > au*	*na odanaḥ* > *naudanaḥ* 'not the rice'
s2.7	*ā̆ + au > au*	*tasya auṣadham* > *tasyauṣadham* 'his medicine'

41 This rule does not apply to dual endings in *-ī* and small interjections e.g. *i Indra* 'hey Indra!'.

42 The sandhi of long *r̥̄* + long *r̥̄* > *r̥̄* exists only theoretically but we do not have any real examples.

Final ī̆, ū̆, r̥̄̆ before dissimilar vowel or diphthong become the respective semivowel

SC	Rule	Example
s3.1	*ī̆ + V > y_V (V≠ ī̆)*[43]	*nārī aikṣata > nāry_aikṣata* 'the woman saw'
s3.2	*ū̆ + V > v_V (V≠ ū̆)*[44]	*astu etat > astv_etat* 'this shall be'
s3.3	*r̥̄̆ + V > r_V (V≠ r̥̄̆)*[45]	*kartr̥ asti > kartr_asti* 'he is active'

Vowel sandhi with *e/o/ai/au* as the first element[46]

SC	Rule	Example
s4.1	*e + V > a_V (V≠ ă)*[47]	*nagare iha > nagara_iha* 'in the city here'
s4.2	*e + V > ay (V≠ ă)*[48]	*yoge ālasyam > yogay_ālasyam* 'laziness in yoga'
s4.3	*e + ă > e '*[49]	*gr̥he agaccham > gr̥he 'gaccham* 'I went into the house'
s4.4	*o + V > a_V (V≠ ă)*[50]	*guro īkṣasva > gura īkṣasva* 'o teacher, look!'
s4.5	*o + V > av (V≠ ă)*[51]	*guro īkṣasva > gurav_īkṣasva* 'o teacher look!'
s4.6	*o + ă > o '*[52]	*prabho atra > prabho 'tra* 'you mighty one here'
s4.7	*ai + V > ā_V*[53]	*īkṣāvahai indum > īkṣāvahā indum* 'we both want to see the moon'
s4.8	*ai + V > āy_V*[54]	*īkṣāvahai indum > īkṣāvahāy_indum* 'we both want to see the moon'
s4.9	*au + V > āv_V*[55]	*tau ubhau > tāv_ubhau* 'these two'
s4.10	*au + V > ā_V*[56]	*nr̥pau ādiśataḥ > nr̥pā_ādiśataḥ* 'the two king command'

Initial *ch* after a final short vowel[57]

SC	Rule	Example
s5.1	*V̆ + ch > V_cch*	*na chāyām vindami > nacchayaṃ_vindāmi* 'I do not find shade'

43 This rule does not apply to dual endings in *-ī* and the pronoun *amī* 'those'.
44 This rule does not apply to dual endings in *-ū*.
45 Final *r̥* occurs seldom.
46 This rule does not apply to dual endings in *-e*.
47 Detailed development: **ai̯_V > a_V*. The starting point is the preform **ai̯* of final *e*. Intervocalic loss of the semivowel **i̯*.
48 This is not a sound change but the preservation of the original sounds.
49 Detailed development **ai̯a > e*. Starting point is the preform **ai̯* of final *e*. Middle Indic development **ai̯a > e*.
50 Detailed development **au̯_V > a_V*. The starting point is the preform **au̯* of final *o*. Intervocalic loss of the semivowel **u̯*.
51 This is not a sound change but the preservation of the original sounds.
52 Detailed development **au̯a > o* which was a Middle Indic regular sound change.
53 Detailed development **āi̯_V > ā_V*. The starting point is the preform **āi̯* of final *ā*. Intervocalic loss of the semivowel **i̯*.
54 This is not a sound change but the preservation of the original sounds.
55 This is not a sound change but the preservation of the original sounds.
56 **āu̯_V > ā_V*. The starting point is the preform **āu̯* of final *au*. Intervocalic loss of the semivowel **u̯*.
57 Also after participles ending in *-mā* and *-ā* as well as occasionally after a long vowel. The sequence *ch* occurs between vowels only as geminated *cch*. This concerns the described sandhi as well as morphological formations like **gʷm̥-sk̂é-ti > gaccháti* 'he walks'.

Sandhi of Final Visarga

Sandhi of etymological final *s/r before voiced sounds

SC	Rule	Example
s6.1	aḥ + V > a _V (V≠a)[58]	ādityaḥ iva > āditya_iva 'like the sun'
s6.2	aḥ + G > o _G[59]	vr̥kṣaḥ rohati > vr̥kṣo_rohati 'the tree grows'
s6.3	aḥ + a > o '[60]	kaḥ api gāyati > ko 'pi gāyati 'someone sings'
s6.4	āḥ + G /V> ā _G/V[61]	nr̥pāḥ jayanti > nr̥pā_jayanti 'the kings overcome'
s6.5	Vḥ + G/V > Vr_G/V (V ≠ a, ā)	agniḥ dahati > agnir_dahati 'the fire burns'
s6.6	Vḥ + r > V̄_r (V ≠ a, ā)[62]	taruḥ rohati > tarū_rohati 'the tree grows'

Sandhi of etymological final *-r before voiced sounds[63]

SC	Rule	Example
s7.1	aḥ + G/V > ar_G/V (G≠r)	prātaḥ gacchati > prātar_gacchati 'he walks in the morning'
s7.2	āḥ + G /V > ār_G/V (G≠r)	dvāḥ dr̥śyate > dvār_dr̥śyate 'the door is seen'

Sandhi of etymological final *-s/r before voiceless sounds

SC	Rule	Example
s8.1	ḥ + k(h) = ḥ_k(h)	aśvaḥ khādati = aśvaḥ_khādati 'the horse eats'
s8.2	ḥ + p(h) = ḥ_p(h)	kapiḥ pibati = kapiḥ_pibati 'the monkey drinks'
s8.2b	ḥ + ṭ(h) > ṣ_ṭ(h)	kapiḥ ṭīkate > kapiṣ_ṭīkate 'the monkey jumps'
s8.2c	ḥ + t(h) > s_t(h)	devaḥ tatra > devas_tatra 'the god over there'
s8.3	ḥ + s/ṣ/ś > ḥ_s/ṣ/ś[64]	arthaḥ sidhyati = arthaḥ_sidhyati 'the matter is successful'
s8.4	ḥ + c > ś _c(h)	kūrmaḥ calati > kūrmaś_calati 'the turtle moves'

Vedic sandhi of original final *-s/r before voiceless sounds

SC	Rule	Example
s9.1	ḥ + ś > ś _ś	suptaḥ śiśuḥ > suptaś_śiśuḥ 'a sleeping child'
s9.2	ḥ + ṣ > ṣ_ṣ	dévīḥ ṣaṭ > dévīṣ_ṣaṭ 'goddesses…six'
s9.3	ḥ + s > s_s	arthaḥ sidhyati = arthas_sidhyati 'the matter is successful'

58 *as_V > *az_V > a_V. Loss of *z without compensatory lengthening. Retention of the short vowel in the ending due to analogical reasons.
59 *as_G > *az_G > *aØ_G > *au̯_G > o_G. Loss of *z. Insertion of the transition consonant *u̯ in order to compensate the lost consonant. Monophthongization of *au̯ > o.
60 *as_a > *az_a > *aØ_a > *au̯_a > o. Loss of *z. Insertion of the transition consonant *u̯ in order to compensate the lost consonant. Middle-Indic development *au̯a > o.
61 *as_G/V > *az_G/V > ā_G/V. Loss of *z with compensatory lengthening.
62 No additional vowel lengthening ofter a long vowel or diphthong.
63 Final etymological –r occurs seldom. It occurs in the voc. of the r̥-declension, pitar 'father!', in prātar 'in the morning', punar 'again', dvār 'door', antar 'inside', svar 'sky', ahar 'day', vār 'water', as well as in some verbal forms ending in -r, the roots of which end in r̥ e.g. 2. sg., 3. sg. ipf. ajāgar from jāgr̥ 'to be awake'.
64 The consonant ṣ is extremely rare in the initial position.

Sandhi of Final Stops

Final dental *t*[65]

SC	Rule	Example
s10.1	*t +c > c_c*	*tat cakram > tac_cakram* 'this wheel'
s10.2	*t +ch > c _ch*	*mr̥t chādayati > mr̥c_chādayati* 'the clay covers (something)'
s10.3	*t +j > j_j*	*tat jalam > taj_jalam* 'this water'
s10.4a	*t + ṭ(h) > ṭ_ṭ(h)*	*suhr̥t ṭīkate > suhr̥ṭ_ṭīkate* 'the friend moves'
s10.4b	*t + ḍ(h) > ḍ_ḍ(h)*	*tat ḍhaukate > taḍ_ḍhaukate* 'it comes nearer'
s10.5	*t +l > l_l*	*tat lokāt labhe > tal_lokāl_labhe* 'that is what I get from the world'
s10.6	*t +ś > c_ch*[66]	*tat śrutvā > tac_chrutvā* 'having this heard'
s10.7	*t +ś > c _ś*[67]	*tat śrutvā > tac_śrutvā* 'having this heard'

Voiceless stops before voiced sounds except before nasals

SC	Rule	Example
s11.1	*k + V/G > g_V/G*	*vaṇik bhaṣate > vaṇig_bhāṣate* 'the merchant speaks'
s11.2	*t + V/G> d_V/G*	*āsīt rājā > āsīd_rāja* 'there was a king'
s11.3	*ṭ + V/G > ḍ_V/G*	*samrāṭ āsīt > samrāḍ_āsīt* 'there was a ruler'
s11.4	*p + V/G > b_V/G*	*kakup api > kakub_api* 'also the direction'

Voiceless stops before nasals

SC	Rule	Example
s12.1	*k +N > ṅ_N*	*vāk me > vāṅ_me* 'my speech'
s12.2	*ṭ + N > ṇ _N*	*madhuliṭ nadati > madhuliṇ_nadati* 'the bee is humming'
s12.3	*t + N > n _N*	*nagarāt nagaram > nagarān_nagaram* 'from city to city'
s12.4	*p + N > m_N*	*kakup mr̥gyate > kapum_mr̥gyate* 'the direction is searched'

Voiceless stops before voiced *h*[68]

SC	Rule	Example
s13.1	*k +h > g_gh*	*vāk harṣayati > vāg_gharṣayati* 'language delights'
s13.2	*t +h > d_dh*	*tat hi > tad_dhi* 'this indeed'
s13.3	*ṭ +h > ḍ_ḍh*	*madhuliṭ hasati > madhuliḍ_ḍhasati* 'the bee laughs'
s13.4	*p +h > b_bh*	*kakup hi > kakub_bhi* 'the direction indeed'

65 The consonants *jh, ṭ, ṭh, ḍ, ḍh* are so rare in the initial position that the following rule nearly only affects initial *c, ch, j*

66 *t_ś* [t̠š] was phonetically too similar to *c* [t̠š] which counted as one consonant only. It became geminated *c_ch* in order to keep up the syllabic structure of two-consonantal *t_ś*.

67 Not as frequent as the sandhi of the preceding rule.

68 The first step was the voicing of the final stop: *k+h > g_h, t+h > d_h, ṭ+h > ḍ_h, p+h > b_h*. The resulting sequences *g_h, d_h, ḍ_h, b_h* were phonetically very near to mono-consonantal *gh, dh, ḍh, bh* which was the reason for their gemination to *g_gh, d_dh, ḍ_ḍh, b_bh* in order to keep up the syllabic structure of the former two-consonantal sequences.

Sandhi of Final Nasals

Sandhi of final nasals

SC	Rule	Example
s14.1	*m +C > ṃ_C*[69]	*pūrvam sattvam > pūrvaṃ_sattvam* 'the former being'
s14.2	*n +ḍ(h) > ṇ_ḍ*	*pakṣin ḍīyasva > pakṣiṇ_ḍīyasva* 'my bird, fly away!'
s14.3	*n + j(h) > ñ_j(h)*	*arīn jayati > arīñ_jayati* 'he overcomes the enemies'
s14.4	*n +ś > ñ_ś*	*tān śaśān > tāñ_śaśān* 'these rabbits'
s14.5	*n +ś > ñ_ch*[70]	*tān śaśān > tāñ_chaśān* 'these rabbits'

Final *n* before voiceless palatal *c, ch*, retroflex *ṭ, ṭh*, dental *t, th* and before *l*

SC	Rule	Example
s15.1	*n+c(h) > ṃś_c(h)*	*abharan ca > abharaṃś_ca* 'and they carried'[71]
s15.2	*n + ṭ(h) > ṃṣ_ṭ(h)*	*tān ṭaṅkān > tāṃṣ_ṭaṅkān* 'these hachets'
s15.3	*n + t(h) > ṃs_t(h)*	*devān tatra > devāṃs_tatra* 'the gods here'
s15.4	*n +l > ṃl_l*[72]	*tān lokān > tāṃl_lokān* 'these worlds'

Final nasals after a short vowel before a vowel[73]

SC	Rule	Example
s16.1	*n > nn / V̆_#V*[74]	*āsan+ atra > āsann_atra* 'they were here'
s16.2	*ṅ > ṅṅ / V̆_#V*[75]	*pratyaṅ āsīnaḥ > pratyaṅ_āsīnaḥ* 'sitting westwards'

Insertion of transition sounds

SC	Rule	Example
s17.1	*n+ś > nt_ś*	*tān śaśān > tāñ_śaśān > tāñ_chaśān* 'these rabbits'
s17.2	*n+s > nt_s*	*tān sahate > tānt_sahate* 'he overcomes them'
s17.3	*ṅ+ś > ṅk_ś*	*prāṅ śete > prāṅk_śete* 'he lies eastwards'

69 This rule also applies to morphological forms.

70 More frequent than the before-going sandhi. Insertion of the phonetical transition sound *t*.

71 Insertion of the homorganic sibilant (*ś, ṣ, s*) between final *-n* and the initial voiceless palatal *c, ch*, retroflex *ṭ, ṭh* and dental *t, th*. Thereby, development of *-n* to anusvāra. As *ṭ, ṭh, ch, th* are very rare in the initial position, this rule nearly only applies to *c* and *t*. In a historic perspective, the ending *-ns* is the oldest and was reduced to *-n* in the absolute final position but remained in sandhi with the assimilation of the nasal to the place of articulation of the consonant following. After the emergence of this rule, it was transferred even onto those cases which had not originated out of *-ns*. The only real change in this sandhi was therefore the development of *m > ṃ / _C* because the etymological *s* was preserved.

72 Even more rare in this phonological context is the spelling with anunāsika *amuṣmiṃ̐l_loke*.

73 This rule is valid after *a* and *i* (theoretically also after *u* and *r̥*). All nasals except *-m* were doubled in this position.

74 Cf. chapter 17.

75 Only in directional adverbs and not before consonants.

A1 Sandhi Overview Tables

Consonant sandhi: changes of the final position

Final	Initial														
	k(h)	***g(h)***	***c(h)***	***j(h)***	***ṭ(h)***	***ḍ(h)***	***t(h)***	***d(h)***	***p(h)***	***b(h)***	***n/m***	***ś***	***l***	***v/y/r***	***h***
k		*g*		*g*		*g*		*g*		*g*	*ṅ*			*g*	*g_(gh)*
ṭ		*ḍ*		*ḍ*		*ḍ*		*ḍ*		*ḍ*	*ṇ*			*ḍ*	*ḍ_(ḍh)*
t		*d*	*c*	*d*	*ṭ*	*d*		*d*		*d*	*n*	*c_(ch)*	*l*	*d*	*d_(dh)*
p		*b*		*b*		*b*		*b*		*b*	*m*			*b*	*b_(bh)*
ṇ															
n			*ṃś_c(h)*	*ñ*	*ṃṣ_ṭ(h)*	*ṇ*	*ṃs_t(h)*					*ñ_(ś/ch)*	*ṃl_(l)*		
m	*ṃ*	*ṃ*	*ṃ*	*ṃ*	*ṃ*	*ṃ*	*ṃ*	*ṃ*	*ṃ*	*ṃ*	*ṃ*	*ṃ*	*ṃ*	*ṃ*	*ṃ*

Final visarga (*V* in *Vḥ* stands for vowels except *a/ā* and *ḥ* stands for etymological **s*)

Final	Initial							
	a	***Vowel***	***n/m/y/l/v/h***	***r***	***g/j/ḍ/d/b(h)***	***c(h)***	***ṭ(h)***	***t(h)***
aḥ	*o ’*	*a*	*o*	*o*	*o*	*aś*	*aṣ*	*as*
āḥ	*ā*	*ā*	*a*	*ā*	*ā*	*āś*	*āṣ*	*ās*
Vḥ	*r*	*r*	*r*	*V̄*	*r*	*ś*	*ṣ*	*s*

Vowel plus vowel (! stands for: if not dual ending.)[76]

Final	Initial										
	a	***ā***	***i***	***ī***	***u***	***ū***	***ṛ***	***e***	***ai***	***o***	***au***
a	*ā*	*a*	*e*	*e*	*o*	*o*	*ar*	*ai*	*ai*	*au*	*au*
ā	*ā*	*ā*	*e*	*e*	*o*	*o*	*ar*	*ai*	*ai*	*au*	*au*
i !	*ya*	*yā*	*ī*	*ī*	*yu*	*yū*	*yṛ*	*ye*	*yai*	*yo*	*yau*
ī !	*ya*	*yā*	*ī*	*ī*	*yu*	*yū*	*yṛ*	*ye*	*yai*	*yo*	*yau*
u !	*va*	*vā*	*vi*	*vī*	*ū*	*ū*	*vṛ*	*ve*	*vai*	*vo*	*vau*
ū !	*va*	*vā*	*vi*	*vī*	*ū*	*ū*	*vṛ*	*ve*	*vai*	*vo*	*vau*
ṛ	*ra*	*rā*	*ri*	*rī*	*ru*	*rū*	*ṝ*	*re*	*rai*	*ro*	*rau*
e !	*e ,*	*a ā*	*a i*	*a ī*	*a u*	*a ū*	*a ṛ*	*a e*	*a ai*	*a o*	*a au*
ai	*ā a*	*ā ā*	*ā i*	*ā ī*	*ā u*	*ā ū*	*ā ṛ*	*ā e*	*ā ai*	*ā o*	*ā au*
o	*o ,*	*avā / a ā*	*avi*	*avī*	*avu*	*avū*	*avṛ*	*ave*	*avai*	*avo*	*avau*
au	*āva*	*āvā*	*āvi*	*āvī*	*āvu*	*āvū*	*āvṛ*	*āve*	*āvai*	*āvo*	*āvau*

APPENDIX

76 From: Dr. Ashok Aklujkar’s “Sanskrit: An Easy Introduction to an Enchanting Language” (Svādhyāya: 2005) Vol. 1B pp. 64–66 https://ubcsanskrit.ca/lesson3/sandhicharts.html.

A2 Vowel Apophony

Similar to the vowel change in English *sing, sang, sung* or *drink, drank, drunk*, we also find a regular vowel change in Sanskrit in related word forms, which is called **ablaut** or **apophony**. The Sanskrit grammarians recognized this linguistic phenomenon and structured it into the following system. The zero grade forms of the basic vowels *ī̆, ū̆, r̥̄̆, l̥* were increased by prefixed *a* which created their full grade forms *ai, au, ar, al*. The diphthongs *ai* and *au* became *e* and *o* before a consonant and *ay* and *av* before a vowel. The process of increasing the vowels by prefixed *a* is then repeated with the full grade forms which created the lengthened grade forms *ai, au, ār, āl*. A special case is the vowel *a* which has *a* as its base form and full grade form.

Base form / Zero Grade	*ī̆*	*ū̆*	*r̥̄̆*	*l̥*	*a*	*ā*
Guṇa grade / Full Grade	*e* < *a*+*ī̆*	*o* < *a*+*ū̆*	*ar* < *a*+*r̥̄̆*	*al* < *a*+*l̥*	*a*	*ā*
Vr̥ddhi grade / Lengthened Grade	*ai* < *a*+*a*+*ī̆*	*au* < *a*+*a*+*ū̆*	*ār* < *a*+*a*+*r*	*āl* < *a*+*a*+*l̥*	*ā*	*ā*

Examples of vowel gradation

The root √*div*- 'to shine' appears in its zero grade in *dívasa*- 'sky, day' and *dívā* 'in the daytime', it appears in its full grade in *deva*- 'god' and *dévana*- 'shining' and it appears in its lengthened grade in *daiva*-, *daivika*-, *daivata*- 'divine'.

The root √*ruc*- 'to shine' appears in its zero grade in *ruci*- 'light' and *ruc*- 'splendor', it appears in its full grade in *rocana*-, *roca*- 'shining' and it appears in its lengthened grade in *raukma*- 'golden' and *raucanika*- 'yellowish'.

The root √*dr̥ś*- 'to see, to watch' appears in its zero grade in *dr̥śi*- 'eye' and *dr̥śīkā́*- 'appearance', it appears in its full grade in *dárśa*- 'watching' and *darśatá*- 'beautiful' and it appears in its lengthened grade in *dārśa*- and *dārśika*- 'new moon'. The same is true for roots with internal *l̥* like √*kl̥p*- 'to fit' but this is the only existing root having this structure.

Sometimes we find *ra, la, rā* for expected *ar, al, ār*. From the root √*dr̥ś*- we find the forms *drakṣyā́mi* 'I will see' and *ádrākṣam* 'I saw' instead of expected ˣ*darkṣyā́mi* and ˣ*ádārkṣam*. From the root √*sr̥j*- 'to release' we find *ásrākṣam* 'I released' instead of ˣ*ásārkṣam* and from √*kl̥p*- we find the form *klapsyate* instead of ˣ*kalpsyate*.

PIE origins of the Sanskrit apophonical system

The foundation of the Sanskrit apophonical system was the Proto-Indo-European apophonical system which is characterized by the presence or absence of the ablaut vowel *e. In the PIE zero grade there is no ablaut vowel *e which corresponds to the Sanskrit zero grade form. The PIE full grade is characterized by the presence of the ablaut vowel *e which corresponds to the Sanskrit full grade form. In the PIE lengthened grade form, the PIE ablaut vowel *e is lengthenend to *ē which corresponds to the Sanskrit lengthened grade form.

	Zero Grade	e-Grade / Full Grade	ē-Grade / Lengthened Grade
PIE	√**dr̥ḱ*-	√**derḱ*-	√**dērḱ*-
Sanskrit	√*dr̥ś*-	√*darś*-	√*dārś*-

Lit.: Ziegler 2012:35–37; Thumb-Hauschild 1958:267; Stiehl 2007:309; Wackernagel 1896:61–68; Meier-Brügger 2000:135ff.

Bibliography

Allen, William Sidney (1953): *Phonetics in Ancient India*. London: Oxford University Press.

Allen, William Sidney (1972): *Sandhi. The Theoretical, Phonetic, and Historical Bases of Word-Junction in Sanskrit*. The Hague-Paris: Mouton.

Burrow, T (1959a): *On the phonological history of Sanskrit kṣám-* 'earth', *ṛ́kṣa- 'bear' and likṣā́-* 'nit'. JAOS 79, 85–90.

Burrow, T (1959b): *Sanskrit kṣi-: Greek* φθίνω. Journal of the American Oriental Society 79, 255–262.

Burrow, T. (1973): *The Sanskrit Language*. London.

Edgerton, Franklin (1946): *Sanskrit Historical Phonology*. New Haven, Conn., American Oriental society.

Grassmann, Hermann (1996): *Wörterbuch zum Rig-Veda. Bearbeitung von Maria Kozianka*. Harrassowitz.

Gonda, Jan (1966): *A Concise Elementary Grammar of the Sanskrit Language*. Brill Archive.

Jain, Danesh and Cardona, George (2007): *The Indo-Aryan-Languages*. Routledge.

Kloekhorst, Alwin (2014): *Proto-Indo-European "thorn"-clusters*. Historical Linguistics: Band 127, Ausgabe 1, 43–67.

Kobayashi, Masato (2004): *Historical Phonology of Old Indo-Aryan Consonants*. Fuchu, Tokyo.

Kümmel, Martin J. (2007): *Konsonantenwandel*. Wiesbaden: Reichert.

Lehmann Thomas (2013): *Sanskrit für Anfänger – Ein Lehr- und Übungsbuch*. Online-Publikation: https://www.sai.uni-heidelberg.de/tamil/.

Liesner, Malte (2006): *Zu den Beziehungen zwischen Heteroklisie und dem Caland-System im Indogermanischen*. Unpublished master's thesis. University of Cologne.

Liesner, Malte (2014): *Latin Historical Phonology Workbook*. Wiesbaden: Reichert.

Liesner, Malte (2015): *Greek Historical Phonology Workbook*. Wiesbaden: Reichert.

Lipp, R. (2009): *Die indogermanischen und einzelsprachlichen Palatale im Indoiranischen. Band I: Neurekonstruktion, Nuristani-Sprachen, Genese der indoarischen Retroflexe, Indoarisch von Mitanni*. Heidelberg.

Lipp, R. (2009): *The indogermanischen and einzelsprachlichen Palatale im Indoiranischen. Band II: Thorn-Problem, indoiranische Laryngalvokalisation*. Heidelberg.

Macdonell, Arthur A. (1916): *A Vedic Grammar for Students*. Oxford: Clarendon Press.

Macdonell, Arthur A. (2007): *A Sanskrit Grammar for Students*. Motilal Banarsidass.

Macdonell, Arthur A. (2010): *Vedic Grammar*. Motilal Banarsidass.

Malzahn, Melanie (2001): *Sandhiphänomene im Rigveda als Reflexe von Archaismen und Dialektismen*. Dissertation zur Erlangung des Doktorgrades der Philosophie an der Geistes- and Kulturwissen schaftlichen Fakultät der Universität Wien.

Mayrhofer, Manfred (1956–1982): *Kurzgefasstes etymologisches Wörterbuch des Sanskrit*. 4 Bände. Winter.

Mayrhofer, Manfred (1978): *Sanskrit-Grammatik*. Berlin: Walter de Gruyter.

Mayrhofer, Manfred (1989): *Vorgeschichte der iranischen Sprachen; Uriranisch*. in Rüdiger Schmitt (ed.) *Compendium Linguarum Iranicarum*. Wiesbaden: Reichert.

Meier-Brügger, Michael (2000): *Indogermanische Sprachwissenschaft*. Berlin: Walter de Gruyter.

Mylius, Klaus (2001): *Sanskrit-Deutsch. Handwörterbuch*. Berlin and München: Langenscheidt.

Renou, L. (1952): *Grammaire de la langue védique*. Lyon-Paris.

Stenzler, Adolf Friedrich (2003). *Elementarbuch der Sanskrit Sprache*. Berlin: Walter De Gruyter.

Stiehl, Ulrich (2007): *Sanskrit-Kompendium*. Heidelberg: Economica.

Thumb, A. (1905): *Handbuch des Sanskrit*. Heidelberg: Carl Winter.

Thumb, A. - Hauschild, R. (1958): *Handbuch des Sanskrit. Bd. I,1. Einleitung and Lautlehre*. Heidelberg: Carl Winter.

Wackernagel, Jacob (1896): *Sanskrit Grammatik, Band I*. Göttingen: Vandenhoeck & Ruprecht. Reprinted in 1957 with Albert Debrunner's Nachträge.

Ziegler, Sabine (2012): *Klassisches Sanskrit*. Wiesbaden: Reichert.

A4 Abbreviations / Notations / Symbols

Languages

AV	Avestan	LAT	Latin	ON	Old Norse
ENG	English	LATV	Latvian	PIE	Proto-Indo-European
GOT	Gothic	LIT	Lithuanian	SKR	Sanskrit
GR	Greek	MHG	Modern High German	TOCH	Tocharian
HIT	Hittite	OCS	Old Church Slavonic	VED	Vedic
IE	Indo-European	OHG	Old High German		
IIR	Indo-Iranian	O-LAT	Old Latin		

Grammatical and Phonetic Terms

acc.	accusative case	gen.	genitive case	pfc.	perfect tense
act.	active	imp.	imperative	pl.	plural
aor.	aorist tense	inf.	infinitive	PPP	perfect passive participle
asp.	aspirated	instr.	instrumental case		
CL	compensatory lengthening	ipf.	imperfect	prs.	present tense
		loc.	locative case	prt.	preterite tense
dat.	dative	masc.	masculine	ps.	person
des.	desiderative	mid.	middle	ptc.	participle
du.	dual	nom.	nominative case	sg.	singular
fem.	feminine	nt.	neuter	subj.	subjunctive
fut.	future	opt.	optative		

Notations and Symbols

-	morpheme boundary	word*	expected word	*V̆*	short vowel
#	word boundary	ˣwort	theoretical word	*V̄*	long vowel
##	absolute final position	*C*	consonant	*V̆̄*	short or long vowel
_	position of derived sound in sound change	C^h	aspiration	L	line
		C^w	labialization	√	root
		G	voiced consonant	cf.	compare / confer
_	sandhi combination	*H*	laryngeal	Lit.	bibliographic information
<	is derived from	SC	sound change		
>	becomes	*R̥*	syllabic resonant	IPA	International Phonetic Alphabet
*word	reconstructed form	*V*	vowel		

Information about the transcription system used in this book

In this book, the voiced palatal sounds SKR *j*, IIR **ǰ*, **j́* are transcribed with [d̲ž] and the voiceless palatal sounds SKR *c*, IIR **ć*, *č* are transcribed with [t̲š] although this is historically not correct because IIR **j́* and **ǰ* as well as IIR **ć* and **č* were pronounced slightly differently in Indo-Iranian which can be seen from their divergent developments in Sanskrit. This transcription system is fully sufficient for this book and employed in order to simplify the explanation of the phonological processes.